Developing Cloud-Native Solutions with Microsoft Azure and .NET

Build Highly Scalable Solutions for the Enterprise

Ashirwad Satapathi
Abhishek Mishra

Apress®

Developing Cloud-Native Solutions with Microsoft Azure and .NET: Build Highly Scalable Solutions for the Enterprise

Ashirwad Satapathi
Gajapati, Odisha, India

Abhishek Mishra
Navi MUmbai, India

ISBN-13 (pbk): 978-1-4842-9003-3
https://doi.org/10.1007/978-1-4842-9004-0

ISBN-13 (electronic): 978-1-4842-9004-0

Managing Director, Apress Media LLC: Welmoed Spahr
Acquisitions Editor: Smriti Srivastava
Development Editor: Laura Berendson
Coordinating Editor: Shrikant Vishwakarma
Copyeditor: William McManus

Cover designed by eStudioCalamar

Cover image by Yaroslav A on Unsplash (www.unsplash.com)

Distributed to the book trade worldwide by Apress Media, LLC, 1 New York Plaza, New York, NY 10004, U.S.A. Phone 1-800-SPRINGER, fax (201) 348-4505, e-mail orders-ny@springer-sbm.com, or visit www.springeronline.com. Apress Media, LLC is a California LLC and the sole member (owner) is Springer Science + Business Media Finance Inc (SSBM Finance Inc). SSBM Finance Inc is a **Delaware** corporation.

For information on translations, please e-mail booktranslations@springernature.com; for reprint, paperback, or audio rights, please e-mail bookpermissions@springernature.com.

Apress titles may be purchased in bulk for academic, corporate, or promotional use. eBook versions and licenses are also available for most titles. For more information, reference our Print and eBook Bulk Sales web page at http://www.apress.com/bulk-sales.

Any source code or other supplementary material referenced by the author in this book is available to readers on GitHub (https://github.com/Apress). For more detailed information, please visit http://www.apress.com/source-code.

Printed on acid-free paper

The book is dedicated to my mother, Mrs. Sabita Panigrahi, for supporting me through every phase of my life.
—Ashirwad Satapathi

This book is dedicated to my parents, wife, and lovely daughter Aaria.
—Abhishek Mishra

Table of Contents

About the Authors

 **Ashirwad Satapathi** is a software developer with a leading IT firm whose expertise is building scalable applications with .NET Core. He has a deep understanding of how to build full-stack applications using .NET and Azure PaaS and serverless offerings. He is an active blogger in the C# Corner developer community. He was awarded the C# Corner MVP (September 2020) for his remarkable contributions to the developer community.

 **Abhishek Mishra** is a cloud architect at a leading organization and has more than 17 years of experience in building and architecting software solutions for large and complex enterprises across the globe. He has deep expertise in enabling digital transformation for his customers using the cloud and artificial intelligence. He speaks at conferences on Azure and has authored five books on Azure prior to writing this new book.

About the Technical Reviewer

As a Cloud Solutions Architect, **Viachaslau Matsukevich** has delivered 20+ DevOps projects for a number of Fortune 500 and Global 2000 enterprises.

Viachaslau has been certified by Microsoft, Google, and the Linux Foundation as a Solutions Architect Expert, Professional Cloud Architect, and Kubernetes Administrator.

He has written many technology articles about Cloud-Native technologies and Kubernetes on *Red Hat Enable Architect, SD Times, Hackernoon, Dzone,* and *Medium's* largest and most followed independent DevOps publication.

Viachaslau has participated as an Industry Expert and Judge for the Globe Awards, including the IT World Awards, Golden Bridge Awards, Disruptor Company Awards, and American Best in Business Awards. He also is the author of online courses about DevOps and Kubernetes tools and is a member of the Leader of Excellence from Harvard Square. You can find him at `www.linkedin.com/in/viachaslau-matsukevich/`.

Acknowledgments

We would like to thank the Apress team for giving us the opportunity to work on this book. Also, thanks to the technical reviewer and the editors for helping us deliver this manuscript.

Introduction

This book will help you learn how to build cloud-native solutions using Microsoft Azure and .NET. It provides step-by-step explanations of essential concepts and practical examples. We will begin by exploring multiple Azure PaaS and serverless offerings by building solutions to solve real-world problems by following the industry best practices.

The books start with Azure fundamentals, followed by scenario-driven chapters on building distributed solutions using Azure Web App and Azure Service Bus. The next set of chapters focuses on building containerized workloads using Azure container-based services. We will explore how to build intelligent applications using Azure AI and IoT services in subsequent chapters. Finally, we will explore ways to deploy our applications using GitHub Actions.

By the end of this book, you will be able to build various types of applications by leveraging Azure PaaS and serverless services and be able to deploy them using Azure GitHub Actions.

This book presents near-production scenarios and provides lab scenarios that deliver the right set of hands-on experience to the reader. The practical approach adopted in the book will help users gain deep proficiency in developing coud-native solutions.

This book is intended for all who wish to get a deep understanding of Azure to build highly scalable and reliable cloud-native applications. It provides a well-illustrated guide for the readers to kickstart their journey with Microsoft Azure.

Source Code

All source code used in this book can be downloaded from `https://github.com/apress/developing-cloud-native-solutions-azure-.net`.

CHAPTER 1

Introduction

Modern applications are being migrated to the cloud like never before. All new applications designed using new-age architectures like microservices, Onion Architecture, and many more are hosted on the cloud. Your applications hosted on the cloud are highly available, fault-tolerant, reliable, and scalable. Cloud computing helps you save infrastructure ownership costs and operational costs to a large extent.

There are many cloud vendors today from which you can rent cloud services. Microsoft Azure is popular among these vendors and is preferred across many industries, such as manufacturing, finance, healthcare, aviation, and others.

In this chapter, we will explore the following Azure-related topics:

- Introduction to cloud computing

- Cloud deployment models

- Cloud service types

- Serverless computing

- A quick tour of Azure services

After studying this chapter, you will understand the fundamentals of cloud computing and the cloud services offered by Azure. Let's start with a brief introduction to what exactly cloud computing is.

Introduction to Cloud Computing

A cloud vendor builds and manages a large number of datacenters. Using virtualization technologies, it spins up virtual machines. It runs many cloud services for hosting applications, storage, databases, artificial intelligence (AI), machine learning (ML), Internet of Things (IoT), and many more. All these services running on the cloud vendor's datacenter are available to the consumers by using a portal or a command-line

© Ashirwad Satapathi and Abhishek Mishra 2023
A. Satapathi and A. Mishra, *Developing Cloud-Native Solutions with Microsoft Azure and .NET*,
https://doi.org/10.1007/978-1-4842-9004-0_1

utility. As a consumer, you can use these services and pay as and when you use them. You just need to request the creation of these services on the cloud vendor datacenter using the portal or the command-line utility. Once the services get created, you can start using them. You get billed for the period you are using it. And when you do not use it, you can decommission these services. Creation and decommission of these services are instantaneous. In a few minutes, you can create and delete these services using the vendor portal or a command-line utility. As soon as you delete the services, your billing stops. Hosting an application on the cloud is more cost-effective than hosting the application on an on-premises server.

The cloud vendor manages the datacenter. The cloud vendor owns the infrastructure and maintains it, saving you the effort and cost of owning and maintaining it. You simply consume the services without worrying about the underlying hosting infrastructure. You save both capital expenditure (CapEx) by not needing to own the infrastructure and operational expenditure (OpEx) by not needing to maintain the cloud infrastructure.

There are industry-standard cloud architectures and practices that you can use to build cloud-based applications. You can execute a service level agreement (SLA) with the vendor for the cloud services you plan to consume. The vendor will guarantee that the applications running on the cloud are highly available, reliable, secured, scalable, and fault-tolerant.

Microsoft Azure, Amazon Web Services (AWS), and Google Cloud Platform are the most popular cloud vendors. However, there are a lot of other cloud vendors that you can rely on.

Cloud Deployment Models

You can deploy your application to the cloud using the following deployment models:

- Public cloud
- Private cloud
- Hybrid cloud

Let's explore each of these deployment models in detail.

Public Cloud

Large cloud vendors have built massive datacenters spread across the globe. They manage these datacenters and have complete control over the datacenter infrastructure. These cloud vendors have enabled a very high degree of virtualization on these datacenters and have developed cloud services running on the virtualized environment on top of the datacenter infrastructure. Anyone across the globe can purchase a subscription for these cloud services and start using them.

As a consumer of these cloud services, you need not worry about owning and managing the underlying infrastructure hosting the cloud services. You just need to pay for the cloud service you are using. The cloud vendor will ensure that the hardware is always up and running and the cloud service is available.

You can create a cloud service on the public cloud in a few minutes, and when you no longer need the service, you can decommission it. Your billing starts when the service gets provisioned, and the billing stops as soon as you decommission the service. You end up paying the cloud vendor only when using the service. This approach saves much cost for you.

Microsoft Azure, Amazon Web Service, and Google Cloud Platform are examples of public cloud providers.

Private Cloud

Large enterprises and organizations execute thousands of customer projects. To cater to the projects they are executing, they can build their datacenter, run the virtualized cloud environment on their datacenter, and host their customer projects. The enterprise owns the datacenter and manages it. It has complete control over the infrastructure and tighter control over the data, network, and infrastructure level security. The projects in the enterprise can host their applications on the private enterprise cloud.

Building and managing a private cloud is costly compared to running the applications on the public cloud. However, the enterprise gets greater control over the cloud infrastructure than it would have over the public cloud.

Hybrid Cloud

A hybrid cloud is a combination of a public cloud and a private cloud. Some application components are hosted on the public cloud and some are hosted on the private cloud.

The public and private cloud components communicate with each other using a dedicated and secured communication channel. For example, you may choose to keep the data on the private cloud and host the application on the public cloud.

Cloud Service Types

There are three types of cloud services:

- Infrastructure-as-a-Service (IaaS)

- Platform-as-a-Service (PaaS)

- Software-as-a-Service (SaaS)

Let's discuss each of the service types in detail.

Infrastructure-as-a-Service

Virtual machines run on cloud-based datacenters. You can build your application and deploy it on a virtual machine. The hosting experience is precisely the same as that in the on-premises server. You get complete control over the virtual machine and its operating system. You can install any software, configure the hosting environment based on your needs, and then run your application without any restriction, just like an on-premises server.

You get greater control over the virtual machine and its environment. However, you will have to spend much operational expenses to keep the virtual machine running. You will have to patch the operating system with the latest security fixes and keep upgrading the installed software and the application-hosting environment.

Platform-as-a-Service

In the case of Platform-as-a-Service, you build your application and data and deploy it to the cloud service without worrying about the underlying hosting infrastructure. The cloud vendor manages all operational aspects of the virtual machine hosting your application and data. You do not have any control over the underlying infrastructure or virtual machine hosting your application. However, you can configure the hosting environment by setting the configuration variables for your application to some extent.

The same virtual machine can host two different applications running on a PaaS-based cloud service in isolation.

Platform-as-a-Service is cheaper than Infrastructure-as-a-Service.

Software-as-a-Service

In the case of Software-as-a-Service, you build your application and host it on the cloud. End users can use an instance of your application by paying a subscription fee for using the application features. You can bill the end users on the number of features and functionalities they choose to use. The end users can configure the data and security for their application instance.

Microsoft 365, Microsoft Dynamics 365, and Netflix are examples of Software-as-a-Service.

Serverless Computing

In the case of serverless computing, you get billed only when the service hosting your code executes. You do not get charged when the service is idle and not doing any job. You can build your application and host it on the serverless service without concern for the underlying hosting infrastructure. The cloud vendor manages the hosting infrastructure, and you have no control over your application's infrastructure. The serverless services scale on their own. You need not set any scale settings. The services will scale automatically, and new service instances will get added or deleted based on the need. You have no control over how the service scales.

Serverless computing is a cheaper hosting option than all the service types we have discussed, if you design it accurately. You get charged for the computing and resources consumed by each service instance. You must design your cloud solution to control the number of service instances that get provisioned when the service scales.

Note   Although serverless computing appears to be the same as Platform-as-a-Service, they are different in some respects. In both cases, you do not have any control over the underlying hosting infrastructure. However, in the case of PaaS, you can control the scaling behavior of the application by setting the manual or automatic scale settings. In the case of serverless services, you do not have any control over how the services scale. In the case of PaaS, your billing starts as soon as you have provisioned the service. You get charged even if the service is idle. However, in the case of serverless services, you get billed only when the service hosting your code is doing some work. You are not billed when the service is idle in the case of serverless computing.

A Quick Tour of Azure Services

Microsoft Azure is a popular cloud choice for many global and large enterprises. It provides a wide range of cloud services suiting your application needs. Using Azure, you can build solutions that are highly reliable, secured, highly available, and fault-tolerant. Let's take a look at some of the service offerings from Azure.

Compute Services

Let us discuss the popular computing services used frequently in cloud-based solutions.

Azure Virtual Machines

Azure Virtual Machines is an IaaS offering. You can host your application on a virtual machine just like you would host it in the on-premises environment. You get greater control over the underlying hardware and the hosting environment. Once your application is ready, you need to spin up the virtual machine with your desired operating system and compute size. You then need to install the hosting software, such as Tomcat or Microsoft Internet Information Services (IIS), and all the application dependencies the application needs to run. Once you are done with these prerequisite steps, you can host your application. You can choose a virtual machine based on the compute size that meets your application needs. If your application is memory intensive, you can choose an Azure D-series, Ds-series, E-series, or M-series virtual machine SKU. If your application is compute intensive, you can choose a high-performance SKU like the H-series, HB-series, or HC-series virtual machine.

Azure App Service

Azure App Service is a PaaS offering. You can build your application using a supported programming language like C# (.NET and .NET Core), Java, PHP, Python, or one of many others, and then host the application on the App Service without concern for the underlying infrastructure. You need to spin up the App Service based on your need and select a plan that meets your computing needs. App Service creates the necessary infrastructure on which you can run your application. Your application runs in a shared environment on a virtual machine. The virtual machine hosts multiple applications, but in isolation from each other. You do not have any control over the virtual machine hosting your application. The underlying Azure platform creates the hosting environment for you, and you need to deploy your application on it. You can set the scale settings that can be either manual or automated.

Azure Functions

Azure Functions is a serverless offering. You need to build your application and host it on the Azure Function. You do not have any access to the underlying hosting environment and the infrastructure running your Function code. You get billed only when the code executes and are not charged when the Function is idle. You do not have control over how the Function scales if you use the consumption or the premium plan. New Function instances will get added or removed based on the incoming traffic load. If you use the dedicated plan, then the Function behaves like an App Service, and you can control the scaling behavior just like in the case of an App Service.

Azure Logic Apps

Azure Logic Apps is a serverless offering. It helps you integrate with a wide range of Azure services, on-premises services, and other cloud services with ease using connectors. You can build graphical workflows without having to write any code. You can trigger these workflows using triggers. Each workflow step performs an action you can configure based on your need. Azure Logic Apps helps you build enterprise-grade integration solutions.

Azure Kubernetes Service

Azure Kubernetes Service (AKS) is managed Kubernetes on Azure that helps you spin up the Kubernetes control plane along with the worker nodes, known as virtual machine scale sets. You can manage the worker nodes, but you do not have any control over the control plane. The underlying Azure platform manages the control plane. The application containers run inside the pods in the worker nodes.

You can scale your application running on the Azure Kubernetes Cluster by adding the number of nodes or pods. Scaling the nodes can be challenging, as the virtual machines may take some time to get added to the virtual machine scale set. To mitigate this challenge, you can use Azure Container Instances as serverless nodes. Azure Container Instances is a container-based offering on Azure and can run a single container.

You can also run Azure Functions inside the Azure Kubernetes Service cluster and bring in serverless capability to the Azure Kubernetes Service by using Kubernetes Event-Driven Autoscaling (KEDA).

Data Services

Now let's discuss the Azure-based data services that are most frequently used.

Azure Storage Account

Azure Storage Account provides blobs, files, queues, and tables to store data. You can use the blob storage to keep blob files like images, text files, videos, and many more types. You can build distributed applications leveraging queues. The distributed application components can communicate using the queues. The sender application component can ingest messages in the queue that the receiver application component can receive and process. Tables store semi-structured data as key/value pairs. Azure Files helps you keep and organize folders and files in a share. You can work with the files using the standard SMB or NFS protocol or HTTP requests. Data stored in the Storage Account is secured using Access Keys.

Azure Data Lake

The first generation of Azure Data Lake was based on HDFS file systems running on Hadoop clusters. Hadoop clusters are expensive. The blob storage in the Azure Storage

Account hosts the second-generation Azure Data Lake. The blob storage is robust enough to support the storage of a huge amount of unstructured data, and you can process the data easily and quickly. You can create a hierarchical folder structure and keep your data.

Azure SQL

Azure SQL is PaaS-based Microsoft SQL Server offering on Azure. You need not own and manage a SQL server to host the SQL database. You can provision the Azure SQL service, and the underlying Azure platform will spin up a SQL Server and give you a database where you can host your data. Azure SQL does not support all features of Microsoft SQL Server, like SQL Server Integration Services (SSIS) and SQL Server Reporting Services (SSRS).

Azure Data Factory

Azure Data Factory helps you connect with different data stores on Azure, on-premises, or in other clouds and process the data. It provides a wide range of connectors with which you can connect to different data stores. You can build pipelines that can get the data from a data store, process it, and keep the processed data in another data store on Azure, on-premises, or in other clouds. You can schedule the pipelines to process the data or trigger the pipelines based on the need.

Azure Synapse

Azure Synapse is a Datawarehouse on Azure. You can perform data integration, data analytics and data visualization, and warehousing of your data. You can work with the Datawarehouse using either Scala, Python, SQL, .NET, or Java. Azure Synapse supports either a SQL or Spark analytics runtime that you can leverage to perform analytics on the big data. You can build pipelines and execute them to perform data processing on a vast amount of data and derive insights from complex datasets. You can also leverage Databricks to process and analyze data managed by Azure Synapse. Azure Synapse provides capabilities to build machine learning solutions based on big data.

Artificial Intelligence– and Machine Learning–Based Services

Now let's discuss the popular offerings on Azure that you can leverage to build complex artificial intelligence– and machine learning–based solutions.

Azure Cognitive Services

Azure Cognitive Services helps you build artificial intelligence solutions easily without needing to build any AI models. Microsoft has already developed these models and hosts them on Azure. You consume these services using REST APIs or client library SDKs. You can perform complex activities like extracting meaningful information from videos and images, analyzing text sentiments and languages, face detection, speech to text and vice versa, language translation, and many more complex AI use cases.

Azure Machine Learning

Azure Machine Learning helps you build and expose custom machine learning models that you can use across your applications. It provides rich capabilities and predefined ML models that you can use to author workflows for your ML model. You need not write much code to build the models. Using Azure Machine Learning Studio, you can use drag-and-drop features to build and train your models.

Azure Bot Service

You can build conversational applications or bots using Azure Bot Framework and host them on Azure Bot Service. You can leverage Azure Cognitive Services and Azure Machine Learning to build intelligent bots that can also process natural user languages.

Other Services

Let's discuss a few other Azure Services we can use in our Azure solutions.

Azure API Management

You can build and host APIs on Azure Functions, Azure App Service, Azure Kubernetes Service, or any other service on Azure. Using Azure API Management, you can manage the hosted APIs. You can set Cross-Origin Resource Sharing (CORS) rules, perform redirection, tweak headers, check for valid access, and conduct many other such API management activities using these services. You can inspect and act on the requests and responses for the APIs.

Azure Active Directory

Azure Active Directory (Azure AD) is an identity and access management offering on Azure. You can perform authentication, authorization, and single sign-on (SSO) for your applications running on Azure, on-premises, or on other clouds. You can create users and roles in Azure AD and even join the on-premises domain controller to Azure AD to integrate on-premises users to Azure. You need not set up any additional infrastructure to handle authentication and authorization for your applications. You need to configure your applications to use Azure AD for authentication and authorization purpose.

Azure Monitor

Azure Monitor helps you collect logs and performance metrics for your application and infrastructure on Azure, on-premises, or on other clouds. You can analyze these logs and metrics for debugging purposes or gather additional insights. You can set performance alerts on the logs and metrics to notify the user if the application fails or performance counters fall below the expected level. Azure Monitor also integrates with IT Service Management (ITSM) tools like ServiceNow and automatically logs tickets in case of performance issues and failures.

Summary

In this chapter, you learned about the basic cloud concepts and the cloud deployment models. We explored the details of the public cloud, private cloud, and hybrid cloud deployment models. We also covered the available cloud service types, including Infrastructure-as-a-Service (IaaS), Platform-as-a-Service (PaaS), and Software-as-a-Service (SaaS), and the concept of serverless computing. We wrapped up by surveying several popular Azure services at a very high level.

In the next chapter, you will learn how to build a Web API that can send messages to Azure Service Bus Queue.

CHAPTER 2

Build a Web API to Send Messages to Azure Service Bus

In the previous chapter, we briefly discussed key Azure services that are used to build resilient, scalable, and secure cloud native solutions. Many of these solutions leverage the power of message brokers to enable inter-application or service communication in an asynchronous manner. There are many such messaging systems available, including Apache Kafka, RabbitMQ, Azure Service Bus, ActiveMQ, and Amazon MQ. The focus of this chapter is to build decoupled solutions using Azure Service Bus, which is the enterprise-grade messaging solution offered by Microsoft Azure.

We will explore the key concepts and features of Azure Service Bus by building solutions using ASP.NET Core Web API for a fictional dental clinic to schedule appointment notifications for patients in a Service Bus Queue. The solution will be able to schedule a message for a future date as well as cancel it if the message has not been enqueued or has not been processed yet.

In this chapter, we will explore the following topics:

- Introduction to Azure Service Bus

- Features of Azure Service Bus

- Getting started with Azure Service Bus: Queue and Topic

- Provision an Azure Service Bus instance

- Build an ASP.NET 6 Web API to send messages to Azure Service Bus Queue

© Ashirwad Satapathi and Abhishek Mishra 2023
A. Satapathi and A. Mishra, *Developing Cloud-Native Solutions with Microsoft Azure and .NET*,
https://doi.org/10.1007/978-1-4842-9004-0_2

After studying this chapter, you should have a solid grasp of the fundamentals of Azure Service Bus, as well as cloud services on Azure.

Introduction to Azure Service Bus

Enterprise messaging software, also known as message-oriented middleware, has been in existence since the late 1980s. Message-oriented middleware is a concept that involves the passing of data between applications using a communication channel that delivers messages from the sender to the receiver. These messages are transferred in an asynchronous manner between the sender and receiver using a message broker. These kinds of messaging systems help in decoupling applications and keeping the sender and receiver anonymous from each other. Azure Service Bus is one such messaging solution offered by Microsoft Azure as part of its cloud suite.

Azure Service Bus is an enterprise-grade, multitenant cloud messaging service of Microsoft Azure. It is a Platform-as-a-Service (PaaS) offering of Azure and is fully managed by Microsoft. As developers, we don't need to worry about tasks such as handling of backups or hardware failures for the services because Azure takes care of it for us. Azure Service Bus supports point-to-point message delivery with Queues and message broadcasting using the publisher-subscriber model with Topics. In a later section of the chapter, we are going to briefly discuss Azure Service Bus Queues and Topics.

Azure Service Bus allows applications to interact or transfer data with each other using messages. It provides an excellent mechanism to build decoupled solutions and make them more scalable, reliable, and resilient. The producer should not be impacted due to the unavailability of the consumer. It supports data in different formats, such as JSON, XML, plain text, and so on, and provides client libraries in different languages to build solutions using it. Apart from that, it offers various advanced features such as message deferral, duplicate detection, and auto-forwarding, to name a few.

When to Use Azure Service Bus

There are various scenarios in which using Azure Service Bus would be appropriate and helpful for the overall function of our application as well as the architecture of the system. Some of them are listed here:

- Increasing scalability of the application

- Replacing RPCs

- Integrating heterogeneous applications

- Reducing the coupling between applications

There are many additional scenarios where Azure Service Bus can be handy to use. Let's discuss how Service Bus can help in the case of heterogeneous applications.

Suppose we have two applications, Application A and Application B. Application A is written in Java while Application B is written in Python. To fulfill some requirements, we want to establish communication between these applications.

Normally, this would be really difficult to do between two applications written in different languages unless you have a common medium of communication between them.

Service Bus helps us do so without a lot of trouble. Service Bus provides clients for multiple languages, including .Net, Python, Ruby, and many more, which helps in sending messages between heterogeneous applications via its message broker.

Features of Azure Service Bus

The following are some of key features of Azure Service Bus:

- Message filtering

- Message sessions

- Message auto-forwarding

- Duplicate detection

- Message expiration

- Message deferral

- Message batching

Let's explore each of these features in detail.

Message Filtering

Azure Service Bus supports message filtering with Topics. It is supported with queues. You can configure subscription rules for Azure Service Bus Topics to deliver messages categorically to different subscribers as per the business requirements. A subscription rule can consist of filter condition or actions. To learn more about the message filtering feature of Azure Service Bus, take a look at `https://docs.microsoft.com/en-us/azure/service-bus-messaging/topic-filters`.

Message Sessions

Azure Service Bus provides a guaranteed reliable delivery of related messages in a particular sequence to the receiver/subscriber application by using message sessions. To leverage this feature, you will have to enable sessions while creating queues/topics. While sending a message to the queue/topic as part of a session, the sender application will also have to set the session ID property. This will help the receiver application to distinguish if a particular message is associated with a particular session or not. To learn more about message sessions of Azure Service Bus, check out `https://docs.microsoft.com/en-us/azure/service-bus-messaging/message-sessions`.

Message Auto-forwarding

Azure Service Bus provides a way to send messages from a particular queue or subscription to another queue or topic within the namespace for the purpose of chaining them. Any messages coming to our source queue/subscription will be removed and moved to the destination queue/topic automatically.

Duplicate Detection

In certain scenarios, a message sent by the sender application may not get delivered within a certain time period, because of which the sender application might resend the message to the service bus queue to be picked up by the receiver application for further processing. Now our receiver application will be processing the same message twice because of the message being resent by the sender. To remove such duplicate messages, Azure Service Bus provides a duplicate detection feature that discards the duplicate message for us.

Message Expiration

While solving real-world problems, we often come across scenarios where the time to live of a message is crucial for the sanity of the message. Some messages can be of no value after a certain threshold. For example, if a notification of an EMI payment to the customer is sent after the due date, it does not add any business value and may result in a bad customer experience. To avoid such scenarios, Azure Service Bus provides a feature to define the maximum time to live of messages for a queue or topic while we are provisioning them.

Message Deferral

Whenever you send a message to a message broker, it gets enqueued in a queue or topic and is available for the receiver application to pick up the message and process it further. But in some scenarios where you might want to schedule a message to be processed at a later date. Azure Service Bus provides a message deferral mechanism to address this scenario. You can schedule a message to be sent at a future date in the queue and the message will only get queued once the scheduled date has come. We are going on a use case for this feature and implement it later in the chapter.

Message Batching

Azure Service Bus provides a mechanism to batch a certain number of messages and send them in a batch to the receiver application to process at one go, which results in better utilization of resources at the receiver's end.

Queues, Topics, and Namespaces

In this section, we are going to discuss the following key components of Azure Service Bus:

- Queues
- Topics
- Namespaces

Queues

Azure Service Bus Queue enables applications to interact with each other using point-to-point messaging. In the point-to-point messaging style, we send messages in a synchronous as well as asynchronous manner using Queues. The message, sent by the sender application, is sent to the receiver application using the queue. Each message is delivered to the queue only once to a single receiver application. If a receiver is not available to process the message, the message stays in the queue until the configured time to live of the message expires.

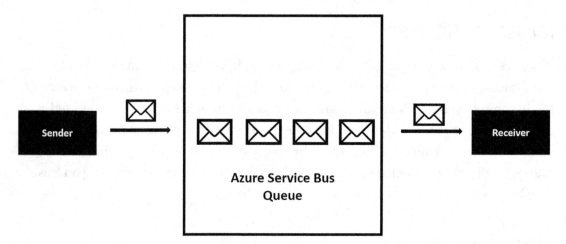

Figure 2-1. *Azure Service Bus Queue*

Topics

Azure Service Bus Topics enables applications to interact with each other using the publisher-subscriber model. In the publisher-subscriber messaging style, sender applications are called *publishers* and receiver applications are called *subscribers*. Here, we use Topics to convey the messages among these sender and receiver applications. A topic can consist of multiple subscriptions. To receive messages, receiver applications need to subscribe to a subscription. Once receivers are registered to the subscription of the topic, every time a message is sent by the sender, all the receivers receive the messages.

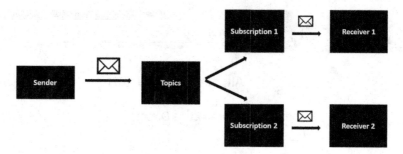

Figure 2-2. *Azure Service Bus Topic*

Namespaces

In Azure Service Bus, Namespaces acts as a logical container for all the queues and topics. To create any queues or topics in Azure Service Bus, you first have to provision an Azure Service Bus Namespace. The number of queues or topics that you can have in a namespace is dependent on the pricing tier that you select while provisioning the namespace.

Working with Azure Service Bus

Now that you have a general understanding of what Azure Service Bus is and what are its key features and components, let's create an Azure Service Bus Queue instance in Azure Portal, a simple message sender application, and a web API to schedule appointments for our fictional dental clinic.

Create an Azure Service Bus Namespace in Azure Portal

Go to the Microsoft Azure portal and search for **Service Bus** in the search box. Click **Service Bus** as shown in Figure 2-3.

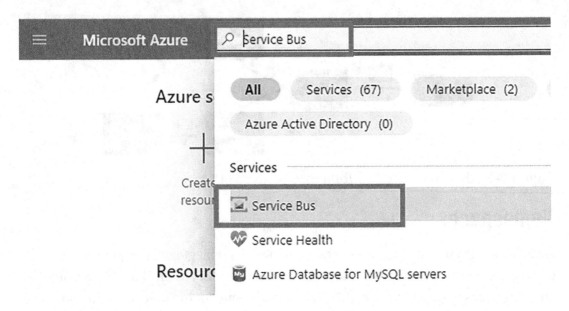

Figure 2-3. *Search for Service Bus*

Click **Create** to provision a new Service Bus namespace, as shown in Figure 2-4.

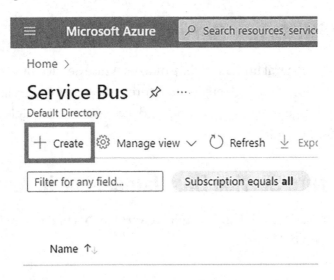

Figure 2-4. *Click Create*

Select the Azure subscription and resource group name from the Subscription and Resource group drop-down lists, respectively, as shown in Figure 2-5. Then provide the namespace name, location, and pricing tier in the corresponding fields. The namespace name needs to be unique globally. After filling in all the required information, click **Review + create**.

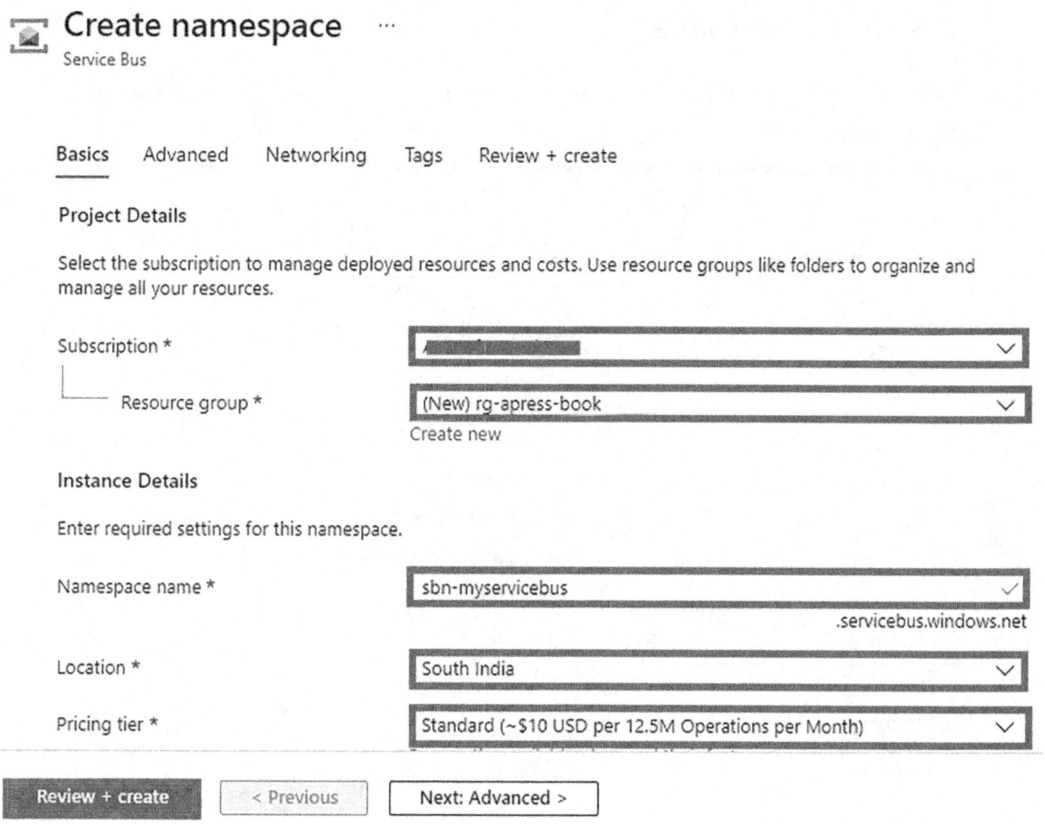

Create namespace ...

Service Bus

Basics   Advanced   Networking   Tags   Review + create

Project Details

Select the subscription to manage deployed resources and costs. Use resource groups like folders to organize and manage all your resources.

Subscription *

Resource group *
(New) rg-apress-book
Create new

Instance Details

Enter required settings for this namespace.

Namespace name *
sbn-myservicebus

.servicebus.windows.net

Location *
South India

Pricing tier *
Standard (~$10 USD per 12.5M Operations per Month)

Review + create   < Previous   Next: Advanced >

Figure 2-5. *Click Review + create*

A validation check will be done in the current page with all the data that you have provided. If all the data is valid (see Figure 2-6), then you will be able to create the namespace. If there was any error, then the particular error will be highlighted in this screen. Once the validation is successful, click **Create**.

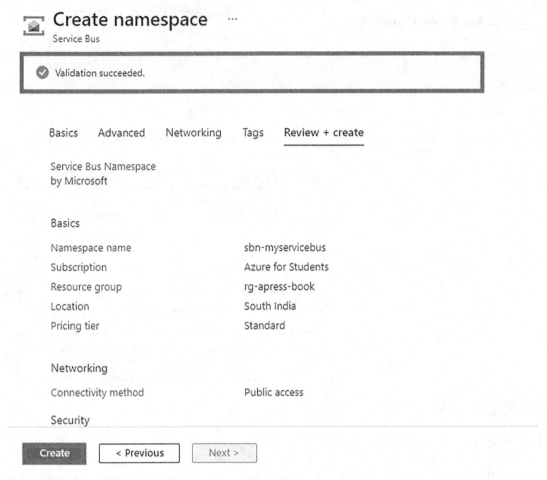

Figure 2-6. *Click Create*

You will be redirected to a page similar to Figure 2-7 that shows the status of the provisioning of your Service Bus namespace. Once the namespace has been created, click **Go to resource**.

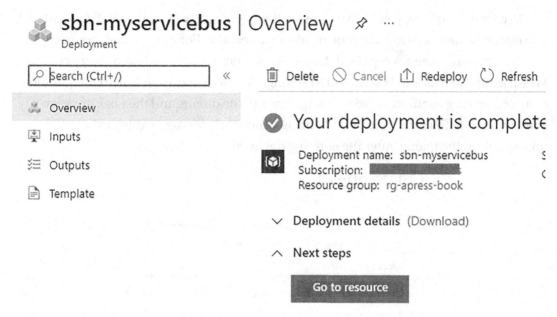

Figure 2-7. *Click Go to resource*

Create an Azure Service Bus Namespace in Azure Portal

To create an Azure Service Queue inside your namespace, click **+ Queue** as highlighted in Figure 2-8.

Figure 2-8. *Click + Queue*

To create the queue, you have to provide the queue name, as shown in Figure 2-9. The queue name needs to be unique inside a namespace. For purposes of this example, use the name **myqueue**. Keep the defaults for the Max queue size, Max delivery count, Message time to live, and Lock duration settings. The Message time to live configuration defines how long an unprocessed message stays in the queue, and the Lock duration configuration defines the time period during which the message is going to be unavailable in the queue. After the entering the details, click **Create**.

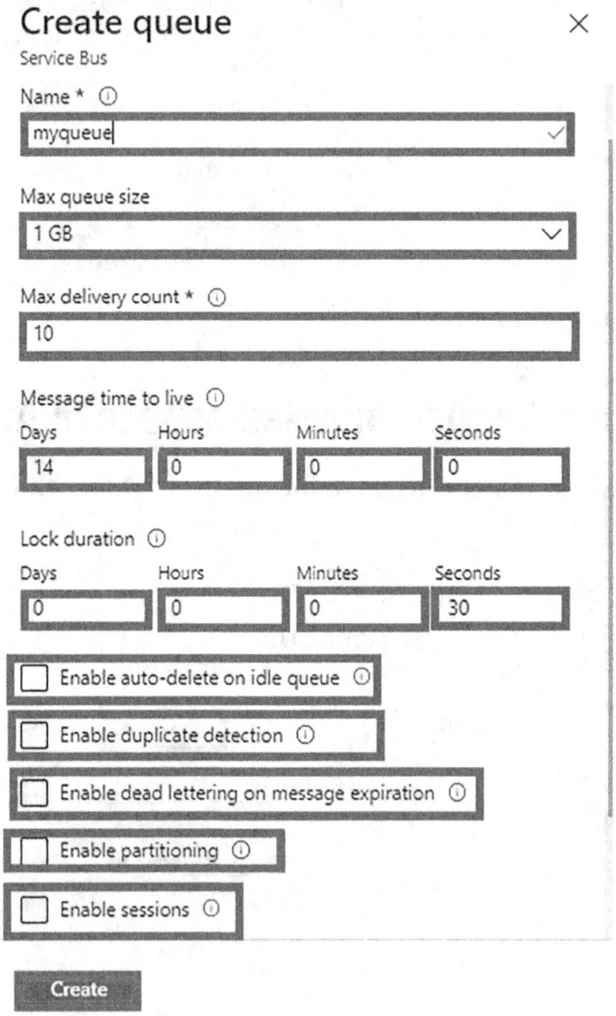

Figure 2-9. Click Create

This creates a Queue inside your Service Bus Namespace. You can view it by clicking **Queues** in the Entities section on the left side of the screen, as shown in Figure 2-10. You will see the list of all the queues present inside the namespace. Currently, you have just one queue, myqueue, as shown on the right in Figure 2-10.

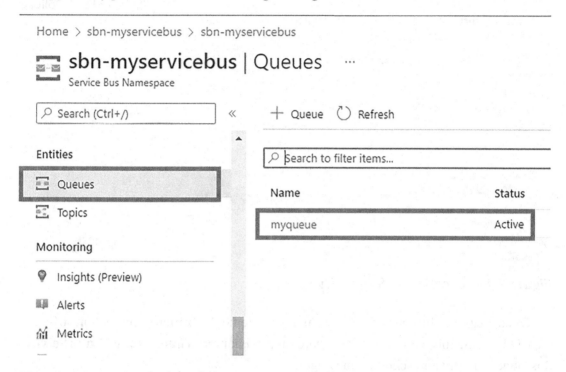

Figure 2-10. *View the list of queues*

Create an SAS Policy to Access the Azure Service Bus Namespace

To access or interact with Azure Service Bus Queues or Topics from our application, we need to authenticate our application's request to the service bus. This can be done in different ways, such as using Azure Active Directory (Azure AD)–based authentication or SAS policies. For the purpose of this book, we will be using SAS policies. For enterprise applications, it is recommended to use Azure AD–based authentication or managed identity if the applications are deployed inside Azure in an Azure Function or App Service by providing necessary role-based access control (RBAC) permissions to the service bus instance.

To create an SAS policy, click **Shared access policies** in the Settings section, as shown in Figure 2-11, and then click **Add** to add a new policy. Enter the policy name in the Policy name box on the right and define the scope of this policy. Following the principle to provide least privilege, click the **Send** check box to assign this policy only the ability to send messages to service bus queues or topics present inside our namespace, and then click **Create**.

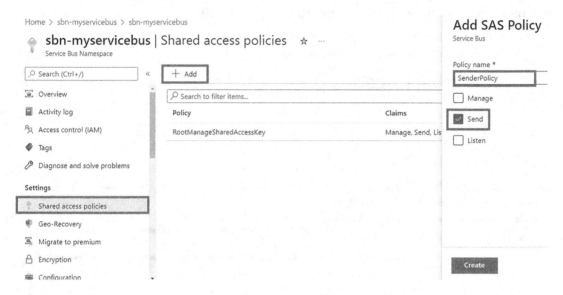

Figure 2-11. *Creating an SAS policy*

Once the policy has been created, you need to fetch the primary connection string. We will be using this connection string later in this chapter to interact with Azure Service Bus Queue to send and schedule messages.

Figure 2-12. *Getting the primary connection string*

Create a Console App to Send Messages to Azure Service Bus Queue

Now that you have provisioned your Azure Service Bus Queue and have fetched the connection string, you are ready to start developing a console app to send messages to Service Bus Queue. Create a Console application project in the IDE of your choice and open the package manager console. Run the following command to install the `Azure.Messaging.ServiceBus` NuGet package:

```
Install-Package Azure.Messaging.ServiceBus
```

This is the Azure software development kit (SDK) for ServiceBus, which allows you to interact with Azure ServiceBus. Once the package has been installed, go to `program.cs` and add the following namespace:

```
using System.Threading.Tasks;
using Azure.Messaging.ServiceBus;
```

Next, create a variable to store the connection string from the SAS policy that you created in the previous section:

```
const string connectionString = "provide-your-connection-string";
```

Create a variable to store the queue name that you created earlier in the chapter:

```
const string queueName = "provide-your-queue-name";
```

Now that you have the connection string and queue name, create the service bus client instances that you need to send messages to the service bus:

```
static ServiceBusClient serviceBusClient = new ServiceBusClient(connecti
onString);
static ServiceBusSender serviceBusSender = serviceBusClient.
CreateSender(queueName);
```

Replace the code present in the main method with the following code snippet, which creates an instance of `ServiceBusBatchMessage` to store ten messages and then uses the `SendMessageAsync` method of `ServiceBusSender` to send the messages to the service bus:

```
// create a batch
using ServiceBusMessageBatch messageBatch = await serviceBusSender.
CreateMessageBatchAsync();
```

```
//Add 10 messages to the messageBatch
for (int i = 1; i <= 10; i++)
{
    // try to add a message to the batch
    if (!messageBatch.TryAddMessage(new ServiceBusMessage($"Message {i}")))
        {
            // if it is too large for the batch
            throw new Exception($"The message {i} is too large to fit in the
            batch.");
        }
}
// Use the serviceBusSender client to send the batch of messages to the
Service Bus queue
await serviceBusSender.SendMessagesAsync(messageBatch);
Console.WriteLine($"A batch of 10 messages has been published to the
queue.");
Console.ReadLine();
// closing the connections and network resources
await serviceBusSender.DisposeAsync();
await serviceBusClient.DisposeAsync();
```

Listing 2-1 shows the complete code for the sender console application.

Listing 2-1. Program.cs

```
using Azure.Messaging.ServiceBus;

namespace ServiceBusConsole
{
    internal class Program
    {
        const string connectionString = "provide-your-connection-string";
        const string queueName = "provide-your-queue-name";
        // Creates the clients, we need to send messages to Azure
        Service Bus
        static ServiceBusClient serviceBusClient = new ServiceBusClient(con
        nectionString);
```

```
static ServiceBusSender serviceBusSender = serviceBusClient.
CreateSender(queueName);
static async Task Main()
{

    // create a batch
    using ServiceBusMessageBatch messageBatch = await
    serviceBusSender.CreateMessageBatchAsync();

    for (int i = 1; i <= 10; i++)
    {
        // try adding a message to the batch
        if (!messageBatch.TryAddMessage(new
        ServiceBusMessage($"Message {i}")))
        {
            // if it is too large for the batch
            throw new Exception($"The message {i} is too large to
            fit in the batch.");
        }
    }
    // Use the producer client to send the batch of messages to the
    Service Bus queue
    await serviceBusSender.SendMessagesAsync(messageBatch);
    Console.WriteLine($"A batch of 10 messages has been published
    to the queue.");
    Console.ReadLine();
        // closing the connections and network resources
    await serviceBusSender.DisposeAsync();
    await serviceBusClient.DisposeAsync();
    }
}
}
```

Now run your console app. Once the application has executed, go to the queue in the Azure portal. Figure 2-13 shows that ten messages were enqueued in the queue.

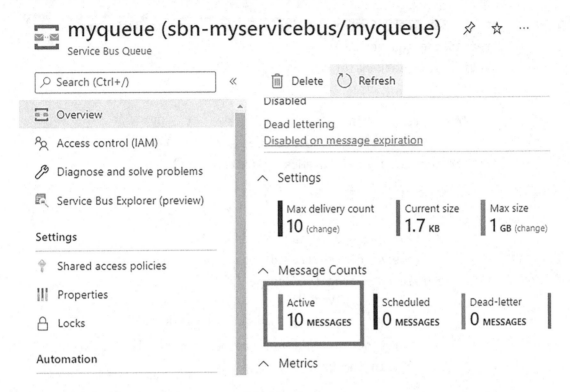

Figure 2-13. *Ten messages were added to the queue*

Create a Web API to Schedule Messages in Azure Service Bus Queue

In the previous section, you learned ways to send messages to the Azure Service Bus queue from your console application. This section focuses on solving the need of a fictional dental clinic to send appointment notifications to its patients. The dental clinic currently has a worker process in place that picks up messages from the service bus queue and processes them to send notifications. Currently, the worker process is processing any messages that are available in the queue, but the clinic doesn't want the worker to send the notification until the right time. The notifications should be sent only three hours before the appointment time. Thus, the message cannot be sent to the queue directly. To solve this problem, we need to build a solution to schedule a message—an appointment reminder in this case—three hours before the appointment time so that the message enqueues in the queue at the scheduled time and then the worker process picks it up to process it and sends the notification to the patient.

We will be building an ASP.NET Core Web API to solve this problem by scheduling messages in the service bus queue by using the message deferral feature of Azure Service Bus. Our web API will provide two essential features: schedule a message to the service bus queue and cancel a scheduled message. There can be business scenarios where a patient can cancel a scheduled appointment and reschedule it for a future date. In such scenarios, the cancel feature will be essential, as we will have to cancel the existing scheduled message because it is no longer valid and may cause a bad customer experience.

As we have covered the business requirement, let's start building our web API. Open Visual Studio 2022 and click **Create a new project**, as shown in Figure 2-14.

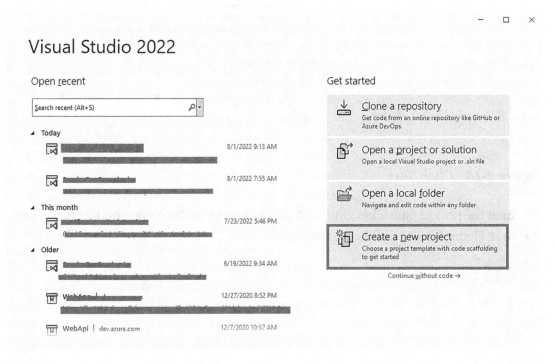

Figure 2-14. *Creating a new project*

Select the **ASP.NET Core Web API** project template, as shown in Figure 2-15, and click **Next**.

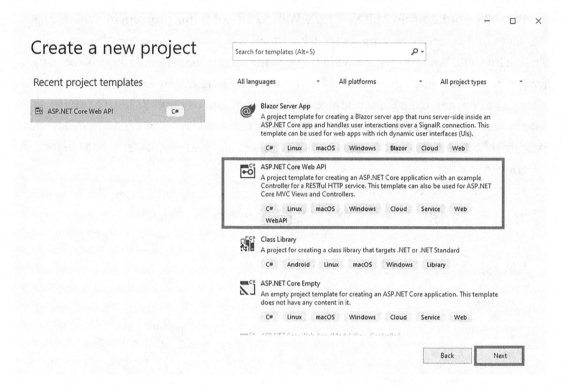

Figure 2-15. *Click Next*

Enter the project name, location, and solution name in the corresponding fields, as shown in Figure 2-16. Click **Next** to continue.

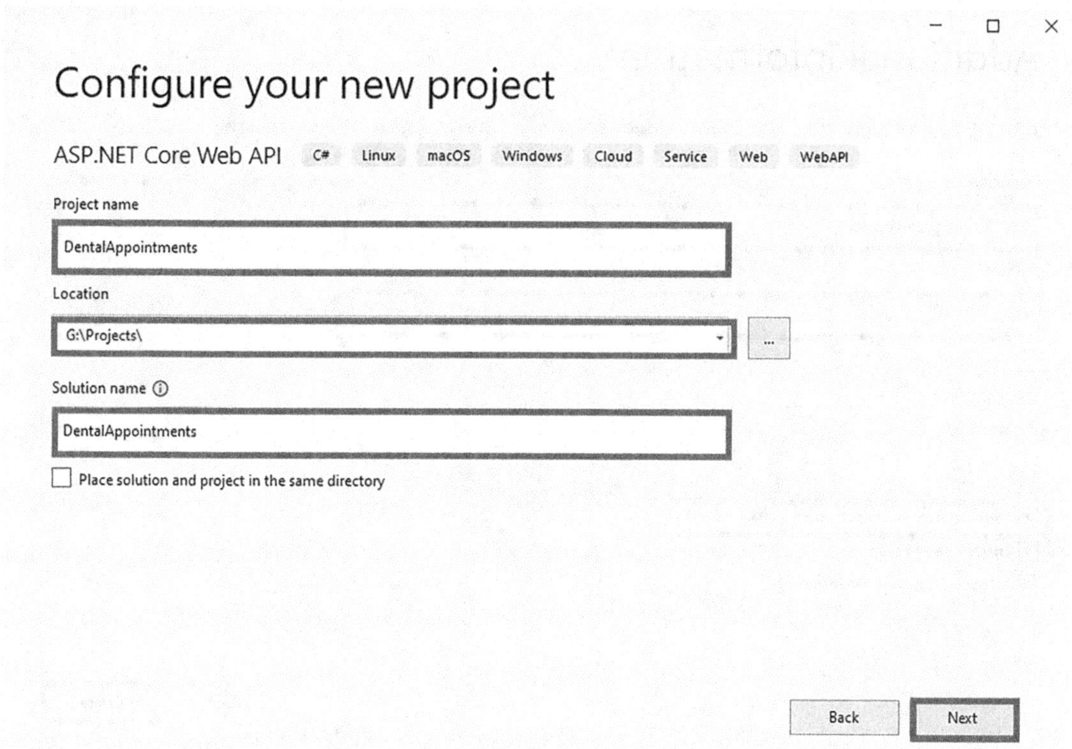

Figure 2-16. *Enter the project name, location, and solution name*

Now check the **Use controllers** check box, as we don't want to use minimal APIs for the project, and keep the other options as shown in Figure 2-17. Click **Create** to create our web API project.

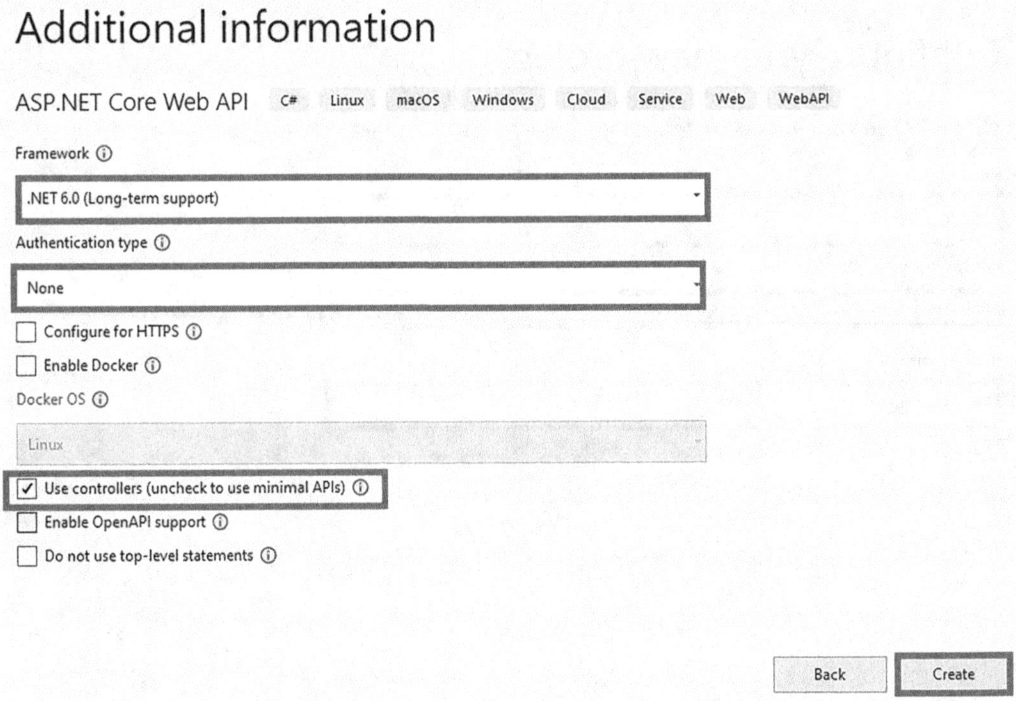

Additional information

ASP.NET Core Web API   C#   Linux   macOS   Windows   Cloud   Service   Web   WebAPI

Framework ⓘ

```
.NET 6.0 (Long-term support)                                    ▾
```

Authentication type ⓘ

```
None                                                           ▾
```

☐ Configure for HTTPS ⓘ

☐ Enable Docker ⓘ

Docker OS ⓘ

```
Linux
```

☑ Use controllers (uncheck to use minimal APIs) ⓘ

☐ Enable OpenAPI support ⓘ

☐ Do not use top-level statements ⓘ

Back   Create

Figure 2-17. *Click Create*

Visual Studio will create a sample API project for us that contains a simple WeatherForecastController, which returns randomly generated weather data to the client. Remove the WeatherForecastController.cs and WeatherForecast.cs files from our project, because we don't need them.

Open the Package Manager Console and run the following command to install the NuGet packages Azure.Messaging.ServiceBus, Microsoft.Extensions.Azure, and Newtonsoft.Json in our project. As discussed earlier in the chapter, Azure.Messaging. ServiceBus is used to communicate with Service Bus. Microsoft.Extensions.Azure is required to inject our Azure Clients inside our dependency container. Newtonsoft.Json will be used for serialization and deserialization of objects.

```
Install-Package Azure.Messaging.ServiceBus
Install-Package Microsoft.Extensions.Azure
Install-Package Newtonsoft.Json
```

Once you have installed the NuGet packages, go to the `appsettings.json` file of our project and add the following key/value pairs. We need to store the service bus connection string in `ServiceBusConn`, our queue name in `queueName`, and the duration before which the message should get scheduled in `enqueueDifference`.

```
"ServiceBusConn": "provide-your-connection-string",
"queueName": "provide-your-queue-name",
"enqueueDifference": -3
```

Open the `program.cs` file and the following namespace:

```
using Microsoft.Extensions.Azure;
```

Now, add the following code in `program.cs` to inject the service bus client in the dependency container of our project. We are using `serviceBusConn` stored in our `appsettings.json` file to create our `ServiceBusClient`.

```
builder.Services.AddAzureClients(
    client => client.AddServiceBusClient(builder.Configuration["service
    BusConn"])
    );
```

For the time being, we are done with the `program.cs` file of our project. Let's create two folders in our project: `Business` and `Models`. The `Business` folder will contain our interface and the classes implementing them. The `Models` folder will contain the classes of our data models.

After creating both folders, create a class called `Appointment.cs` in the `Models` folder and paste the following code. This class represents the appointment data that we receive in the request payload. We have used data annotations to mark the necessary fields as required.

```
public class Appointment
    {
        [Required]
        public int AppointmentId { get; set; }
        [Required]
        public int PatientId { get; set; }
        [Required]
        public string? PatientName { get; set; }
        [Required]
        public string? PatientEmail { get; set; }
```

```
    [Required]
    public int CaretakerId { get; set; }
    [Required]
    public DateTime ScheduledAt { get; set; }
}
```

Now that our model is ready, create an interface called `INotificationBusiness.cs` in the `Business` folder and add the method definitions. As you can see in the following code snippet, our interface contains two method definitions: `ScheduleAppointmentNotification` and `CancelAppointmentNotification`. The `ScheduleAppointmentNotification` method will be responsible for taking the appointment data coming from the request payload and scheduling it as a message for a future date in the service bus queue. The `CancelAppointmentNotification` method is responsible for canceling a scheduled message in the service queue. It takes the `sequenceNumber` as a parameter (i.e., `messageSequenceNumber`) and cancels the scheduled message.

```
public interface INotificationBusiness
    {
        public Task<long> ScheduleAppointmentNotification(Appointment
        appointment);
        public Task CancelAppointmentNotification(long id);
    }
```

Now that you know what each of the methods is designed to perform, create a class called `NotificationBusiness.cs` to implement the `INotificationBusiness` interface. Before implementing the interface, add the following properties:

```
public IConfiguration _configuration { get; set; }
public ServiceBusClient _serviceBusClient { get; set; }
public ServiceBusSender _serviceBusSender { get; set; }
```

Now, instantiate the properties by using constructor injection. Replace your constructor with the following code:

```
public NotificationBusiness(ServiceBusClient serviceBusClient,
IConfiguration configuration)
        {
            _configuration = configuration;
```

```
    _serviceBusClient = serviceBusClient;
    _serviceBusSender = _serviceBusClient.CreateSender(_
    configuration.GetValue<String>("queueName"));

}
```

In the preceding code snippet, we are leveraging the `ServiceBusClient` that we had injected in the DI container in our `program.cs` file and we are using it to instantiate the `_serviceBusSender` client to interact with the Azure Service Bus Queue whose name is stored with the key name as queueName in our `appsetting.json` file.

Now let's implement the methods of the `INotificationBusiness` interface in the class. Let's add the following code snippet to implement the methods.

The `ScheduleAppointmentNotification` converts the `appointment` object coming in the parameter of the method to a `string` type and then converts it into a service bus message. Then we calculate the time when we want to schedule it by subtracting three hours from the value passed in the `ScheduledAt` property of our `appointment` object in the parameter of our method and store it in the `enqueueTime` variable. It might be confusing at first glance when you see that enqueueTime will have three hours subtracted while we are using the `AddHours` method. It is happening as such because the value of enqueueDifference in our `appsettings.json` file is -3. We then use the `ScheduleMessageAsync` method of the `ServiceBusSender` client to schedule the message by passing our `serviceBusMessage` and `enqueueTime` as parameters. This method returns the sequence number of the scheduled message in the service bus queue.

Add the following code as the implementation for the `ScheduleAppointmentNotification` method in our `NotificationBusiness` class:

```
public async Task<long> ScheduleAppointmentNotification(Appointment
appointment)
{
//Serialize the appointment object
String serializedContent = JsonConvert.SerializeObject(appointment);
//Create a service bus message which contains the serialized
appointment data
ServiceBusMessage serviceBusMessage = new ServiceBusMessage(serialize
dContent);

var enqueueTime = appointment.ScheduledAt.AddHours(_configuration.GetValue<
int>("enqueueDifference"));
```

37

```
//Schedules the message in the service bus queue
var messageSequenceNumber = await _serviceBusSender
            .ScheduleMessageAsync(serviceBusMessage, enqueueTime);
//Returns the message sequence number of the scheduled message in service
bus queue
return messageSequenceNumber;
}
```

The CancelAppointmentNotification method takes a long value
(i.e., messageSequenceNumber) as a parameter and then uses the
CancelScheduledMessageAsync method of the serviceBusSender client to cancel
the method.

Add the following code as the implementation for the
CancelAppointmentNotification method in our NotificationBusiness class:

```
public async Task CancelAppointmentNotification(long messageSequenceNumber)
{
//Cancels a message
await _serviceBusSender.CancelScheduledMessageAsync(messageSequenceNumber);
}
```

As we have added the implementation of both the methods defined in our interface,
let's go to our program.cs file and add a singleton service in our DI container by adding
the following code snippet:

```
builder.Services.AddSingleton<INotificationBusiness,
NotificationBusiness>();
```

Now, let's add an empty API controller called AppointmentController.cs in the
controllers folder and then add the following constructor code in our controller to
inject the NotificationBusiness object to our _notificationBusiness property using
constructor dependency injection:

```
public INotificationBusiness _notificationBusiness { get; set; }
public AppointmentController(INotificationBusiness notificationBusiness)
      {
            _notificationBusiness = notificationBusiness;
      }
```

Let's add our actions in our AppointmentController. We are going to have two actions: ScheduledAppointmentNotificationInQueue and CancelAppointmentNotificationFromQueue.

The purpose of the ScheduledAppointmentNotificationInQueue action is to schedule a message in our service bus queue. It makes a call to the ScheduleAppointmentNotification method of our NotificationBusiness class by passing the payload coming from the request body to complete the action.

- *URL route*: http://localhost:5010/api/Appointment/ Notification/schedule

- *HTTP verb*: POST

Add the following code snippet to add the ScheduledAppointmentNotificationInQueue action in our controller:

```
[HttpPost("Notification/Schedule")]
public async Task<IActionResult> ScheduledAppointmentNotificationInQueue([F
romBody] Appointment appointment)
{
    try
    {
        long msgSequenceNumber = await _notificationBusiness.ScheduleAppoin
        tmentNotification(appointment);

        return new OkObjectResult(new { MessageSequenceNumber =
        msgSequenceNumber });
    }
    catch (Exception ex)
    {
        return StatusCode(StatusCodes.Status500InternalServerError,
        ex.Message);
    }
}
```

The purpose of the second action in our AppointmentController, CancelAppointmentNotificationFromQueue, is to cancel a scheduled message in the service bus queue by the using the messageSequenceNumber. It makes a call to the

CancelAppointmentNotification method of our NotificationBusiness class by passing the messageSequenceNumber coming in the URL to compete this action.

- *URL route*: http://localhost:5010/api/Appointment/ Notification/Cancel/{messageSequenceNumber}

- *HTTP verb*: DELETE

Add the following code snippet to add the CancelAppointmentNotificationFromQueue action in our controller:

```
[HttpDelete("Notification/Cancel/{messageSequenceNumber:long}")]
public async Task<IActionResult> CancelAppointmentNotificationFromQueue([Fr
omRoute] int messageSequenceNumber)
{
    try
    {
        if (messageSequenceNumber < 0)
        {
            eturn new BadRequestObjectResult("Invalid value of
            messageSequenceNumber");
        }
        await _notificationBusiness.CancelAppointmentNotification(messageSe
        quenceNumber);
        return new OkObjectResult("Scheduled message has been discarded.");
    }
    catch (Exception ex)
    {
        return StatusCode(StatusCodes.Status500InternalServerError,
        ex.Message);
    }

}
```

And with this our API project to schedule notifications for our fictional dental clinic is complete. Press Ctrl+F5 to build and run our project. The complete source code of this API project can be found at the following GitHub repository: https://github.com/ AshirwadSatapathi/DentalAppointments.

In the next section, we will test our API using Postman, which is an API testing tool.

Test APIs Using Postman

Now that we have developed our APIs and have run them locally, let's perform
a sanity test on the functionalities of our API. Let's open Postman and create a
collection for our requests. After creating the collection, add a request to test the
ScheduledAppointmentNotificationInQueue API. Now define the request method as
POST and define the route as http://localhost:5010/api/Appointment/Notification/
schedule and then click the **Body** tab to add the appointment information in the
payload in key/value pairs. After you add the preceding information, click **Send** to send
a request to our API. The API will now receive a request, process this information, and
schedule this message in the service bus queue. Once the message has been scheduled,
it will return a 200 response code along with the messageSequenceNumber as shown in
Figure 2-18.

Figure 2-18. Sending a request to schedule a message

We can now go to our queue in the service bus and see that a message has been scheduled, as shown in Figure 2-19.

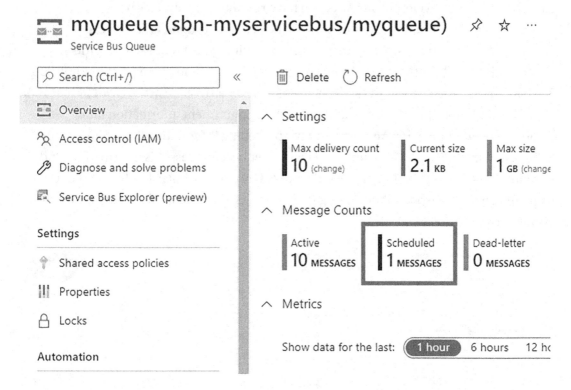

Figure 2-19. A message has been scheduled in the service bus queue

Now that we have tested the ScheduledAppointmentNotificationInQueue API, let's create a request in our collection to the CancelAppointmentNotificationFromQueue API. We will cancel the message that was scheduled as part of our test for the ScheduledAppointmentNotificationInQueue API. We will do this by passing the messageSequenceNumber of the scheduled message that was returned by our ScheduledAppointmentNotificationInQueue API as response i.e., 11. After creating a new request, define the request method as DELETE and define the API URL as http://localhost:5010/api/Appointment/Notification/Cancel/11. To test this API, just click **Send** and our CancelAppointmentNotificationFromQueue API will cancel the message and it won't be able go to the queue anymore. Upon successful execution, our API would return 200 OK as the status code with the message *Scheduled message has been discarded*, as shown in Figure 2-20.

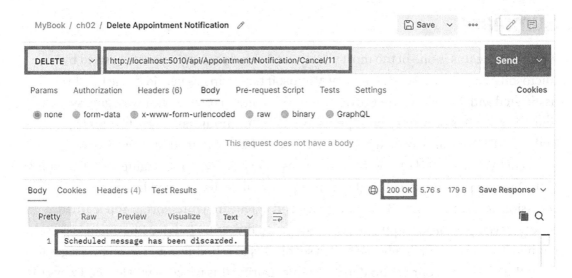

Figure 2-20. *Sending a request to cancel a scheduled message*

We can now go to our queue in the service bus and see that a message has been discarded and we have no scheduled message, as can be seen in Figure 2-21.

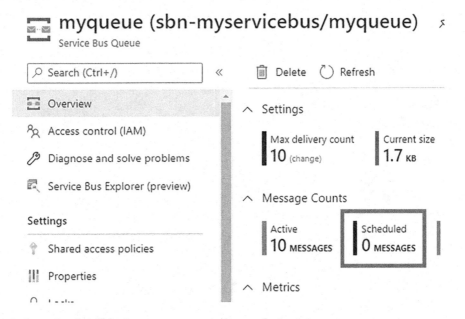

Figure 2-21. *A scheduled message was discarded*

Summary

Azure Service Bus is one of the most widely used cloud messaging services used by Microsoft Azure. It is a PaaS offering of Microsoft that helps us get rid of the hassles associated with infrastructure provisioning and maintenance of our messaging systems. Azure Service Bus provides rich support for SDKs in various languages like Node.js, Python .NET, Java, and forth. It supports protocols like Advanced Message Queuing Protocol (AMQP) and HTTP\REST. It provides us two styles of messaging: point-to-point with Queues and publish-subscribe with Topics. In this chapter, you learned ways to provision an Azure Service Bus Namespace and Queue in Azure Portal. You learned how to develop a console app to send messages to the Azure Service Bus queue using a connection string. And finally, we built a set of APIs to schedule and cancel messages to solve the problem of our fictional dental clinic. During this process, you learned ways to leverage the Azure Service Bus SDK for .NET to build applications by implementing the message deferral feature of Service Bus.

CHAPTER 3

Build a Worker Service to Process Messages from Azure Service Bus

In the previous chapter, we discussed the enterprise Azure Service Bus and its key features. We explored ways to provision a service bus instance in the Microsoft Azure portal and interact with a service bus queue using our ASP.NET Core web application. You learned about ways to send as schedule a message to the service bus queue. In this chapter, we will build upon the knowledge gained from the previous chapter and explore ways to receive and process messages from the service bus queue.

We will be exploring ways to process messages from the service bus queue by building a .NET Core Worker Service for our fictional dental clinic to send email alerts for the scheduled appointment notifications to the clinic's patients. The solution will be able to process the enqueued messages in the service bus queue and send an email alert to a patient to remind them about their scheduled appointment at our fictional dental clinic.

Structure

In this chapter, we will explore the following Azure-related topics:

- Introduction to worker services
- Build a .NET Core worker service to process messages to Azure Service Bus Queue
- Deploy the worker service to Azure WebJobs

© Ashirwad Satapathi and Abhishek Mishra 2023
A. Satapathi and A. Mishra, *Developing Cloud-Native Solutions with Microsoft Azure and .NET*,
https://doi.org/10.1007/978-1-4842-9004-0_3

Objectives

After studying this chapter, you should be able to

- Understand the fundamentals of worker services

- Deploy worker services to Azure WebJobs

Introduction to .NET Core Worker Services

Often, we come across scenarios where we would like to perform certain operations which can or cannot be memory intensive by our applications. Many times these operations don't require a user interface (UI) and are run as background services that run on a schedule or perform operations continuously. Some examples of such example can be to generate reports and send email alerts to the end users periodically or process messages from a message queue. These kinds of scenarios can be handled using background services that run either 24×7 or periodically to perform business requirements.

Along with ASP.NET Core 3.0, a new application template was introduced, the Worker Service template. This template allows us to create an out-of-the-box project to create background services with .NET Core with some boilerplate code. We can create cross-platform background services with the Worker Service template, which can be configured to run as Windows services or Linux daemons. These services can be configured to run and execute the business logic periodically over time or continuously as per the requirement.

The following are some of the scenarios where background services are helpful:

- Long-running processes

- CPU-intensive operations

- Performing scheduled tasks

- Processing messages asynchronously

Now that we have covered what the Worker Service template is and its use cases, we will explore the life-cycle methods of worker services.

Life-Cycle Methods of Worker Services

Worker classes are added as hosted services using the AddHostedService method in the program.cs class. A worker class implements the BackgroundService abstract class and the BackgroundService class implements the IHostedService interface. Any functionality that we want our worker class to perform needs to be implemented inside the ExecuteAsync method. This method is an abstract method present in the BackgroundService abstract class that is implemented by the worker class.

Apart from ExecuteAsync, there are two other methods, StartAsync and StopAsync, that can be overridden by a worker service to explicitly handle scenarios where we are concerned about activities that need to be performed at the start or end of the worker service. The BackgroundService class provides an implementation of StartAsync and StopAsync methods by default, but we can always override them as per the requirement in our respective worker class.

Problem Statement

As discussed in the previous chapter, our fictional dental clinic wants to send notifications to its customers to remind them about their upcoming appointments. As part of the work performed in the previous chapter, we are able to schedule messages in our service bus queue. But so far, we haven't been able to do anything with the messages scheduled in the service queue. We need to send email alerts to the patients of our fictional dental clinic about their scheduled appointments to solve the problem statement.

Proposed Solution

Now that you have a brief understanding of background services and have the problem statement at hand, we will be working toward designing and developing a solution to complete the requirements of our fictional dental clinic. We have completed the part of scheduling the appointments in a service bus queue in the previous chapter, but we have yet to find a solution to process these appointments scheduled as messages in the queue. There are various ways we can process the messages, like using a background service or a function app. That solves one part of our requirement, which is to process messages. Now we need to solve one more puzzle: How do we send email notifications to the patients? Well, we have many solutions available to solve this problem. We can use the Gmail SMTP server or use third-party services like SendGrid to send emails to the clinic's patients.

As we have found quite a few options to solve our problem statement, let's walk through the approach that we have decided to use to solve the problem statement. We plan to build a background service using the Worker Service template, which will poll for messages continuously and send email alerts to customers using the Gmail SMTP server. We will later deploy this background service to an Azure WebJob and test the functionality by sending a message to the service bus queue by using the Service Bus Explorer in the Azure portal.

Before we start building the background service, we need a couple of things in place. The following are the prerequisites to start development activities:

- Create a Listener SAS policy in Azure Service Bus Queue

- Generate the app password for your Gmail account

Once we have these two things in place, we will start building our background service using the Worker Service template in Visual Studio 2022.

Create an SAS Policy to Access the Azure Service Bus Namespace

As discussed in Chapter 2, to access or interact with Azure Service Bus Queues or Topics from our application, we need to authenticate our application's request to the service bus. This can be done in different ways, such as using Azure Active Directory (Azure AD)–based authentication or SAS policies. For the purpose of this book, we will be using SAS policies. For enterprise applications, it is recommended to use Azure AD–based authentication or managed identity if the applications are deployed inside Azure in an Azure Function or App Service by providing necessary RBAC permissions to the service bus instance.

To create an SAS policy, click **Shared access policies** in the **Settings** section, as shown in Figure 3-1, and then click **Add** to add a new policy. Enter the policy name in the Policy name box on the right and define the scope of this policy. Following the principle to provide least privilege, click the **Listen** check box to assign this policy only the ability to listen to messages to service bus queues or topics present inside our namespace, and then click **Create**.

Figure 3-1. *Creating an SAS policy*

Once the policy has been created, you need to fetch the primary connection string (see Figure 3-2). We will be using this connection string later in this chapter to interact with Azure Service Bus Queue to process the enqueued messages.

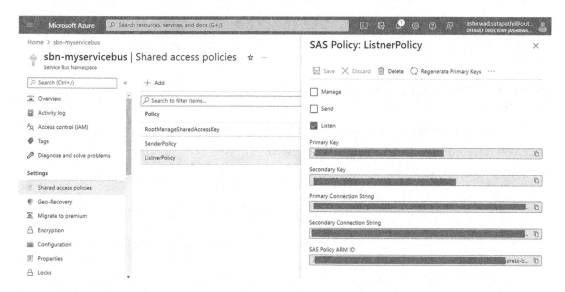

Figure 3-2. *Getting the primary connection string*

Generate an App Password in our GMAIL account

As discussed earlier, we plan to use the Gmail SMTP server to send emails to the clinic's patients to remind them about their appointments. To send emails using your Gmail account, you have to generate an app password. We will be using this app password for authentication purposes of our SMTP client in our application. To generate the app password, go to the **Security** section of your Google Account and click **App passwords**, as shown in Figure 3-3.

Figure 3-3. *Click App passwords*

You have to enter your password to validate your credentials, as shown in Figure 3-4. Once you have entered the password, click **Next**.

Figure 3-4. *Enter your password and click Next*

As shown in Figure 3-5, I already have an app password created, EmailSender. To create a new app password, select the app type as **other(Custom Name)**. Now, enter the name of your choice for the app and click **Generate** to create the app password.

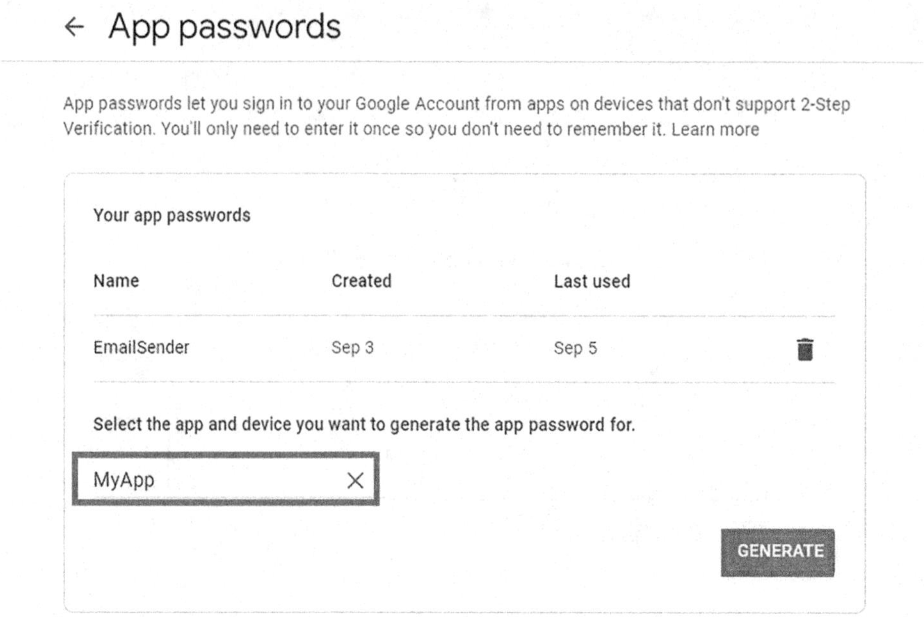

← App passwords

App passwords let you sign in to your Google Account from apps on devices that don't support 2-Step Verification. You'll only need to enter it once so you don't need to remember it. Learn more

Your app passwords

Name	Created	Last used	
EmailSender	Sep 3	Sep 5	🗑

Select the app and device you want to generate the app password for.

MyApp	×

GENERATE

Figure 3-5. *Click Generate*

This opens a pop-up message that has the app password generated for you, as shown in Figure 3-6. You need to copy it and store it to use it in your applications. Once copied, click Done.

Generated app password

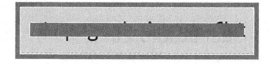

Your app password for your device

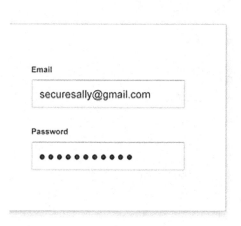

How to use it

Go to the settings for your Google Account in the application or device you are trying to set up. Replace your password with the 16-character password shown above.
Just like your normal password, this app password grants complete access to your Google Account. You won't need to remember it, so don't write it down or share it with anyone.

Figure 3-6. *Copy the app password for future use*

Now that we have the connection string and password necessary to build our background service, we will start developing the solution using the Worker Service template in the next section.

Create a Worker Service to Process Scheduled Messages in Azure Service Bus Queue

In the previous section, you learned about worker services. The focus of this section is to solve the need of a fictional dental clinic to send appointment notifications to its patients by using the Worker Service template. The clinic currently has an API that schedules appointments as messages in the service bus queue. As part of this section, we will build a background service that polls for messages continuously and sends email alerts to the patients about their scheduled appointments.

As we have covered the business requirement, let's start building our background service using the Worker Service template. Open Visual Studio 2022 and click **Create a new project**, as shown in Figure 3-7.

Figure 3-7. *Creating a new project*

Select the **Worker Service** project template, as shown in Figure 3-8, and click **Next**.

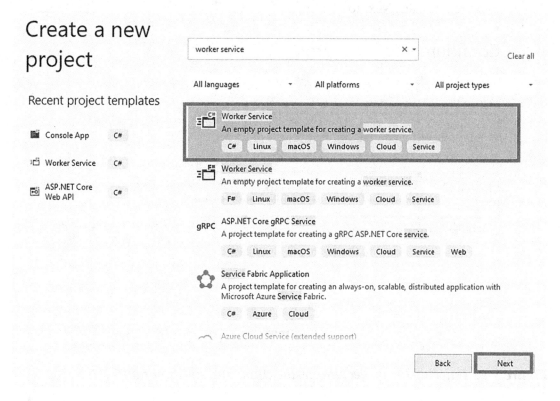

Figure 3-8. *Click Next*

Enter the project name, location, and solution name in the corresponding fields, as shown in Figure 3-9. Click **Next** to continue.

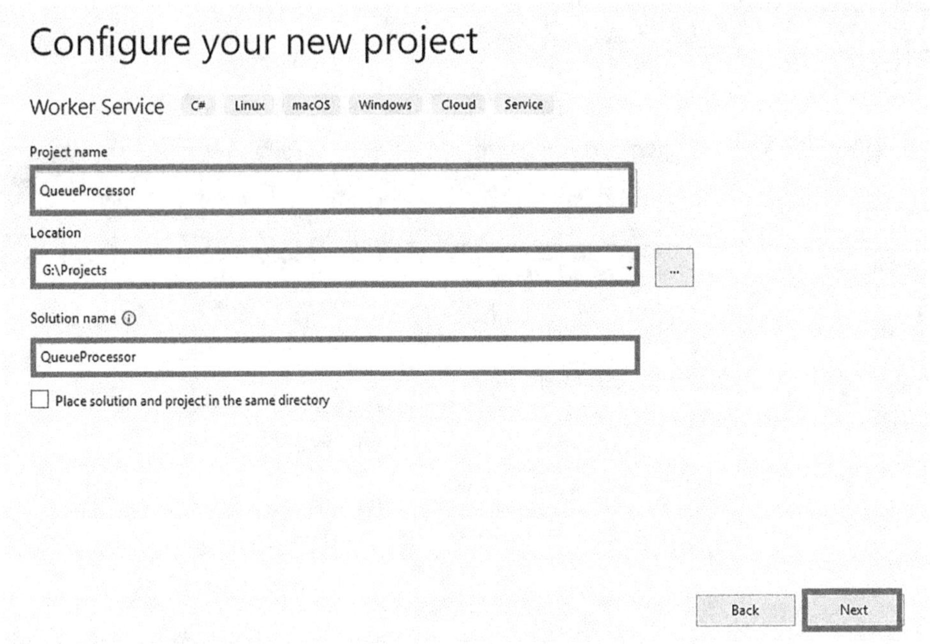

Configure your new project

Worker Service   C#   Linux   macOS   Windows   Cloud   Service

Project name

QueueProcessor

Location

G:\Projects

Solution name ⓘ

QueueProcessor

☐ Place solution and project in the same directory

Back   Next

Figure 3-9. *Entering the project name, location, and solution name*

Now check the **Do not use top-level statements** check box and keep the other option as shown in Figure 3-10. Click **Create** to create our Worker Service project.

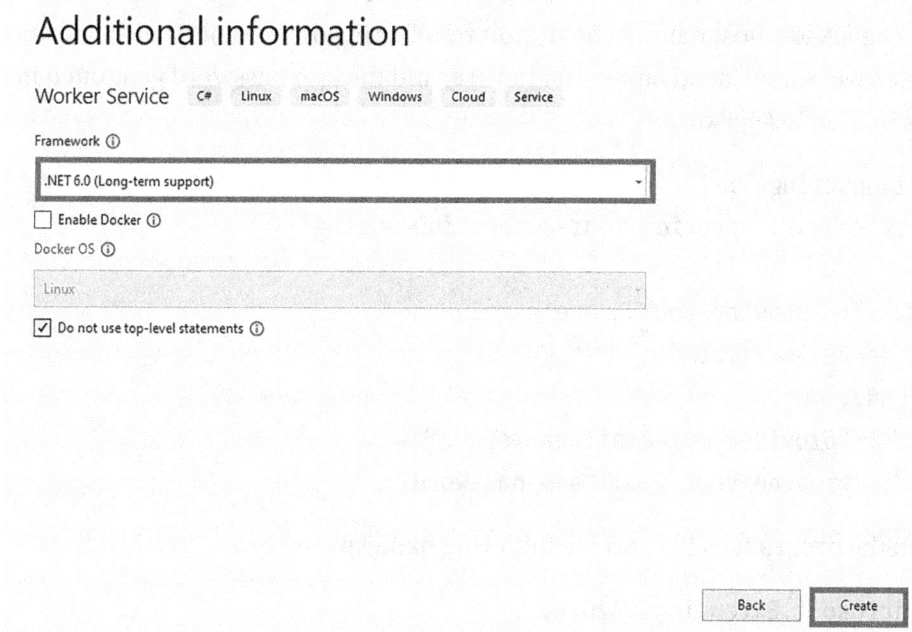

Additional information

Worker Service   C#   Linux   macOS   Windows   Cloud   Service

Framework ⓘ

.NET 6.0 (Long-term support)

☐ Enable Docker ⓘ

Docker OS ⓘ

Linux

☑ Do not use top-level statements ⓘ

Back   Create

Figure 3-10. *Click Create*

Now Visual Studio will create a sample Worker Service project for us that will contain a simple worker service that inherits the BackgroundService abstract class and provides an implementation to the ExecuteAsync method, which logs a message every one second.

Open the Package Manager Console and run the following command to install the NuGet packages Azure.Messaging.ServiceBus, Microsoft.Extensions.Azure, and Newtonsoft.Json in our project. As discussed earlier in the chapter, Azure.Messaging. ServiceBus is used to communicate with Service Bus. Microsoft.Extensions.Azure is required to inject our Azure Clients inside our dependency container, and Newtonsoft. Json will be used for serialization and deserialization of objects.

```
Install-Package Azure.Messaging.ServiceBus
Install-Package Microsoft.Extensions.Azure
Install-Package Newtonsoft.Json
```

Once you have installed the NuGet packages, go to the `appsettings.json` file of our project and add the following key/value pairs. We need to store the service bus connection string in the `ServiceBus` key of the `connectionStrings` node, our queue name in `queueName`, host name in `host`, port number in `port`, email ID of the account from which we want to send emails in `emailId`, and the app password generated in the previous section in `AppPwd`.

```
"ConnectionStrings": {
    "ServiceBus": "provide-your-connection-string"
  },
"queueName": "provide-your-queue-name",
"host": "smtp.gmail.com",
"port": 587,
"emailId": "provide-your-email-address",
"AppPwd": "provide-your-gmail-app-password"
```

Open the `program.cs` file and the following namespace:

```
using Microsoft.Extensions.Azure;
```

Now, add the following code in `program.cs` to inject the service bus client in the dependency container of our project. We are using the `serviceBusConn` stored in our `appsettings.json` file to create our `ServiceBusClient`.

```
services.AddAzureClients(builder
                    => builder.AddServiceBusClient(
                        host.Configuration.GetConnectionString("Se
                        rviceBus")
                        )
                    );
```

For the time being, we are done with the `program.cs` file of our project. Let's create two folders in our project: `Business` and `Models`. The `Business` folder will contain our interface and the classes implementing them. The `Models` folder will contain the classes of our data models.

After creating both folders, create a class called `Appointment.cs` in the `Models` folder and paste the following code. This class represents the appointment data that we receive in the request payload. We have used data annotations to mark the necessary fields as required.

```
public class Appointment
    {
        [Required]
        public int AppointmentId { get; set; }
        [Required]
        public int PatientId { get; set; }
        [Required]
        public string? PatientName { get; set; }
        [Required]
        public string? PatientEmail { get; set; }
        [Required]
        public int CaretakerId { get; set; }
        [Required]
        public DateTime ScheduledAt { get; set; }
    }
```

Now that our model is ready, create an interface called IMailService.cs in the
Business folder and add the method definitions. As shown in the following code snippet,
our interface contains one method definition, sendEmail. The sendEmail method will
be responsible for taking the appointment data coming from the message payload and
sending an email alert to patients by using an HTML template.

```
public interface IMailService
{
    void SendEmail(Appointment appointment);
}
```

Now that you know the purpose of the method, create a class called MailService.
cs to implement the IMailService interface. Before implementing the interface, add the
following property:

```
private readonly IConfiguration _configuration;
```

Now, instantiate the property by using constructor injection. Replace your constructor with the following code:

```
public MailService(IConfiguration configuration)
{
    _configuration = configuration;
}
```

In the preceding code snippet, we are instantiating an instance of the IConfiguration interface to access the values that we earlier stored in our appsetting. json file.

Now let's implement the methods of the **IMailService** interface in the class. Let's add the following code snippet to implement the methods.

The SendEmail takes the appointment object coming in the parameter of the method and then uses the PatientName and PatientEmail properties of the appointment object to send an email notification. We are defining an object of type MailMessage and provide values of required properties for our case i.e., recipient and sender's email, Subject, Body. We have created a simple HTML template for the email body. You can customize it to be more elegant using CSS. After instantiating the MailMessage instance, we create an SMTP client using the configuration we stored in our appsettings.json file to send out emails to the patients of our fictional dental clinic

Add the following code as the implementation for the SendEmail method in our MailService class:

```
public void SendEmail(Appointment appointment)
{
    MailMessage mail = new MailMessage();
    mail.To.Add(appointment.PatientEmail);
    mail.Subject = $"You have a appointment scheduled at {appointment.
    ScheduledAt.ToString("g")}";
    mail.Body = $"<p>Hello there {appointment.PatientName}!" +
        $"<br /><br />You have a dental appointment scheduled at
        {appointment.ScheduledAt.ToString("g")}." +
        $"<br /><br />Thanks" +
        $"<br />Ashirwad</p>";
    mail.IsBodyHtml = true;
```

```
mail.From = new MailAddress(_configuration.
GetValue<String>("emailId"));

using (var smtpClient = new SmtpClient())
{
    smtpClient.Host = _configuration.GetValue<string>("host");
    smtpClient.Port = _configuration.GetValue<int>("port");
    smtpClient.EnableSsl = true;
    smtpClient.UseDefaultCredentials = false;
    smtpClient.Credentials = new System.Net.NetworkCredential(_
    configuration.GetValue<String>("emailId"), _configuration.
    GetValue<String>("AppPwd"));
    smtpClient.Send(mail);
}
}
```

As we have added the implementation of the SendEmail method defined in our interface, let's go to our program.cs file and add a singleton service in our DI container by adding the following code snippet:

```
services.AddSingleton<IMailService, MailService>();
```

Now, let's add the following constructor code in our worker class to inject the ILogger, IMailService, ServiceBusClient object to our _logger, _mailService, and _sbClient property using constructor dependency injection and, finally, instantiate the ServiceBusReceiver client using the _sbClient object:

```
private readonly ILogger<Worker> _logger;
private readonly ServiceBusClient _sbClient;
private readonly ServiceBusReceiver _receiver;
private readonly IMailService _mailService;

public Worker(ILogger<Worker> logger, ServiceBusClient serviceBusClient,
IConfiguration configuration, IMailService mailService)
{
    _logger = logger;
    _sbClient = serviceBusClient;
```

```
_receiver = _sbClient.CreateReceiver(configuration.GetValue<String>("qu
eueName"));
_mailService = mailService;
}
```

Let's add our logic to integrate the logic to send email in our worker service. We are going to perform three actions:

- Fetch messages from the service bus queue using the service bus receiver client

- Deserialize the content of the message coming from the service bus queue

- Make a call to the SendEmail method of the MailService to send an email notification to the patients

To do so, we need to replace the ExecuteAsync method with the following snippet:

```
protected override async Task ExecuteAsync(CancellationToken stoppingToken)
{
    while (!stoppingToken.IsCancellationRequested)
    {
        _logger.LogInformation("Worker running at: {time}",
        DateTimeOffset.Now);
        _logger.LogInformation($"FullyQualifiedNamespace is {_receiver.
        FullyQualifiedNamespace}");
        try
        {
            var message = await _receiver.ReceiveMessageAsync();
            while (message != null)
            {
                _logger.LogInformation(message.Body.ToString());
                Appointment? data = JsonConvert.DeserializeObject<Appointme
                nt>(message.Body.ToString());
                if (data == null)
                {
                    _logger.LogError("Message content was null");
                }
```

```
                if (String.IsNullOrWhiteSpace(data.PatientEmail))
                {
                    _logger.LogError("Patient's email does not exist in the
                    payload.");
                }
                _mailService.SendEmail(data);
                await _receiver.CompleteMessageAsync(message);
                message = await _receiver.ReceiveMessageAsync();
            }
            _logger.LogInformation("Waiting for 2 mins now.");
            await Task.Delay(120000);

        }
        catch (Exception ex)
        {
            _logger.LogError(ex.Message);
        }
    }
}
```

And with this our background service to process the scheduled notification for our fictional dental clinic is complete. Press Ctrl+F5 to build and run our project. The complete source code of this background service project can be found at the following GitHub repository: https://github.com/AshirwadSatapathi/QueueProcessor.

In the next section, we will deploy and test our worker service.

Deploy and Test the Worker Service

Now that we have developed our worker service, let's deploy it to Azure and perform a sanity test. We can deploy a worker service to Azure in multiple ways, like deploying it to a WebJobs or Azure Container Instance or Azure Container Apps. For the purpose of this chapter, we will be using Azure WebJobs, a feature of Azure App Service that allows us to run scripts or programs in the web app instance. WebJobs are used to run background tasks in Azure and are of two types: continuous and triggered.

Continuous WebJobs are used for background tasks that run on an endless loop and start immediately when the WebJob is created. Triggered WebJobs are used for background tasks that need to run when they are triggered manually or are triggered on a scheduled basis. Continuous WebJobs support remote debugging, which is not supported for triggered WebJobs.

Now that you know what Azure WebJobs are, let's see how we can deploy a worker service to it using Visual Studio.

To initiate the deployment, you first have to create a publish profile. To do so, right-click the project name and click **Publish**, as shown in Figure 3-11.

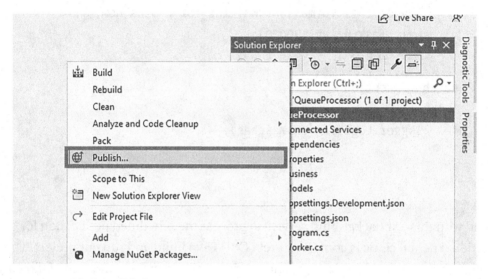

Figure 3-11. *Click Publish*

Select **Azure** as the **Target**, as shown in Figure 3-12, and click **Next**.

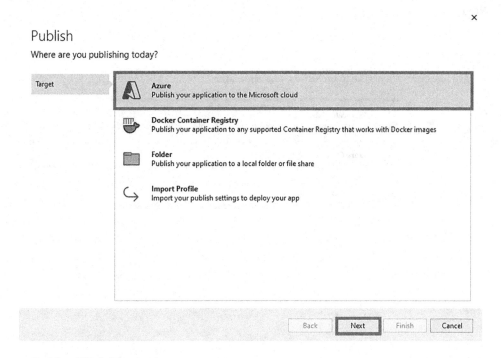

Figure 3-12. *Click Next*

Select **Azure WebJobs** as the **Specific Target**, as shown in Figure 3-13, and click **Next**.

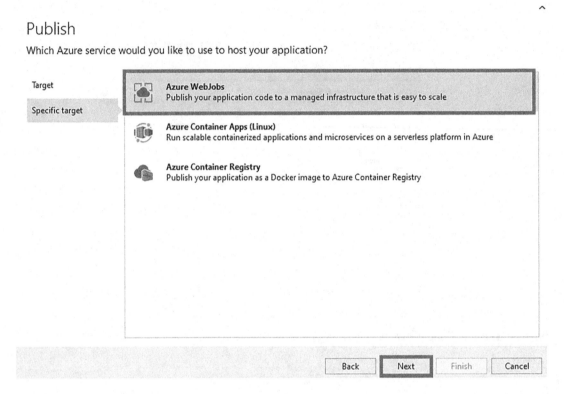

Figure 3-13. *Select Azure WebJobs*

Click the + icon (see Figure 3-14) to create a new App Service to host our worker service.

Publish

Select existing or create a new Azure WebJob

Microsoft account
ashirwad.satapathi@outlook.co...

Target	Subscription name
	Azure for Students
Specific target	View
Azure WebJobs	Resource group
	Search
	App Service instances
	▷ 📁 rg-apress-book

Back   Next   Finish   Cancel

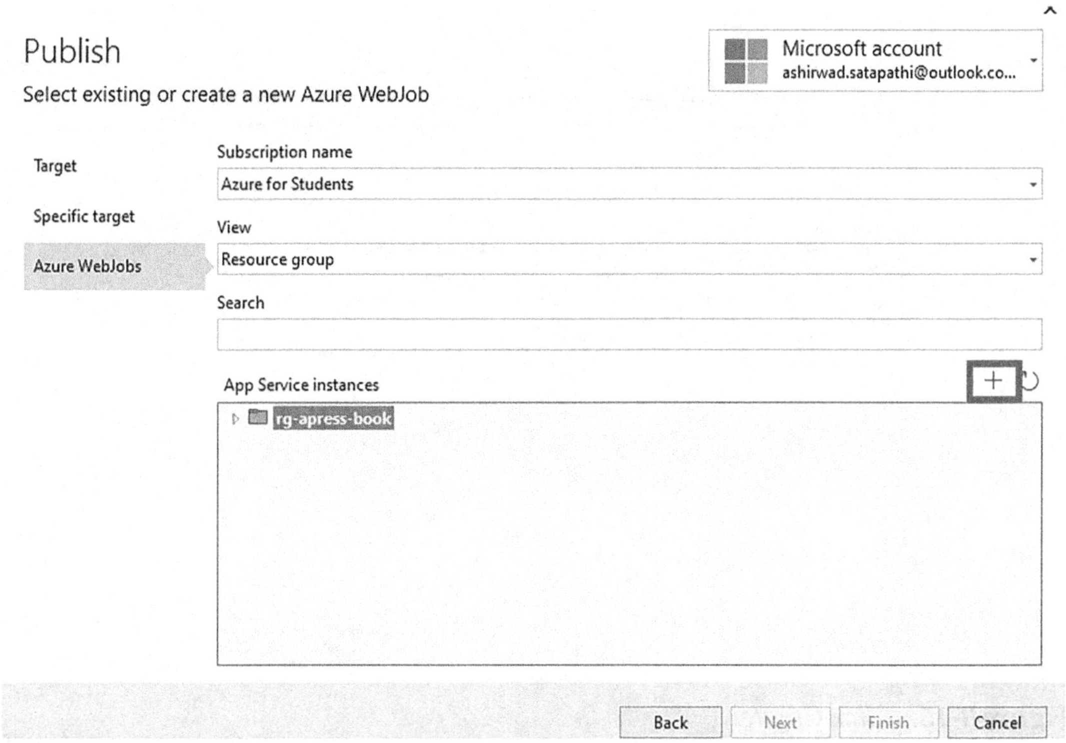

Figure 3-14. *Click the + icon*

Enter the App Service name, subscription name, resource group, and hosting plan in the respective fields as shown in Figure 3-15. Once you have filled in the required information, click **Create**. This will create an App Service that will host our worker service.

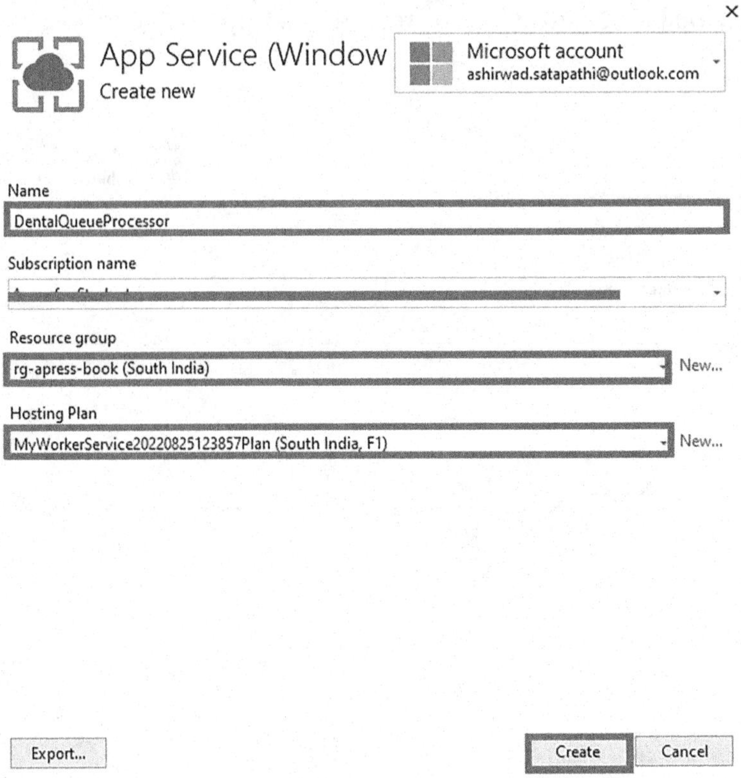

Figure 3-15. *Click Create*

As the resource to host our worker service has been provisioned, as shown in Figure 3-16, click **Finish** to create the publish profile. We will use this to deploy our worker service to the Azure WebJobs running as part of the new App Service we recently provisioned.

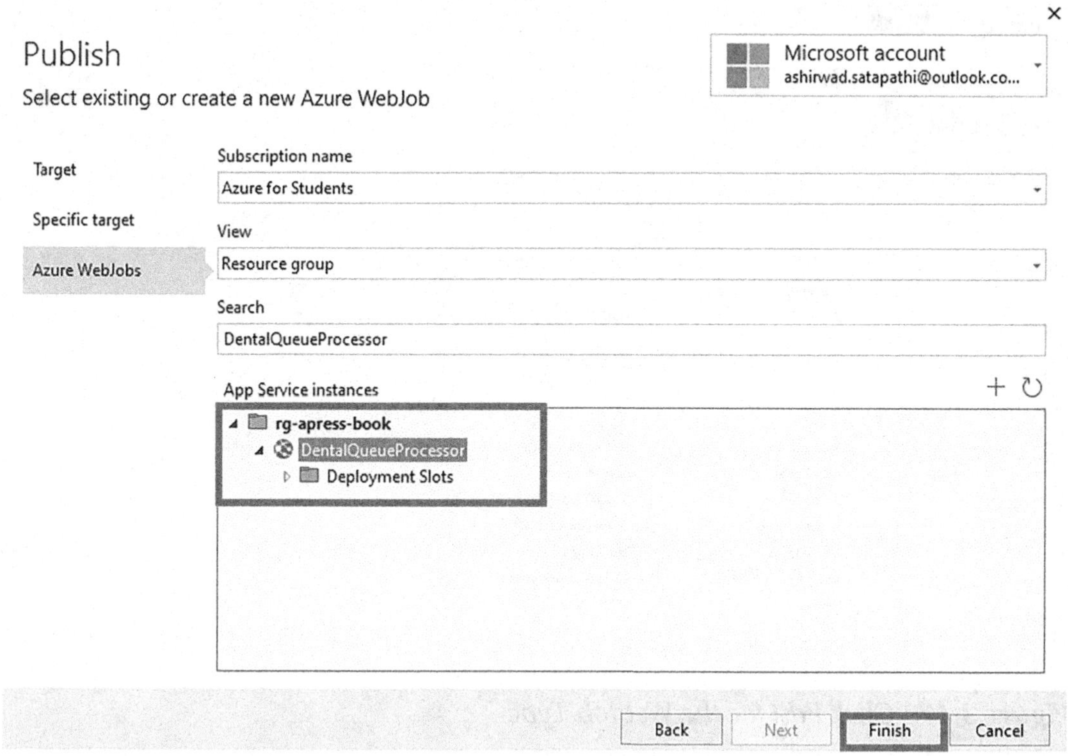

Figure 3-16. *Click Finish*

Now, we want to poll messages continuously, so we have to configure our WebJob type to be continuous. By default, the WebJob type is triggered. To modify it, click the edit button as highlighted in Figure 3-17.

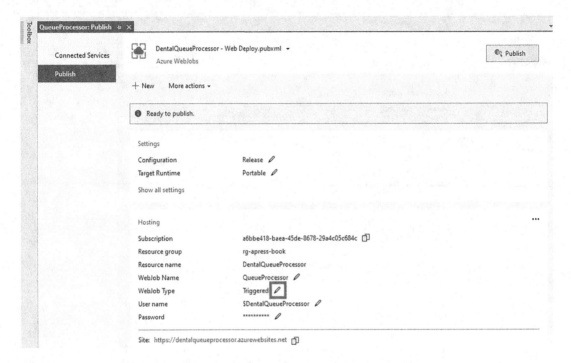

Figure 3-17. *Click Edit for the WebJob Type*

In the dialog box that opens, shown in Figure 3-18, select the **WebJob Type** as **Continuous** and click **Save**.

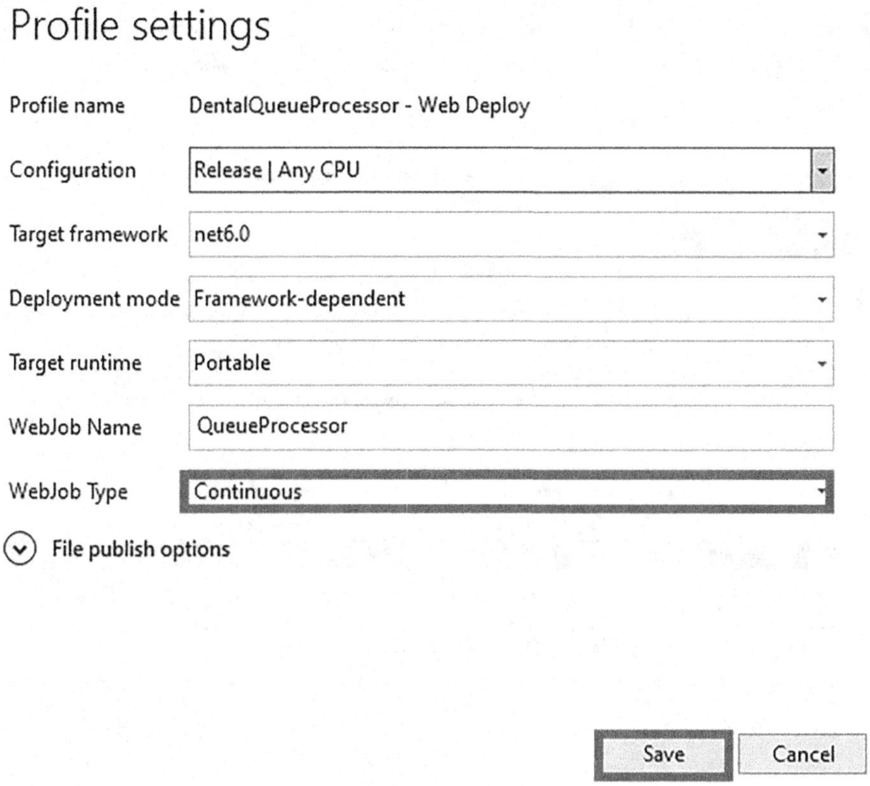

Profile settings

Profile name   DentalQueueProcessor - Web Deploy

Configuration   Release | Any CPU

Target framework   net6.0

Deployment mode   Framework-dependent

Target runtime   Portable

WebJob Name   QueueProcessor

WebJob Type   Continuous

⌄ File publish options

Save   Cancel

Figure 3-18. *Click Save*

As we have configured the required settings, click **Publish** to initiate the deployment of our worker service. We can view the deployment status by looking at the Output pane. Once the build and publish have succeeded, we see a message in the pane as shown in Figure 3-19.

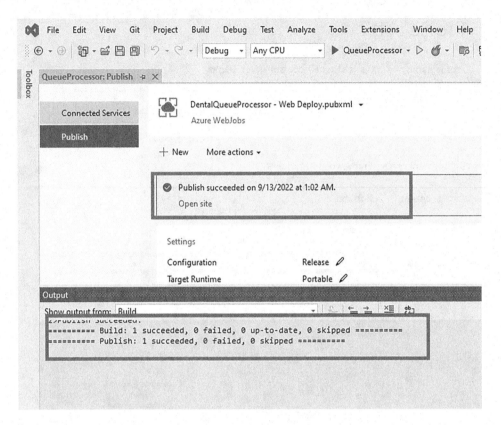

Figure 3-19. *Click Publish*

Now that we have deployed the worker service to our App Service, let's go to our resource group in Azure and click the web app instance we provisioned, as shown in Figure 3-20.

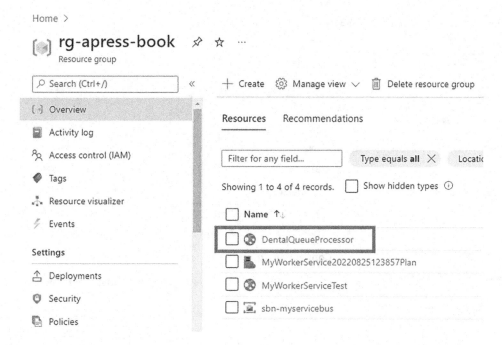

Figure 3-20. *Click DentalQueueProcessor*

Right now, our worker service may not be functional because we haven't configured the application setting with the required key/value pairs. To do so, go to the Configuration window of the App Service, shown in Figure 3-21, and add the AppPwd, emailId, host, port, and queueName in the application settings and ServiceBus key/value pair in the Connection strings section. Once done, click **Save**. Ideally, it is recommended to keep any kind of connection string or app secrets in a key vault instead of storing the values as is in the application settings of the Configuration section of our App Service.

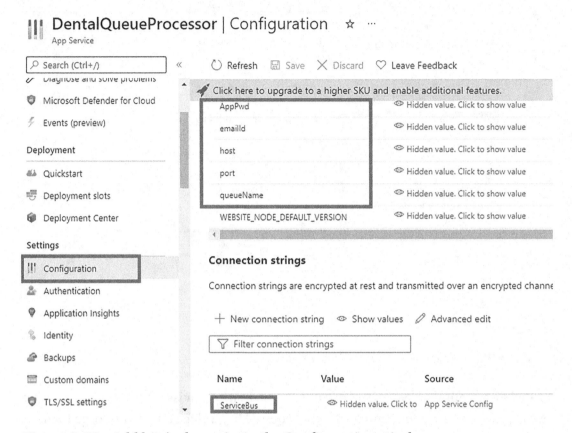

Figure 3-21. *Add key/value pairs in the Configuration window*

Now that we have configured the key/value pair, our worker service should be fully functional. We can view the WebJobs by going to the WebJobs section of the App Service, as shown in Figure 3-22. Here, we can start, stop, or delete a WebJob. We can view the logs by clicking the Logs button.

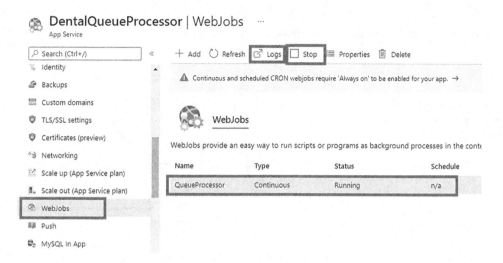

Figure 3-22. *View the deployed WebJobs*

As our WebJob is fully functional, we can start testing the functionality by sending an appointment payload to the service bus queue as a message. We will be leveraging the service bus queue that we created in Chapter 2. Go to the Queues section of our service bus namespace in the Azure portal and click **myqueue**, as shown in Figure 3-23.

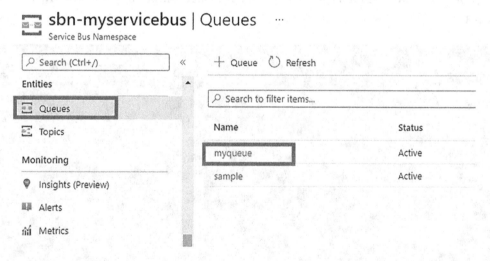

Figure 3-23. *Go to the service bus queue*

Now, click the **Service Bus Explorer (Preview)** section and click **Send messages**. We need to provide the appointment payload in the Message Body and define the Content type as **application/json**, as shown in Figure 3-24. Once done, click **Send** to enqueue a message to the service bus queue.

Figure 3-24. *Enqueue a message in Service Bus Queue*

As soon the message gets enqueued in the service bus queue, our worker service running in the WebJob will find it and will start processing. Once the message has been processed, the WebJob is going to send a message similar to the one shown in Figure 3-25.

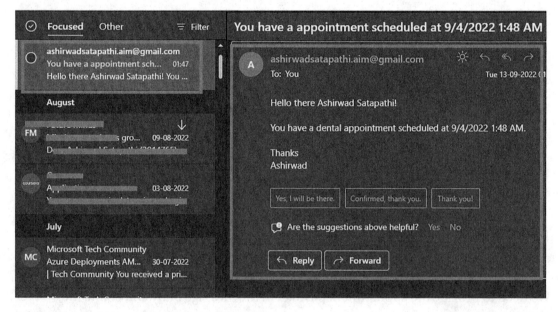

Figure 3-25. *Email alert sent to the patients*

As you can see, we were able to send an email alert to the patients and solve the problem statement of out fictional dental clinic.

Summary

The Worker Service template provides an out-of-the-box template for building background services in .NET Core. Background services are useful for a variety of scenarios. We can leverage them to build long-running processes to execute continuously or on a scheduled basis. In this chapter, we explored ways to integrate capabilities in our worker service to receive and process messages in our background service by leveraging the powerful Azure Service Bus SDK and used the SMTP client to send email alerts to patients. We saw ways to create a Listener policy in the Azure Service queue and explored ways to create an app password for a Gmail account that can be used to authenticate operations. At the end of the chapter, you learned about ways to deploy our worker service to an Azure WebJob and test it using the Service Bus Explorer provided in the Azure portal for Azure Service Bus Queue.

CHAPTER 4

Building a Microservice Using .NET and Azure Kubernetes Service

Microservices-based applications are widely adopted today. You can build a purely distributed application with loosely coupled components. You can manage the design concerns like availability, reliability, scalability, and availability for each application component independently and more efficiently. Development, testing, deployment, and maintenance of the application components become easy. Each application component can be containerized as Docker images and run on a container orchestration platform like Azure Kubernetes Service (AKS).

In this chapter, you will learn how to host a microservices-based application on Azure Kubernetes Service and become familiar with the basics of Azure Kubernetes Service.

In this chapter, we will explore the following topics related to microservices and Azure Kubernetes Service:

- Introduction to Azure Kubernetes Service and Azure Container Registry

- Build a microservice using .NET

- Create Azure Kubernetes Service and an Azure container registry

- Containerize the microservice and push it to the Azure container registry

- Run the microservice on Azure Kubernetes Service

© Ashirwad Satapathi and Abhishek Mishra 2023
A. Satapathi and A. Mishra, *Developing Cloud-Native Solutions with Microsoft Azure and .NET*,
https://doi.org/10.1007/978-1-4842-9004-0_4

After studying this chapter, you will understand the fundamentals of Azure Kubernetes Service and how to host .NET-based microservices on Azure Kubernetes Service.

Let's start things off with an introduction to Azure Kubernetes Service and Azure Container Registry.

Introduction to Azure Kubernetes Service and Azure Container Registry

You develop and deploy an application across multiple environments, including development, test, user acceptance, and production. Once the application is ready, you host it on a virtual machine or a physical server. Traditionally (prior to containerization), before hosting the application, you install all necessary hosting software and dependencies required by the application to run. You may debug and troubleshoot installation and setup issues while preparing the hosting environment. The entire process takes a reasonable amount of time. You must repeat this process for the other hosting environments and expend the same effort.

With the introduction of containers, you no longer need to set up a hosting environment. Containers make the process much simpler and reusable. Instead, you can package all your application dependencies and hosting software along with the application in a Docker container image, keep it in a container registry, and run the container image in the target environment. You pull the image from the container registry and run it in the target environment. You may externalize configurations based on the environment and keep them in a database or some configuration store.

Managing a single container hosting a single monolith application is easy. You may choose to have multiple containers running application copies and sitting behind a load balancer. If one container crashes, you have other containers to serve the application. However, microservices consist of multiple services each running in a separate container. You may end up having hundreds of containers. You must manage the availability, reliability, security, and other architectural challenges of these services inside the containers. This approach can become challenging. To make life easy here, we have container orchestrators like Docker Swarm and Kubernetes. They orchestrate, manage, monitor, and execute the containers. They guarantee high availability, reliability, fault tolerance, security, and many other architectural concerns.

Kubernetes is a container orchestrator developed by Google. It is one of the most widely used container orchestrators. The Kubernetes cluster has a master node (a.k.a. control plane) that manages and runs containers on the worker nodes. The containers run inside pods in the worker nodes. A worker node can have multiple pods, and a pod usually has a single container. However, in some complex scenarios, you can have a container running as a sidecar along with the application container. You define a Kubernetes manifest that specifies the container images to run and other cluster specifications. You use utilities like kubectl and provide the instruction to the control plane to install the manifest. The control plane interprets the manifest, runs the container, and sets up the cluster based on the information provided in the manifest file.

The control plane consists of the following components:

- API server

- Scheduler

- Controller manager

- Etcd

You work with the Azure Kubernetes Service using the API server. Once you have the Kubernetes manifest ready, you pass it to the API server. The controller manager gets the Kubernetes manifest from the API server. The scheduler determines the worker nodes on which it can run the pods. The controller manager manages the replication of pods, deployment, and many more such activities. Etcd is a key-value store that can store all the cluster data along with secret values used in the Kubernetes cluster.

The worker nodes consist of the following components:

- kubelet

- Pod

- kube-proxy

The kubelet is a communication agent and facilitates communication between the control plane and the worker nodes. It makes the worker nodes discoverable to the control plane. The Pod runs the container inside it. The kube-proxy takes care of the cluster networking. You usually define replica sets for your pods. A replica set consists of replicas or identical pods running the exact copy of the container. If one replica goes down, the other replicas can serve the requests until another replica is created to replace the failed replica. The pods communicate with each other inside the cluster and with components outside the cluster using services.

The following are the services available in the Kubernetes cluster:

- Cluster IP

- Node Port

- Load Balancer

The pods sitting behind the Cluster IP can communicate within the cluster. They are not accessible by components outside the cluster. Pods behind the Node Port and the Load Balancer can communicate with the external world. The Load Balancer operates on a standard HTTP port, but the Node Port services operate using ports within the range 30000 to 32767.

Setting up a Kubernetes control plane can be tricky sometimes, and you may need days to set it up. To make life easy, cloud vendors offer managed Kubernetes where they create and manage the control plane, and the control plane is abstracted from you. You have no control over the control plane in the case of managed Kubernetes. Azure Kubernetes Service is a managed Kubernetes offering on Azure. You create the control plane and the worker nodes when creating an Azure Kubernetes Service. You can manage the worker nodes but have no control over the control plane.

You build the containers and push them to the container registry. The worker nodes pull the container images from the container registry and run them inside the pods. The container registry can either be a private registry or a public registry. In the case of a private registry, only those with access to the container registry can pull the image. In the case of a public container registry, anyone can pull the image as the access is anonymous. Azure Container Registry is a private container registry on Azure.

Note   You build Kubernetes manifest files that define the Kubernetes cluster's state and how the application will run in the cluster. The control plane ensures that the cluster state is always maintained as defined in the manifest file. If there are any changes, a pod dies. For example, a new pod gets created to replace the pod that died. You use the `kubectl` command to deploy this manifest file. If you have a bunch of Kubernetes manifest files, you can package them in a Helm Chart and deploy the Helm Chart.

Build a Microservice Using .NET

Now let's build a simple Math Microservice with three services, as depicted in Figure 4-1. The Math API receives the user request to perform either an addition or a subtraction action and then sends it to the Add or Subtract API. The Add or Subtract API performs the operation and returns the result to the Math API, and the Math API sends it back to the user.

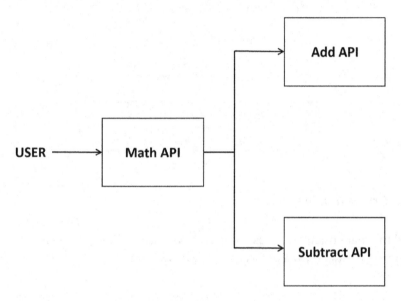

Figure 4-1. *Math Microservice architecture*

We'll build the APIs using Visual Studio. Open Visual Studio and click **Create a new project** as shown in Figure 4-2.

Figure 4-2. *Create a new project*

We need to create microservices using ASP.NET Core Web API. Search for **Web API** and click **ASP.NET Core Web API** as shown in Figure 4-3.

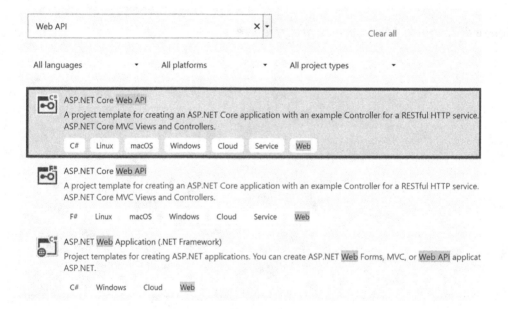

Figure 4-3. *Select ASP.NET Core Web API*

Give the project the name **MathAPI** as shown in Figure 4-4. Click **Next**. Provide the folder location where you want to create the solution.

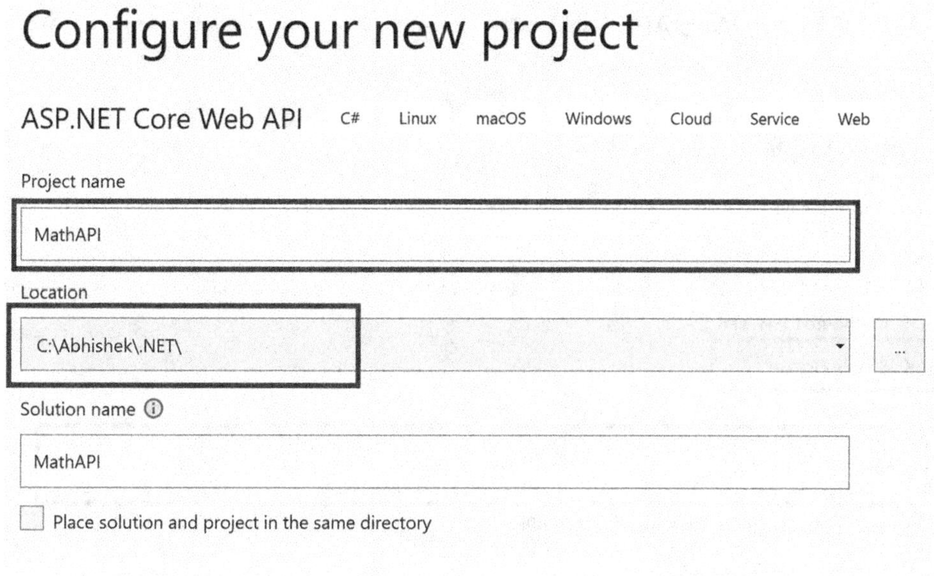

Configure your new project

ASP.NET Core Web API   C#   Linux   macOS   Windows   Cloud   Service   Web

Project name

MathAPI

Location

C:\Abhishek\.NET\

Solution name ⓘ

MathAPI

☐ Place solution and project in the same directory

Figure 4-4. *Provide a project name*

We need to containerize the API and run it on the Azure Kubernetes Service Cluster. Ensure you generate the Docker file as shown in Figure 4-5. Click **Create**. The MathAPI project in the MathAPI solution will get created.

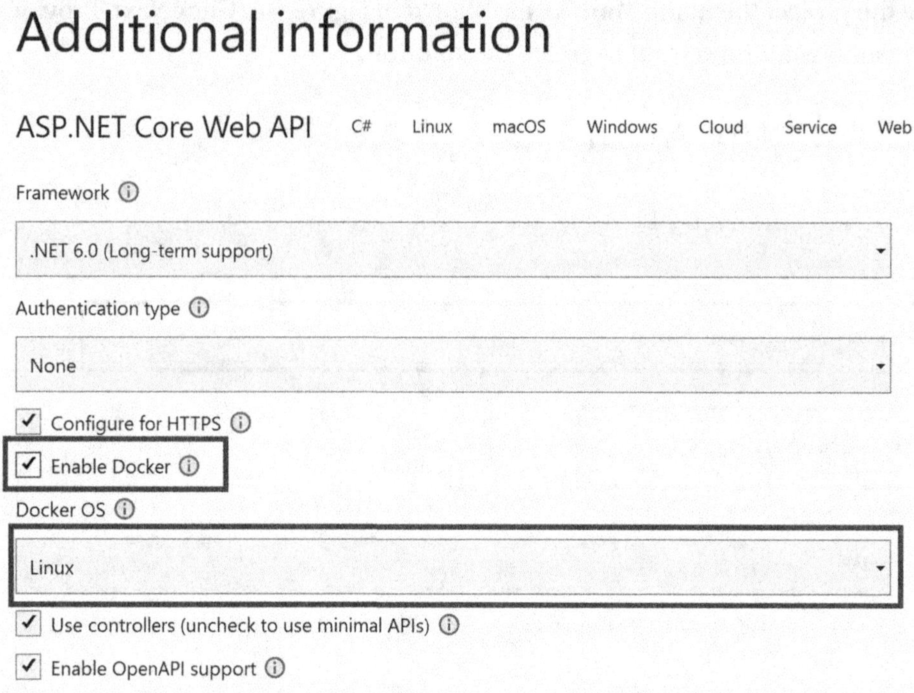

Additional information

ASP.NET Core Web API   C#   Linux   macOS   Windows   Cloud   Service   Web

Framework ⓘ

.NET 6.0 (Long-term support)	▾

Authentication type ⓘ

None	▾

☑ Configure for HTTPS ⓘ

☑ Enable Docker ⓘ

Docker OS ⓘ

Linux	▾

☑ Use controllers (uncheck to use minimal APIs) ⓘ

☑ Enable OpenAPI support ⓘ

Figure 4-5. *Enable Docker support*

We need to create two more Web API projects for the Add API and the Subtract API. Right-click the solution in the Solution Explorer, click **Add**, and then click **New Project** as shown in Figure 4-6. Create a new Web API project with the name **AddAPI**.

Figure 4-6. *Create Add API*

Similarly, create another Web API project and name it **SubtractAPI**. Ensure you generate the Docker file for both projects while creating them.

Now go to the AddAPI project and add a new controller. Right-click the **Controllers** folder, click **Add**, and then click **Controller** as shown in Figure 4-7.

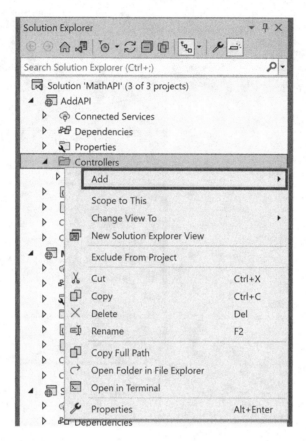

Figure 4-7. *Add a new controller*

Select **MVC Controller – Empty** as shown in Figure 4-8. We will add the controller code later. Name the controller **AddController**.

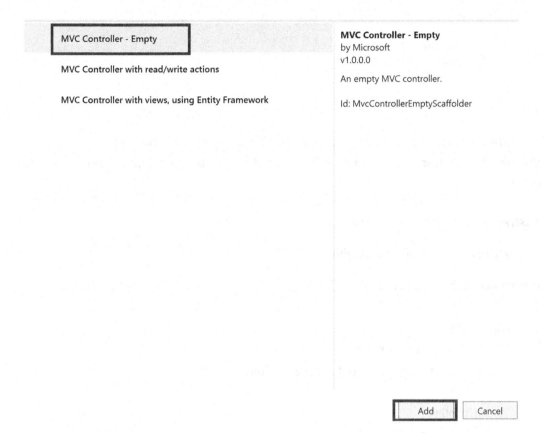

Figure 4-8. *Add API controller*

Replace the code in the AddController.cs file you created with the code in Listing 4-1.

Listing 4-1. AddController.cs

```
using Microsoft.AspNetCore.Mvc;

namespace AddAPI.Controllers
{
    [ApiController]
    [Route("[controller]")]
    public class AddController : Controller
    {
        [HttpGet]
        public int Add(int a, int b)
```

```
    {
        return a + b;
    }
  }
}
```

Now go to the SubtractAPI project and add a new controller named
SubtractController. Add the code in Listing 4-2 to the SubtractController.cs file you
created.

Listing 4-2. SubtractController.cs

```
using Microsoft.AspNetCore.Mvc;

namespace SubtractAPI.Controllers
{
    [ApiController]
    [Route("[controller]")]
    public class SubtractController : Controller
    {
        [HttpGet]
        public int Add(int a, int b)
        {
            return a - b;
        }
    }
}
```

Build the solution and make sure that there is no error. Make sure you delete the
additional code for the WeatherController generated by default. This makes our
codebase look clean. We will work with the MathAPI project once we have deployed the
AddAPI and SubtractAPI to the Azure Kubernetes Service. The AddAPI and SubtractAPI
should not be accessible from outside the cluster and should be accessible only to the
MathAPI. We need the IP address of the ClusterIP service for both the AddAPI and
SubtractAPI so that the MathAPI can access these services. So, we need to defer working
on the MathAPI once the SubtractAPI and the AddAPI are up and running in the Azure
Kubernetes Cluster.

Note   There are better ways to manage the service discovery and ingress using Open Service Mesh (OSM) or Istio. We will configure a ClusterIP for both services to prevent exposing these APIs outside the AKS cluster. However, to keep things simple for first-time learners, we will be accessing the AddAPI and SubtractAPI from the MathAPI using the IP address of their ClusterIP. We will expose the MathAPI to the user using the LoadBalancer service. We will discuss the detailed deployment architecture for the microservices before deploying them to the Azure Kubernetes Service cluster.

Create Azure Kubernetes Service and Azure Container Registry

Let's go to the Azure portal and create an Azure container registry. We will push the containerized API services here. The Azure Kubernetes Service will pull these images and orchestrate the API services from this container registry. Once you have opened the Azure portal, click **Create a resource**, as shown in Figure 4-9.

Figure 4-9. *Create a resource*

You will be navigated to the Azure Marketplace. Click **Container Registry** in the **Containers** tab as shown in Figure 4-10. This takes you to the screen where you can provide the basic details for the container registry.

Figure 4-10. *Click Container Registry*

Provide the subscription details, resource group, registry name, location, and SKU for the container registry in the corresponding fields, as shown in Figure 4-11. We have selected the **Basic** SKU, which is the cheapest among other available tiers like Standard and Premium. Click **Review + create** as shown in Figure 4-11.

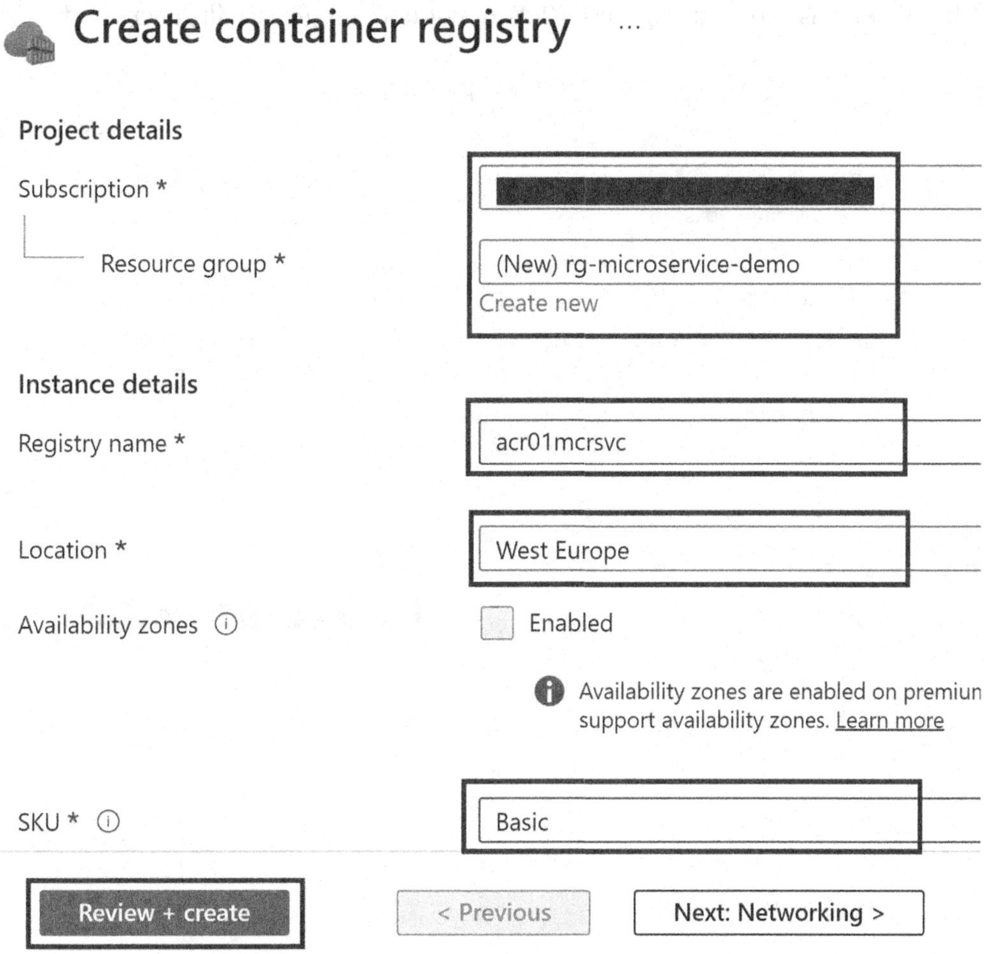

 # Create container registry ...

Project details

Subscription *

    └───── Resource group *

       (New) rg-microservice-demo
       Create new

Instance details

Registry name *

    acr01mcrsvc

Location *

    West Europe

Availability zones ⓘ

    ☐ Enabled

       🛈 Availability zones are enabled on premiun
          support availability zones. Learn more

SKU * ⓘ

    Basic

[Review + create]   [< Previous]   [Next: Networking >]

Figure 4-11. *Click Review + create*

Click **Create** as shown in Figure 4-12. Your container registry will get created.

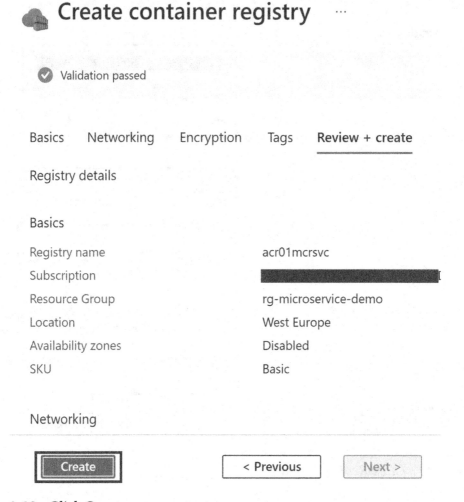

Figure 4-12. *Click Create*

Now that we have created the container registry, let's create the Azure Kubernetes Service, where we will run the microservice. Go to the Azure portal and click **Create a resource** as shown in Figure 4-13.

Microsoft Azure
Search resources, services,
Azure services
Create a resource
Resource groups
Subscriptions

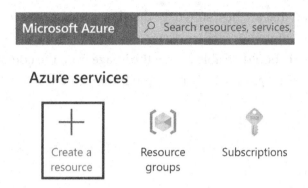

Figure 4-13. *Create a resource*

Click **Kubernetes Service** on the **Containers** tab as shown in Figure 4-14. You will be navigated to a screen where you can provide the basic details for the Kubernetes Service cluster.

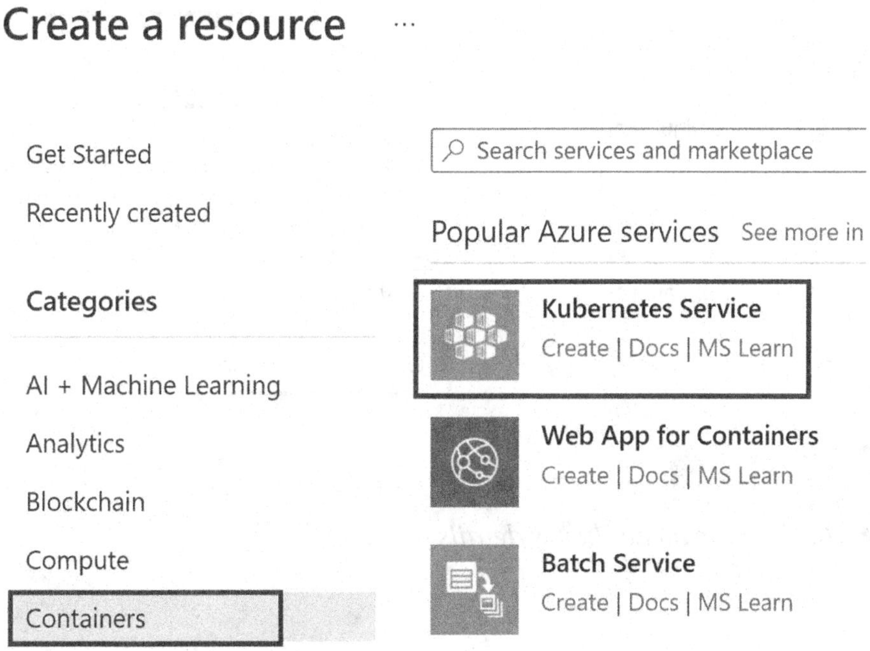

Create a resource ...
Get Started
Recently created
Categories
AI + Machine Learning
Analytics
Blockchain
Compute
Containers
Search services and marketplace
Popular Azure services
See more in
Kubernetes Service
Create | Docs | MS Learn
Web App for Containers
Create | Docs | MS Learn
Batch Service
Create | Docs | MS Learn

Figure 4-14. *Click Kubernetes Service*

Provide the subscription details, resource group, cluster name, location, and cluster preset configuration for the Kubernetes Service in the corresponding fields, as shown in Figure 4-15. We have selected the **Dev/Test** as the cluster preset configuration here, which will save cost for us. The nodes that will get created for us will be virtual machines of lower configuration that are best suited for development and test activities. We need to integrate the Azure container registry we created earlier with the Kubernetes cluster. The pods in the cluster should be able to pull the image from the container registry. You can achieve this in the Integrations tab. Click the **Integrations** tab.

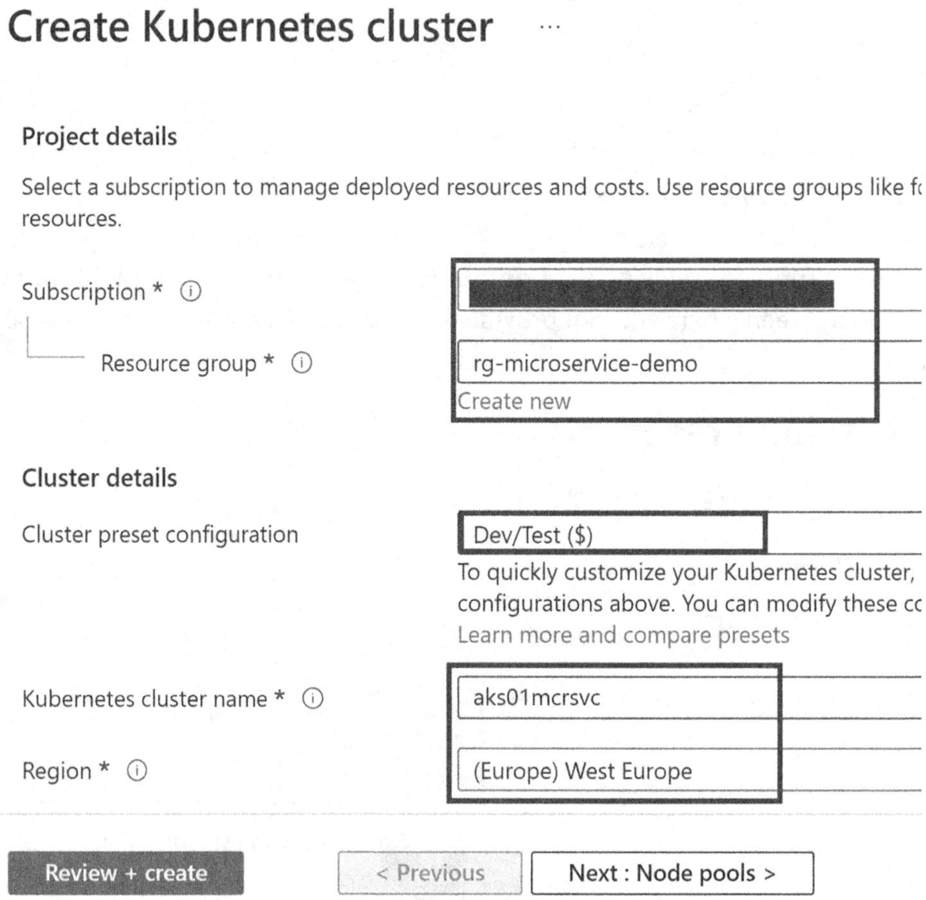

Create Kubernetes cluster   ⋯

Project details

Select a subscription to manage deployed resources and costs. Use resource groups like f
resources.

Subscription *   ⓘ

└──── Resource group *   ⓘ   rg-microservice-demo

Create new

Cluster details

Cluster preset configuration   Dev/Test ($)

To quickly customize your Kubernetes cluster,
configurations above. You can modify these cc
Learn more and compare presets

Kubernetes cluster name *   ⓘ   aks01mcrsvc

Region *   ⓘ   (Europe) West Europe

Review + create   < Previous   Next : Node pools >

Figure 4-15. *Provide basic cluster details*

On the Integrations tab, select the container registry and click **Review + create** as shown in Figure 4-16.

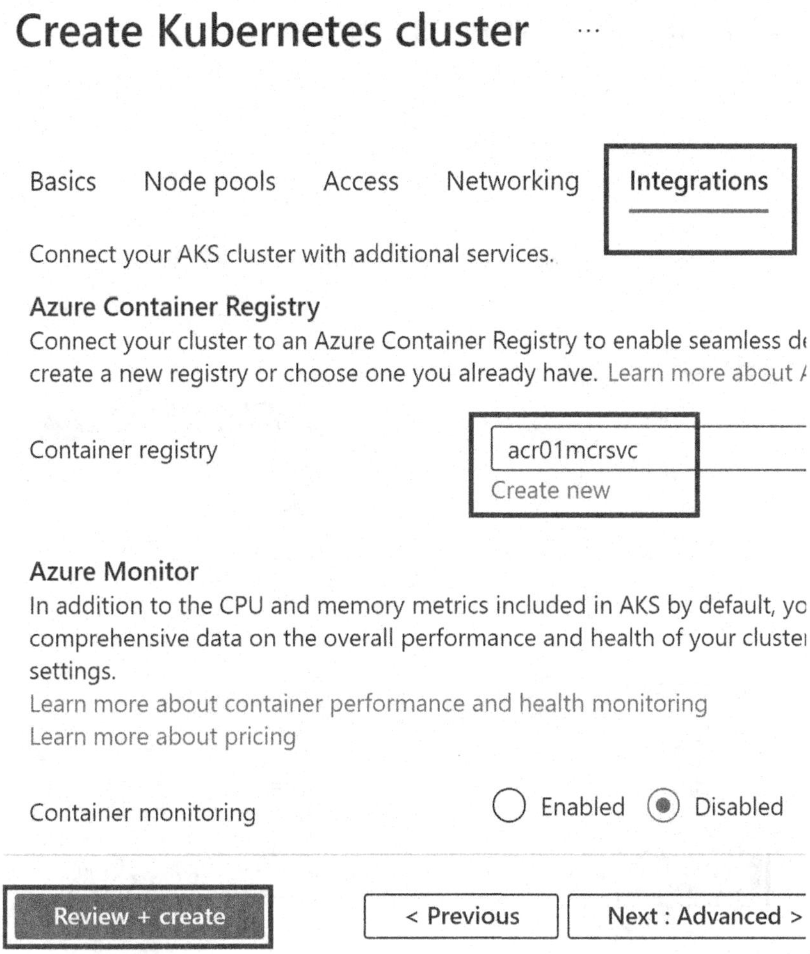

Create Kubernetes cluster ⋯

Basics   Node pools   Access   Networking | **Integrations** |

Connect your AKS cluster with additional services.

Azure Container Registry
Connect your cluster to an Azure Container Registry to enable seamless de create a new registry or choose one you already have. Learn more about /

Container registry   acr01mcrsvc
                            Create new

Azure Monitor
In addition to the CPU and memory metrics included in AKS by default, yo comprehensive data on the overall performance and health of your cluster settings.
Learn more about container performance and health monitoring
Learn more about pricing

Container monitoring   ◯ Enabled   ◉ Disabled

| Review + create | | < Previous | | Next : Advanced > |

Figure 4-16. Click Review + create

Click **Create** as shown in Figure 4-17, and the Azure Kubernetes Service will get created.

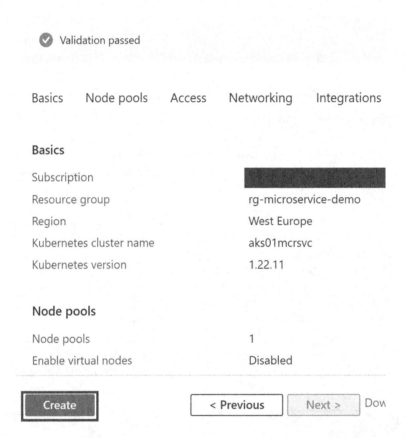

Create Kubernetes cluster ...

✓ Validation passed

Basics   Node pools   Access   Networking   Integrations

Basics

Subscription

Resource group   rg-microservice-demo

Region   West Europe

Kubernetes cluster name   aks01mcrsvc

Kubernetes version   1.22.11

Node pools

Node pools   1

Enable virtual nodes   Disabled

Create   < Previous   Next >   Dow

Figure 4-17. Click Create

Containerize the Microservice and Push It to the Azure Kubernetes Service

Now let's containerize the Add API and the Subtract API we created earlier. To follow the steps in this section you should have Docker Desktop installed on your system. Go to the Add API and copy the generated Docker file to the folder where the .NET solution file (.sln) is present, as shown in Figure 4-18.

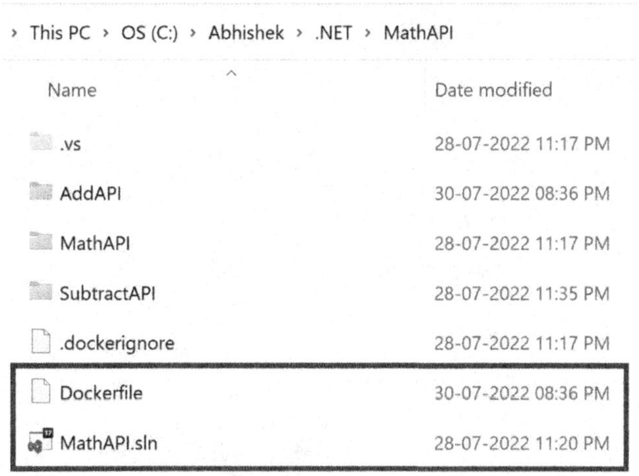

> This PC > OS (C:) > Abhishek > .NET > MathAPI

Name	Date modified
.vs	28-07-2022 11:17 PM
AddAPI	30-07-2022 08:36 PM
MathAPI	28-07-2022 11:17 PM
SubtractAPI	28-07-2022 11:35 PM
.dockerignore	28-07-2022 11:17 PM
Dockerfile	30-07-2022 08:36 PM
MathAPI.sln	28-07-2022 11:20 PM

Figure 4-18. *Dockerfile location*

As a prerequisite, you should have the Azure command-line interface (CLI) installed. Open the command prompt and execute the command in Listing 4-3 to log in to Azure.

Listing 4-3. Log In to Azure and Select Your Subscription

```
az login
az account set -s "[Provide your Subscription Name or Subscription ID]."
```

You will be prompted to provide your credentials as shown in Figure 4-19. Provide the credentials and sign in.

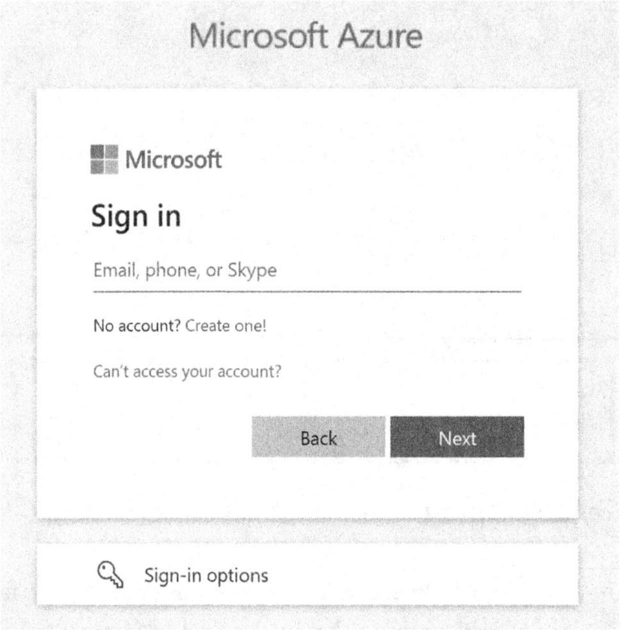

Figure 4-19. *Sign in to Azure*

To containerize the API, we will use the Azure CLI command to build the image and push it to the Azure container registry. We need not run any Docker command to achieve it. However, as a prerequisite, you should have the Docker desktop installed on your system. Navigate to the .NET solution (`.sln`) folder in the command prompt where you have copied the Docker file for the Add API. Execute the command shown in Listing 4-4. The Add API will get containerized and pushed to the Azure container registry. In the command, replace `acr01mcrsvc` with the name of your container registry (`acr01mcrsvc` is the name of the container registry created earlier in this demonstration).

Listing 4-4. Containerize and Push Add API

```
az acr build -t add:ver01 -r acr01mcrsvc .
```

Now we can containerize the Subtract API. Copy the generated Docker file to the folder where the solution file (`.sln`) is present and execute the command shown in Listing 4-5. The Subtract API will get containerized and pushed to the Azure container registry. In the command, replace `acr01mcrsvc` with the name of your container registry (again, acr01mcrsvc is the name of the container registry created in this demonstration).

Listing 4-5. Containerize and Push Subtract API

```
az acr build -t sub:ver01 -r acr01mcrsvc .
```

You can verify if the images are pushed in the Repositories tab of the Container Registry as shown in Figure 4-20.

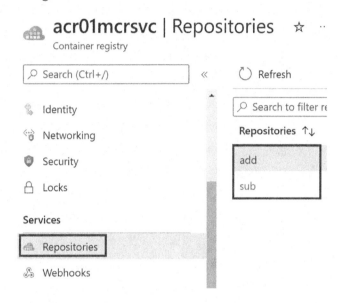

Figure 4-20. *Add API and Subtract API images in the container registry*

We will deal with the Math API later once we have the Add API and the Subtract API running inside the Azure Kubernetes Service Cluster.

Run the Microservice on Azure Kubernetes Service

Now that we have containerized the Add API and the Subtract API, let's create a Kubernetes manifest file and deploy the Add API. Listing 4-6 depicts the manifest file for Add API. Ensure that you specify the correct container registry and the image name you created. We are adding a service named add, which is a Cluster IP service. The Add API container pod will not be accessible outside the cluster. However, it will be accessible inside the cluster. You can save the manifest file as kubernetes-manifest-add.yaml.

Listing 4-6. Kubernetes-manifest-add.yaml

```yaml
apiVersion: apps/v1
kind: Deployment
metadata:
 name: add
 labels:
   app: add
spec:
 selector:
   matchLabels:
     app: add
 replicas: 1
 template:
   metadata:
     labels:
       app: add
   spec:
     containers:
     - name: add
       image: acr01mcrsvc.azurecr.io/add:ver01
       resources:
         requests:
           cpu: 100m
           memory: 100Mi
         limits:
           cpu: 200m
           memory: 200Mi
       ports:
       - containerPort: 80
---
apiVersion: v1
kind: Service
metadata:
 name: add
spec:
```

```
ports:
- port: 80
selector:
  app: add
---
```

Listing 4-7 depicts the manifest file for the Subtract API. You can save the manifest file as kubernetes-manifest-subtract.yaml. Make sure you specify the right container registry and the image name for the Subtract API.

Listing 4-7. Kubernetes-manifest-subtract.yaml

```
apiVersion: apps/v1
kind: Deployment
metadata:
 name: subtract
 labels:
   app: subtract
spec:
 selector:
   matchLabels:
     app: subtract
 replicas: 1
 template:
   metadata:
     labels:
       app: subtract
   spec:
     containers:
     - name: subtract
       image: acr01mcrsvc.azurecr.io/sub:ver01
       resources:
         requests:
           cpu: 100m
           memory: 100Mi
         limits:
           cpu: 200m
```

103

```
        memory: 200Mi
    ports:
    - containerPort: 80
---
apiVersion: v1
kind: Service
metadata:
 name: subtract
spec:
 ports:
 - port: 80
 selector:
   app: subtract
---
```

Now let's apply these manifest files to the AKS cluster. Open a command prompt or bash prompt and execute the command shown in Listing 4-8 to log in to Azure. You will be prompted to provide your credentials. Provide the credentials and sign in.

Listing 4-8. Log In to Azure and Select Your Subscription

```
az login
az account set -s "[Provide your Subscription Name or Subscription ID]"
```

Execute the command shown in Listing 4-9 to get the Kubernetes cluster credentials locally so that you can access the cluster.

Listing 4-9. Get AKS Credentials

```
az aks get-credentials -n [Provide AKS Name] -g [Provide Resource
Group Name]
```

Execute the commands shown in Listing 4-10 to apply the Kubernetes manifest files we created to the AKS cluster.

Listing 4-10. Apply Kubernetes Manifest to AKS Cluster

```
kubectl apply -f kubernetes-manifest-add.yaml
kubectl apply -f kubernetes-manifest-subtract.yaml
```

Execute the command shown in Listing 4-11 to check if the Add and Subtract pods are running successfully. It may take some time for the pods to transition from *Pending* to *Running* state.

Listing 4-11. Get Pods

```
kubectl get pods
```

You can see in Figure 4-21 that the add and subtract pods are in the Running state.

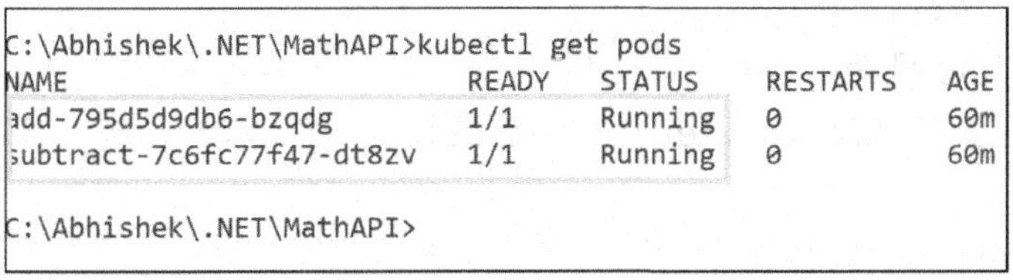

```
C:\Abhishek\.NET\MathAPI>kubectl get pods
NAME                         READY   STATUS    RESTARTS   AGE
add-795d5d9db6-bzqdg         1/1     Running   0          60m
subtract-7c6fc77f47-dt8zv    1/1     Running   0          60m

C:\Abhishek\.NET\MathAPI>
```

Figure 4-21. *kubectl get pods*

Execute the command shown in Listing 4-12 to get the Cluster IP addresses for the add and subtract pods. We will need this information while creating the Math API. The Math API will access the Add API and Subtract API using these IP addresses.

Listing 4-12. Get Services

```
kubectl get services
```

Figure 4-22 depicts the services running in the cluster. You need to copy the CLUSTER-IP values for the add service and the subtract service. We will use it in the Math API .NET controller code.

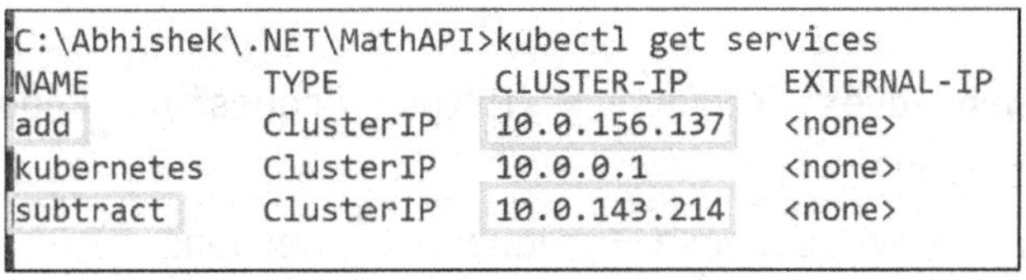

```
C:\Abhishek\.NET\MathAPI>kubectl get services
NAME         TYPE        CLUSTER-IP      EXTERNAL-IP
add          ClusterIP   10.0.156.137    <none>
kubernetes   ClusterIP   10.0.0.1        <none>
subtract     ClusterIP   10.0.143.214    <none>
```

Figure 4-22. *kubectl get services*

Now let's modify the MathAPI project. Create a new controller named **MathController.cs**. Replace the code in `MathController.cs` with the code in Listing 4-13. Make sure you replace the IP address in the Add and the Subtract API URL with the cluster IP address of the Add and Subtract API running in the AKS cluster.

Listing 4-13. MathController.cs

```
using Microsoft.AspNetCore.Mvc;
using System.Net;
using System.Net.Http.Headers;
using System.Text;

namespace MathAPI.Controllers
{
    [ApiController]
    [Route("[controller]")]
    public class MathController : Controller
    {
        [HttpGet("Get")]
        public string Get(string ops, int a,int b)
        {
            string result = "";
            string url = "";
            string queryStr = "?a=" + a + "&b=" + b;

            if (ops == "add")
            {
                url = "http://10.0.156.137/add" + queryStr;
            }
            else
            {
                url = "http://10.0.143.214/subtract" + queryStr; ;
            }
            HttpWebRequest request = (HttpWebRequest)WebRequest.
            Create(url);
            WebResponse response = request.GetResponse();
            using (Stream responseStream = response.GetResponseStream())
            {
                StreamReader reader = new StreamReader(responseStream,
                Encoding.UTF8);
                result = reader.ReadToEnd();
            }
```

```
        return result;
      }
   }
}
```

Now we can containerize the Math API. Copy the generated Docker file to the folder where the solution file (.sln) is present and execute the command shown in Listing 4-14. The Math API will get containerized and pushed to the Azure container registry. In the command, replace acr01mcrsvc (the name of the container registry created earlier) with the name of your container registry.

Listing 4-14. Containerize and Push Math API

```
az acr build -t math:ver01 -r acr01mcrsvc .
```

Listing 4-15 depicts the manifest file for the Math API. Make sure you specify the right container registry and the image name for the Subtract API. You can save the manifest file as kubernetes-manifest-math.yaml.

Listing 4-15. Kubernetes-manifest-math.yaml

```
apiVersion: apps/v1
kind: Deployment
metadata:
 name: math
 labels:
   app: math
spec:
 selector:
   matchLabels:
     app: math
 replicas: 1
 template:
   metadata:
     labels:
       app: math
   spec:
     containers:
```

```
    - name: math
      image: acr01mcrsvc.azurecr.io/math:ver01
      resources:
        requests:
          cpu: 100m
          memory: 100Mi
        limits:
          cpu: 200m
          memory: 200Mi
      ports:
      - containerPort: 80
---
apiVersion: v1
kind: Service
metadata:
 name: math
spec:
 type: LoadBalancer
 ports:
 - port: 80
 selector:
    app: math
---
```

Execute the command shown in Listing 4-16 to apply the Math API Kubernetes manifest file we created to the AKS cluster.

Listing 4-16. Apply Kubernetes Manifest File to AKS Cluster

```
kubectl apply -f kubernetes-manifest-math.yaml
```

Now let's check if the math pod is running. To check the pod state, execute the command shown in Listing 4-17.

Listing 4-17. Get Pods

```
kubectl get pods
```

You can see in Figure 4-23 that the add, subtract, and math pods are in the
Running state.

```
C:\Abhishek\.NET\MathAPI>kubectl get pods
NAME                      READY   STATUS    RESTARTS   AGE
add-795d5d9db6-bzqdg      1/1     Running   0          54m
math-6566657db4-hpb6m     1/1     Running   0          16m
subtract-7c6fc77f47-dt8zv 1/1     Running   0          54m

C:\Abhishek\.NET\MathAPI>
```

Figure 4-23. *kubectl get pods*

Let's copy the External-IP address for the Load Balancer service for the Math
API. Execute the command shown in Listing 4-18 to list the services in the cluster.

Listing 4-18. Get Services

```
kubectl get services
```

Figure 4-24 depicts the services running in the cluster. You need to copy the
EXTERNAL-IP value for the math service. We will use it to browse the Math API from the
browser. Pods behind the Load Balancer service are exposed outside the cluster.

```
C:\Abhishek\.NET\MathAPI>kubectl get services
NAME        TYPE           CLUSTER-IP     EXTERNAL-IP
add         ClusterIP      10.0.156.137   <none>
kubernetes  ClusterIP      10.0.0.1       <none>
math        LoadBalancer   10.0.125.0     20.82.24.81
subtract    ClusterIP      10.0.143.214   <none>
```

Figure 4-24. *kubectl get service*

Now let's browse the URL as shown in Listing 4-19. Replace [EXTERNAL-IP] with
the EXTERNAL-IP address of the math API running in the cluster. We are adding two
numbers, 3 and 5.

Listing 4-19. Browse Math API for Add Operation

```
http://[EXTERNAL-IP]/math/get?ops=add&a=3&b=5
```

Figure 4-25 depicts the output in the browser. The browser renders the addition result.

8

Figure 4-25. *Add operation output*

Now browse the URL as shown in Listing 4-20. Replace [EXTERNAL-IP] with the EXTERNAL-IP address of the math API running in the cluster. We are subtracting two numbers, 3 and 5.

Listing 4-20. Browse Math API for Subtract Operation

```
http://[EXTERNAL-IP]/math/get?ops=subtract&a=3&b=5
```

Figure 4-26 depicts the output in the browser. The browser renders the subtract result.

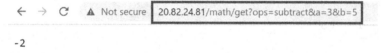

-2

Figure 4-26. *Subtract operation output*

Summary

In this chapter, you learned the basic concepts of Kubernetes. We explored Azure Kubernetes Service and Azure Container Registry. Then, we created a simple Math microservice and containerized it. We created an Azure container registry and pushed the containerized microservice to it. We created an Azure Kubernetes Service and hosted the microservices containers in its worker nodes.

In the next chapter you will learn how to secure the microservice running inside AKS using Azure AD.

CHAPTER 5

Secure Microservice with Azure AD

You must secure the microservices-based applications you are building. Only authorized users and applications who have access to the microservices should be allowed to access them. Azure Active Directory (Azure AD) is an Identity-as-a-Service (iDaaS) offering that you can use to configure authentication for your microservices. You can easily configure Azure AD for your application and use it for authentication and authorization purposes. In the previous chapter we developed a simple Math microservices application and orchestrated it in the Azure Kubernetes Service. However, we did not secure it and anyone could access the application.

In this chapter, you will learn how to secure the Math microservices application using Azure AD. We will also explore the basics of Azure AD.

In this chapter, we will explore the following topics related to microservices and Azure AD:

- Introduction to Azure AD

- Create an application in Azure AD

- Create scopes for the Azure AD application

- Configure authentication and authorization for the Math microservices application running in Azure Kubernetes Service

After completing this chapter, you'll understand the fundamentals of Azure AD and be able to secure containerized .NET-based microservices applications running inside Azure Kubernetes Service.

© Ashirwad Satapathi and Abhishek Mishra 2023
A. Satapathi and A. Mishra, *Developing Cloud-Native Solutions with Microsoft Azure and .NET*,
https://doi.org/10.1007/978-1-4842-9004-0_5

Introduction to Azure AD

As mentioned, Azure AD is an iDaaS offering on Azure. Azure AD is completely managed by the underlying Azure platform. You need not create any additional infrastructure to manage identity and authentication for your application running on Azure. You can configure authentication and authorization for your application with ease. You need to register your application in Azure AD and then you can create users who can use your application. You can also let the application users authenticate using third-party authentication providers like Google, Facebook, and many more. Application users can authenticate using SAML, OAuth, Open ID Connect, or WS-Federation. Azure AD supports modern authentication features like single sign-on (SSO) and multifactor authentication (MFA).

You can integrate applications running on the on-premises server or Azure or any other supported cloud with Azure AD. You can integrate on-premises Active Directory with Azure AD using Azure AD Connect. Both on-premises users and users created in Azure AD can authenticate to applications registered with Azure AD. Using Azure AD, you can configure business-to-business (B2B) scenarios where the businesses can authenticate and authorize their applications and resources. You can also configure business-to-consumer (B2C) scenarios where the end users can authenticate their applications.

Azure AD can help you as a domain controller and you can join your virtual machines to Azure AD that works as domain controller. You can join the on-premises Active Directory and sync the on-premises users and roles to Azure AD. Azure AD is a multitenant directory management service.

You need to complete the following steps to configure your microservices-based application for Azure AD–based authentication:

1. Register an application with Azure AD.

2. Create scopes for the application created in Azure AD to perform authorization.

3. Create a secret for your registered application.

4. Configure your microservices-based application with an Azure AD application ID, secret, and tenant ID.

We will follow these steps and configure authentication for the Math microservices application that we developed in Chapter 4.

Register an Application in Azure AD

Let's go to the Azure portal and register an application in Azure AD default tenant. Click **Azure Active Directory** as in Figure 5-1.

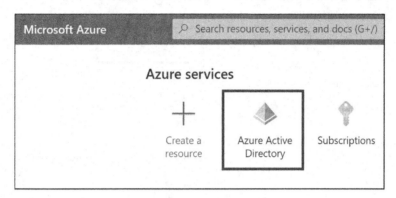

Figure 5-1. *Click Azure Active Directory*

Click **App registrations** and then click **New registration** as shown in Figure 5-2. This enables us to register a new application in Azure AD.

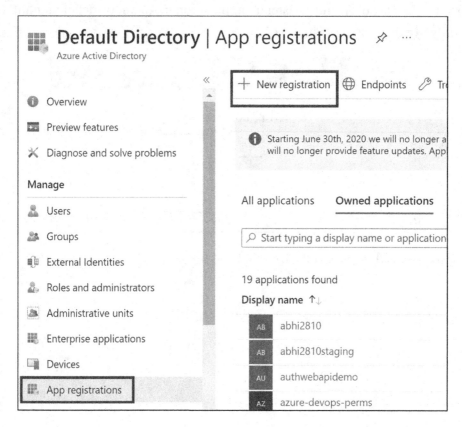

Figure 5-2. *Click App registrations*

Provide a name for the application you need to register and then click **Register** as shown in Figure 5-3.

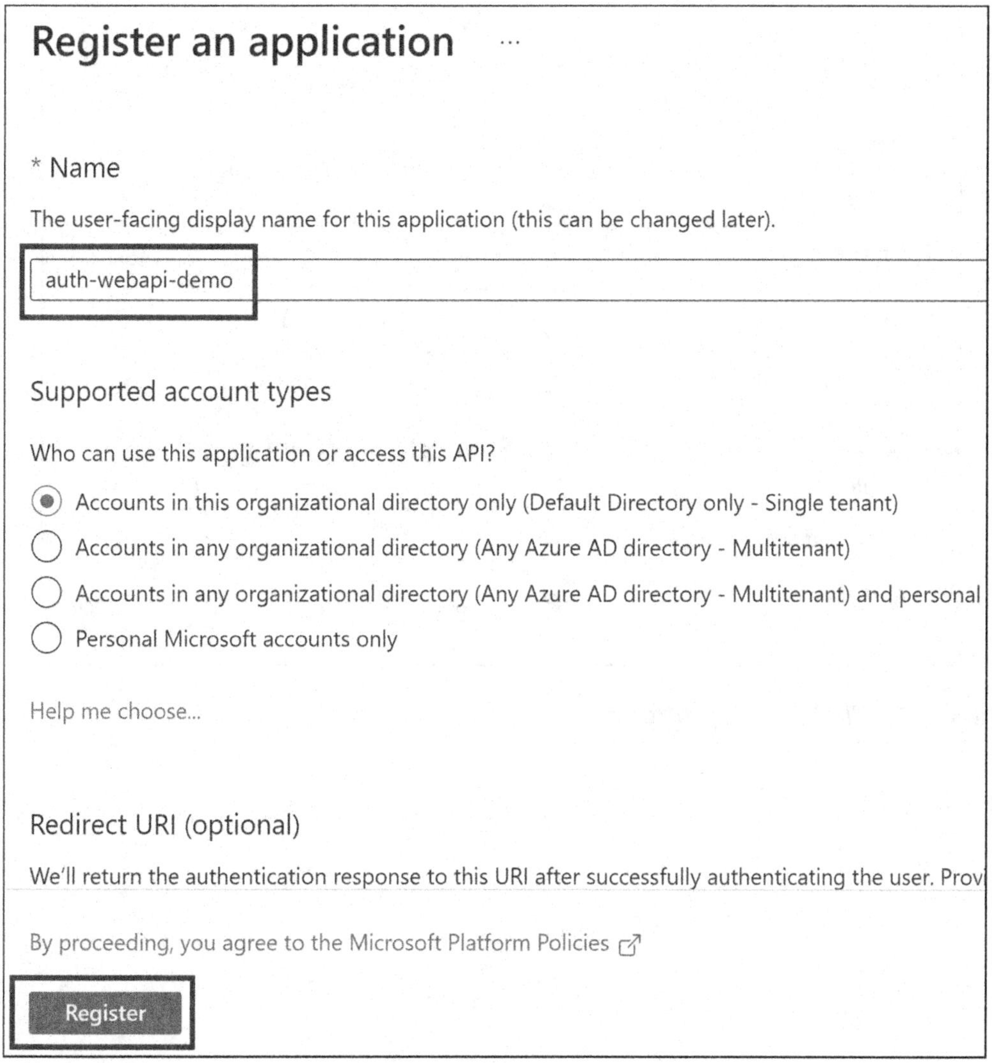

Register an application   ⋯

* Name

The user-facing display name for this application (this can be changed later).

auth-webapi-demo

Supported account types

Who can use this application or access this API?

◉ Accounts in this organizational directory only (Default Directory only - Single tenant)

◯ Accounts in any organizational directory (Any Azure AD directory - Multitenant)

◯ Accounts in any organizational directory (Any Azure AD directory - Multitenant) and personal

◯ Personal Microsoft accounts only

Help me choose...

Redirect URI (optional)

We'll return the authentication response to this URI after successfully authenticating the user. Prov

By proceeding, you agree to the Microsoft Platform Policies ⧉

Register

Figure 5-3.   *Click Register*

The application will get registered. Click **Authentication** and then click **Add platform** as shown in Figure 5-4. We need to add a web platform because we need to use this application to authenticate the MathAPI.

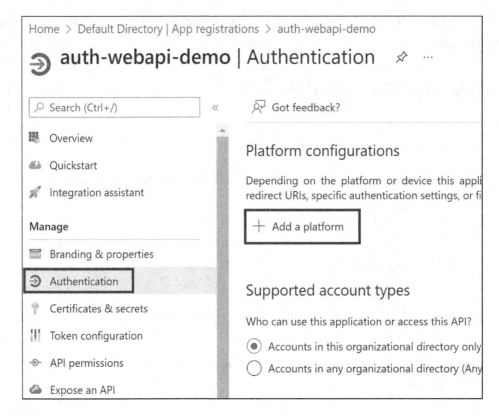

Figure 5-4. *Click Add a platform*

Select **Web** as shown in Figure 5-5. We need to authenticate a WebAPI.

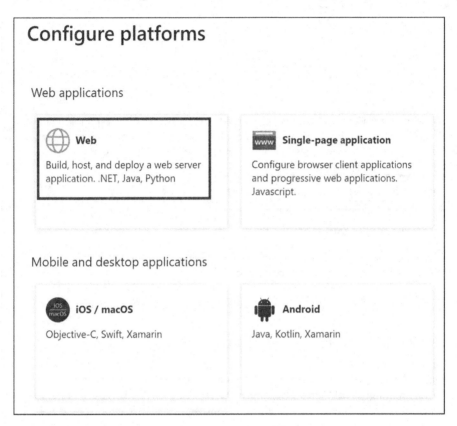

Figure 5-5. *Select Web*

We are going to access the application from Postman, so we need to provide the redirect URI of Postman. Once the authentication is successful, the response will get redirected to the Postman from where you are invoking the application. Provide the Postman URL as the redirect URI as shown in Figure 5-6. The URL will standard for all the calls from Postman. You can use the URL as is without any modifications. Click **Configure** as shown in Figure 5-6.

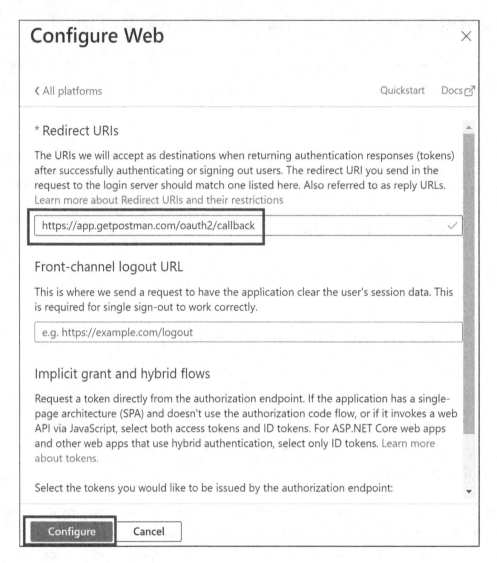

Figure 5-6. *Click Configure*

Create the Application Scope

We can use the scope for the registered application to restrict access to the application. To create the application scope, click **Expose an API** and then click **Add a scope** as shown in Figure 5-7.

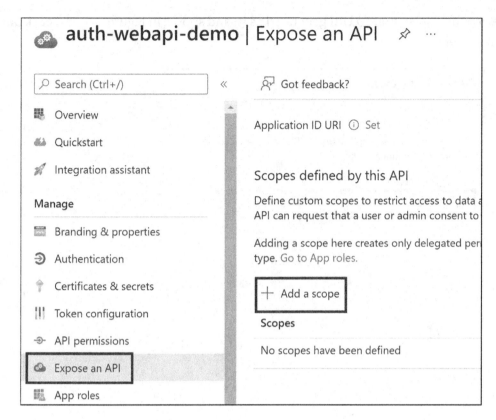

Figure 5-7. *Click Add a scope*

Keep the application ID URI generated as is, and shown in Figure 5-8, and click **Save and continue**.

Figure 5-8. Click Save and continue

Provide a name for the scope and other required values as shown in Figure 5-9. Click
Add scope. The scope will get added.

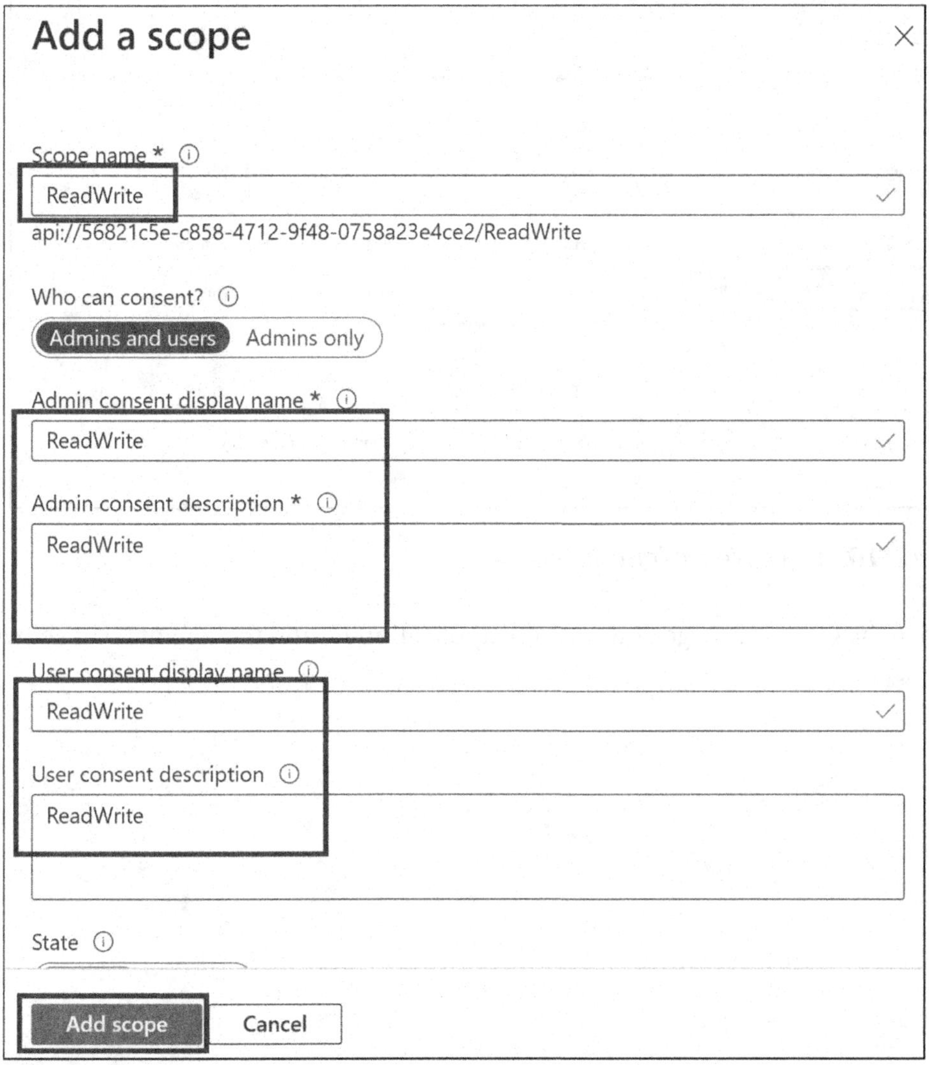

Figure 5-9. *Click Add scope*

Create the Application Secret

We'll use the secret for the application to access the application from the client, which
is Postman in our case. To create the application secret, click **Certificates & secrets** and
then click **New client secret** as shown in Figure 5-10. Copy the secret value. We will use
the secret value later.

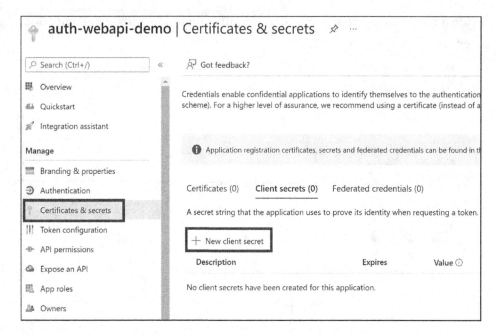

Figure 5-10. *Click New client secret*

Go to the Overview page and copy the application ID and the tenant ID as shown in Figure 5-11.

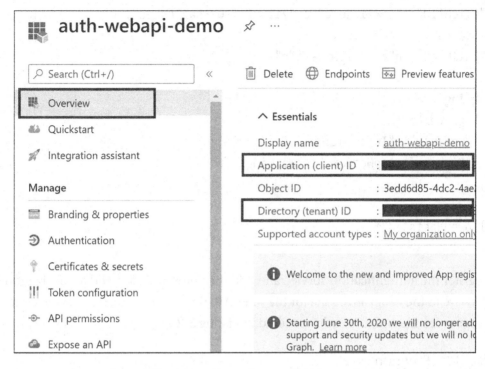

Figure 5-11. *Copy the application ID and tenant ID*

Configure MathAPI for Authentication and Authorization

Now we'll modify the MathAPI project we created in Chapter 4. MathAPI invokes the AddAPI and SubtractAPI services. The AddAPI and SubtractAPI services are not exposed outside the Kubernetes cluster. We can enable authentication for the MathAPI and need not make any changes for AddAPI and SubtractAPI. Open the appsettings.json file in the MathAPI project and add the tenant ID, client ID, scope, and other necessary values as shown in Listing 5-1.

Listing 5-1. Appsettings.json

```
{
  "AzureAd": {
    "Instance": "https://login.microsoftonline.com/",
    "TenantId": "112a00d5-bc7e-4c48-856c-281cff2328bf",
```

```json
    "ClientId": "56821c5e-c858-4712-9f48-0758a23e4ce2",
    "Scopes": "ReadWrite",
    "CallbackPath": "/signin-oidc"
  },
  "Logging": {
    "LogLevel": {
      "Default": "Information",
      "Microsoft.AspNetCore": "Warning"
    }
  },
  "AllowedHosts": "*"
}
```

Register the authentication service and add the authentication and authorization middleware in the Program.cs file for the MathAPI project. You can replace the code in the Program.cs file with the code specified in Listing 5-2.

Listing 5-2. Program.cs

```csharp
using Microsoft.AspNetCore.Authentication;
using Microsoft.AspNetCore.Authentication.JwtBearer;
using Microsoft.Identity.Web;

var builder = WebApplication.CreateBuilder(args);

// Add services to the container.

//Register authentication service
builder.Services.AddAuthentication(JwtBearerDefaults.AuthenticationScheme)
    .AddMicrosoftIdentityWebApi(builder.Configuration.
GetSection("AzureAd"));

builder.Services.AddControllers();
// Learn more about configuring Swagger/OpenAPI at https://aka.ms/
aspnetcore/swashbuckle
builder.Services.AddEndpointsApiExplorer();
builder.Services.AddSwaggerGen();

var app = builder.Build();
```

```
// Configure the HTTP request pipeline.
if (app.Environment.IsDevelopment())
{
    app.UseSwagger();
    app.UseSwaggerUI();
}

app.UseHttpsRedirection();

//Enable Authentication and authorization middleware
app.UseAuthentication();
app.UseAuthorization();

app.MapControllers();


app.Run();
```

Add the Authorize attribute for the MathController. You can replace
MathController.cs file with code as in Listing 5-3. This enables authentication for the
MathAPI.

Listing 5-3. MathController.cs

```
using Microsoft.AspNetCore.Authorization;
using Microsoft.AspNetCore.Mvc;
using System.Net;
using System.Net.Http.Headers;
using System.Text;

namespace MathAPI.Controllers
{
    [Authorize]
    [ApiController]
    [Route("[controller]")]
    public class MathController : Controller
    {
        [HttpGet("Get")]
        public string Get(string ops, int a,int b)
        {
```

```
        string result = "";
        string url = "";
        string queryStr = "?a=" + a + "&b=" + b;

        if (ops == "add")
        {
            url = "http:// 10.0.156.137/Add" + queryStr;
        }
        else
        {
            url = "http://10.0.143.214/subtract" + queryStr; ;
        }
        HttpWebRequest request = (HttpWebRequest)WebRequest.
        Create(url);
        WebResponse response = request.GetResponse();
        using (Stream responseStream = response.GetResponseStream())
        {
            StreamReader reader = new StreamReader(responseStream,
            Encoding.UTF8);
            result = reader.ReadToEnd();
        }
        return result;
    }
  }
}
```

We can use the same Azure Kubernetes Service cluster that we have created earlier and have deployed the APIs in Chapter 4. We need to containerize the MathAPI and push it to Azure Container Registry. You need not redeploy the AddAPI and the SubtractAPI to the Kubernetes cluster. We need to deploy the MathAPI service to the cluster. If you have deleted the Azure container registry and the Azure Kubernetes Service, you can follow the instructions provided in Chapter 4 to re-create them. And then deploy the AddAPI and SubtractAPI to the Kubernetes cluster. Follow the steps illustrated in Chapter 4 to containerize and deploy the MathAPI to the Azure Kubernetes Service cluster.

Once the MathAPI deployment is complete, we can use the Postman tool to test the deployed API. Get the External IP address of the MathAPI using the kubectl command as shown in Listing 5-4.

Listing 5-4. Get Services in the Cluster

```
kubectl get services
```

Figure 5-12 depicts the response for the command in Listing 5-4.

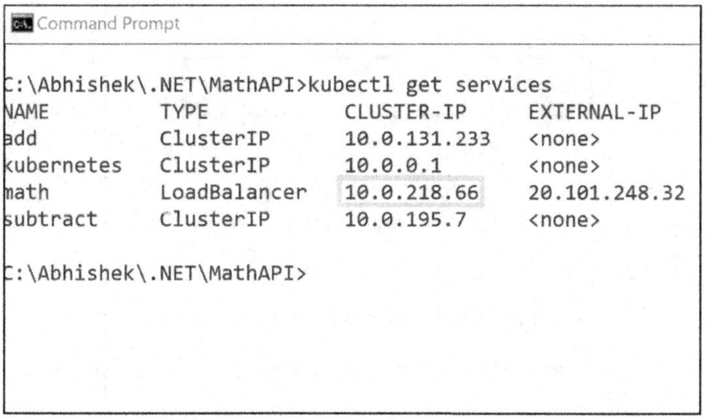

```
C:\Abhishek\.NET\MathAPI>kubectl get services
NAME          TYPE          CLUSTER-IP       EXTERNAL-IP
add           ClusterIP     10.0.131.233     <none>
kubernetes    ClusterIP     10.0.0.1         <none>
math          LoadBalancer  10.0.218.66      20.101.248.32
subtract      ClusterIP     10.0.195.7       <none>

C:\Abhishek\.NET\MathAPI>
```

Figure 5-12. *Services in Kubernetes cluster*

We can use the URL shown in Listing 5-5 to browse the math service.

Listing 5-5. MathAPI URL in Kubernetes Cluster

```
http://[External-IP]/Math/Get?ops=subtract&a=4&b=6
```

Open Postman and create a new request. Click the **Authorization** tab and select Type as **OAuth 2.0** as shown in Figure 5-13.

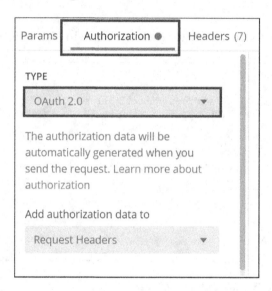

Figure 5-13. *Postman authorization*

Provide Auth URL as shown in Listing 5-6. Replace [Tenant ID] with your Tenant ID for Azure AD.

Listing 5-6. Postman Auth URL

```
https://login.microsoftonline.com/[Tenant ID]/oauth2/v2.0/authorize
```

Provide the Access Token URL as shown in Listing 5-7. Replace [Tenant ID] with your Tenant ID for Azure AD.

Listing 5-7. Postman Access Token URL

```
https://login.microsoftonline.com/[Tenant Id]/oauth2/v2.0/token
```

As shown in Figure 5-14, provide in the Client ID, Client Secret, and Scope fields the information for your application registered in Azure AD. Click **Get New Access Token**. You will be prompted for your Azure credentials.

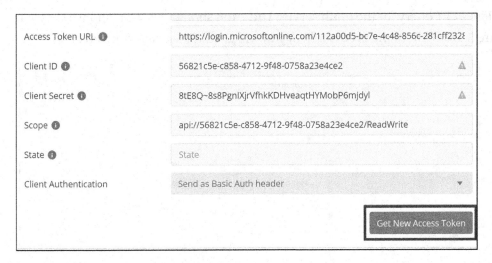

Figure 5-14. *Click Get New Access Token*

Once the authentication is successful, the access token will get generated. Click **Use Token** as shown in Figure 5-15.

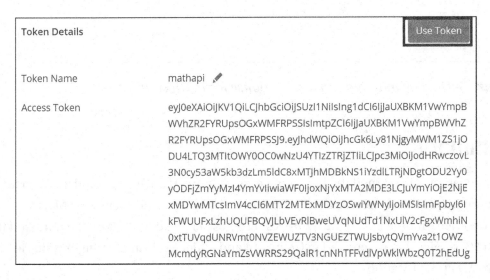

Figure 5-15. *Click Use Token*

Fire a GET query for the math service URL. You should get the response shown in Figure 5-16. Without the access token, you will get a 401 – Unauthorized error.

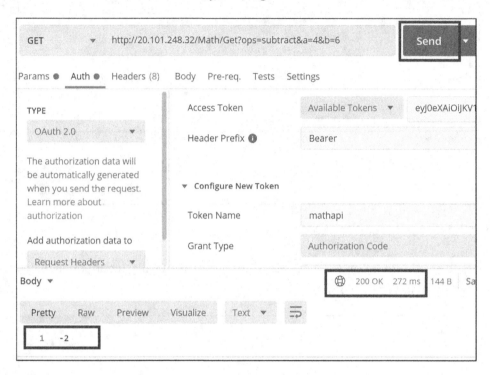

Figure 5-16. *Postman request and response for math service*

Summary

In this chapter, you learned the basic concepts of Azure AD. We registered an application in Azure AD and made necessary configurations in Azure AD to secure the Math microservice running inside the Azure Kubernetes Service cluster. We then modified the MathAPI service that we created in Chapter 4 and added code and configurations for Azure AD authentication.

In the next chapter we will explore how to run APIs in Azure Container Apps.

CHAPTER 6

Running APIs on Azure Container Apps

Azure Container Apps helps you to run containerized applications and microservices with ease in an underlying Kubernetes environment. You only need to focus on building, containerizing, and deploying the application to the Azure Container Apps Environment. All the complexities involved with the Kubernetes cluster are abstracted from you. You need not worry about building a Kubernetes deployment manifest file and running `kubectl` or `helm` commands to deploy the manifest file on the underlying Kubernetes platform.

In this chapter, you will learn how to deploy the Math microservices application to Azure Container Apps. We will also explore the basics of Azure Container Apps.

In this chapter, we will explore the following topics related to Azure Container Apps:

- Introduction to Azure Container Apps

- Create an Azure Container Apps Environment with the Add API and Subtract API

- Modify the Math API and push it to Azure Container Registry

- Deploy the Math API to the Azure Container Apps Environment

After completing this chapter, you should understand the fundamentals of Azure Container Apps and be able to run .NET-based microservices on Azure Container Apps.

Introduction to Azure Container Apps

Azure Container Apps is a serverless container offering on Azure that is built on top of Kubernetes. It abstracts all complexities involved in deploying and managing

© Ashirwad Satapathi and Abhishek Mishra 2023
A. Satapathi and A. Mishra, *Developing Cloud-Native Solutions with Microsoft Azure and .NET*,
https://doi.org/10.1007/978-1-4842-9004-0_6

the Kubernetes cluster, enabling you to focus on building your application and containerizing it. You can deploy your application containers with ease without needing to write any Kubernetes deployment manifest files. However, you do not have any control over the underlying Kubernetes cluster and there is no mechanism that will help you in running `kubectl` commands to interact with the Kubernetes cluster.

Because Azure Container Apps is a serverless offering, it can scale based on the incoming traffic. It supports event-driven scaling using Kubernetes Event-Driven Autoscaling (KEDA). For example, Azure Container Apps can scale when the number of items in the service bus queue increases. When the number of queue item increases, it fires an event that drives autoscaling for Azure Container Apps. Whenever there is no workload, you do not get charged. For example, if there are no items in the Service Bus queue to be processed, no container pod will be created and you will not get charged. Azure Container Apps can scale based on any of the following. In contrast, Azure Kubernetes Service can scale based on CPU or memory usage only.

- CPU or memory usage

- HTTP requests

- Events like items in Azure Service Bus Queue

- KEDA-supported events

Multiple Azure container apps run inside an Azure Container Apps Environment. Each of the container apps runs multiple containers in a replica, as shown in Figure 6-1. It can also execute multiple versions or revisions of containers, and you can define the traffic percentage that will hit each of the container versions.

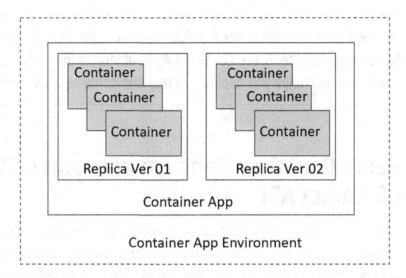

Figure 6-1. *Azure Container Apps*

You can configure Ingress for the application running inside Container Apps and expose the access to the Internet. You may choose to restrict access to the container to the other container apps running inside the Azure Container Apps Environment. Figure 6-2 demonstrates an Azure Container Apps Environment hosting three Azure container apps. The container app running the Math API is exposed outside the Container Apps Environment for consumption. The Add API container app and Subtract API container app are accessible within the Container Apps Environment. The Math API container app can access the Add API container app and Subtract API container app.

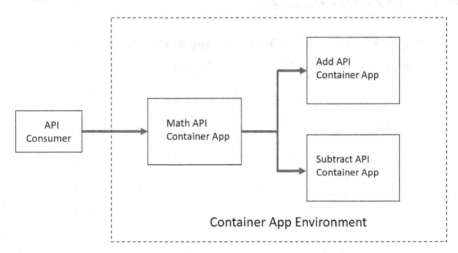

Figure 6-2. *Math Microservice on Azure Container Apps*

> **Note**   If you need greater control over the Kubernetes cluster, then you should use Azure Kubernetes Service. Azure Container Apps abstracts the underlying Kubernetes platform and helps you deploy and manage containers with ease.

Create Azure Container Apps Environment with Add API and Subtract API

Let's create an Azure Container Apps Environment with a container app for the Add API and a container app for the Subtract API. We need to limit access to the container apps inside the Container Apps Environment and they should not be exposed to the Internet. Go to the Azure portal and click **Create a resource** as shown in Figure 6-3.

Figure 6-3. *Click Create a resource*

Click **Containers** and then click **Container App** as shown in Figure 6-4. You get all container offerings on Azure in the Containers category.

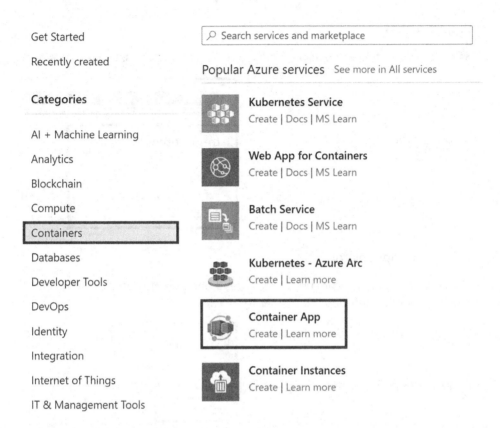

Figure 6-4. *Click Container App*

In the respective fields shown in Figure 6-5, provide the subscription details, resource group, container app name, and the location where you want to create the container app. We need to create the container app inside a Container Apps Environment, so click **Create new** as shown in Figure 6-5 to create a Container Apps Environment.

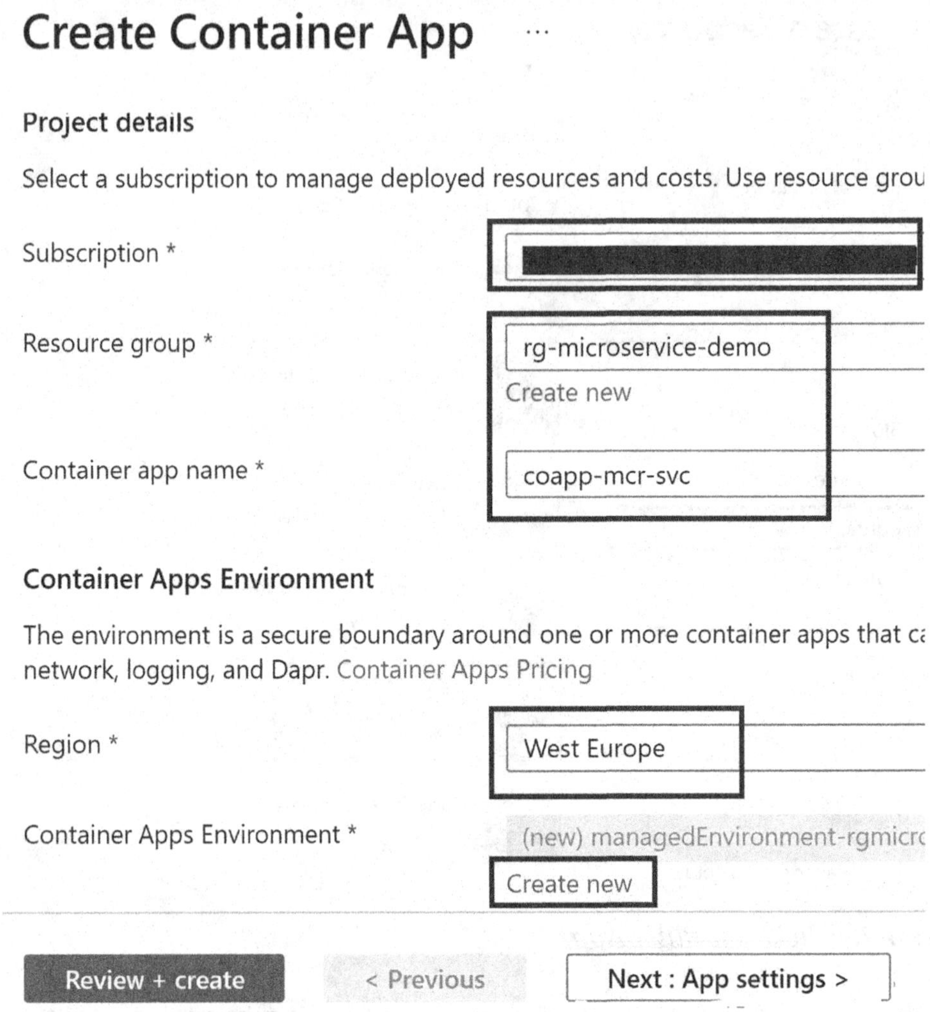

Create Container App   ...

Project details

Select a subscription to manage deployed resources and costs. Use resource grou

Subscription *

Resource group *

rg-microservice-demo

Create new

Container app name *

coapp-mcr-svc

Container Apps Environment

The environment is a secure boundary around one or more container apps that ca
network, logging, and Dapr. Container Apps Pricing

Region *

West Europe

Container Apps Environment *

(new) managedEnvironment-rgmicrc

Create new

Review + create   < Previous   Next : App settings >

Figure 6-5. *Provide basic details*

Provide the container environment name and click **Create** as shown in Figure 6-6.

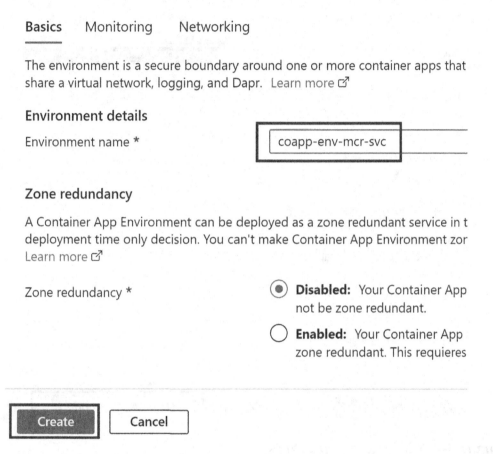

Create Container Apps Environment ···

Basics   Monitoring   Networking

The environment is a secure boundary around one or more container apps that share a virtual network, logging, and Dapr. Learn more ☐

Environment details

Environment name *   coapp-env-mcr-svc

Zone redundancy

A Container App Environment can be deployed as a zone redundant service in t deployment time only decision. You can't make Container App Environment zor Learn more ☐

Zone redundancy *   ⦿ **Disabled:** Your Container App
                                         not be zone redundant.

                                    ○ **Enabled:** Your Container App
                                         zone redundant. This requieres

Create   Cancel

Figure 6-6. *Click Create*

We need to select the container image that we have in the Azure container registry. We have containerized the Add API and the Subtract API in Chapter 4 and have pushed them to Azure Container Registry. Click **Next : App settings** as shown in Figure 6-7 to select the container image.

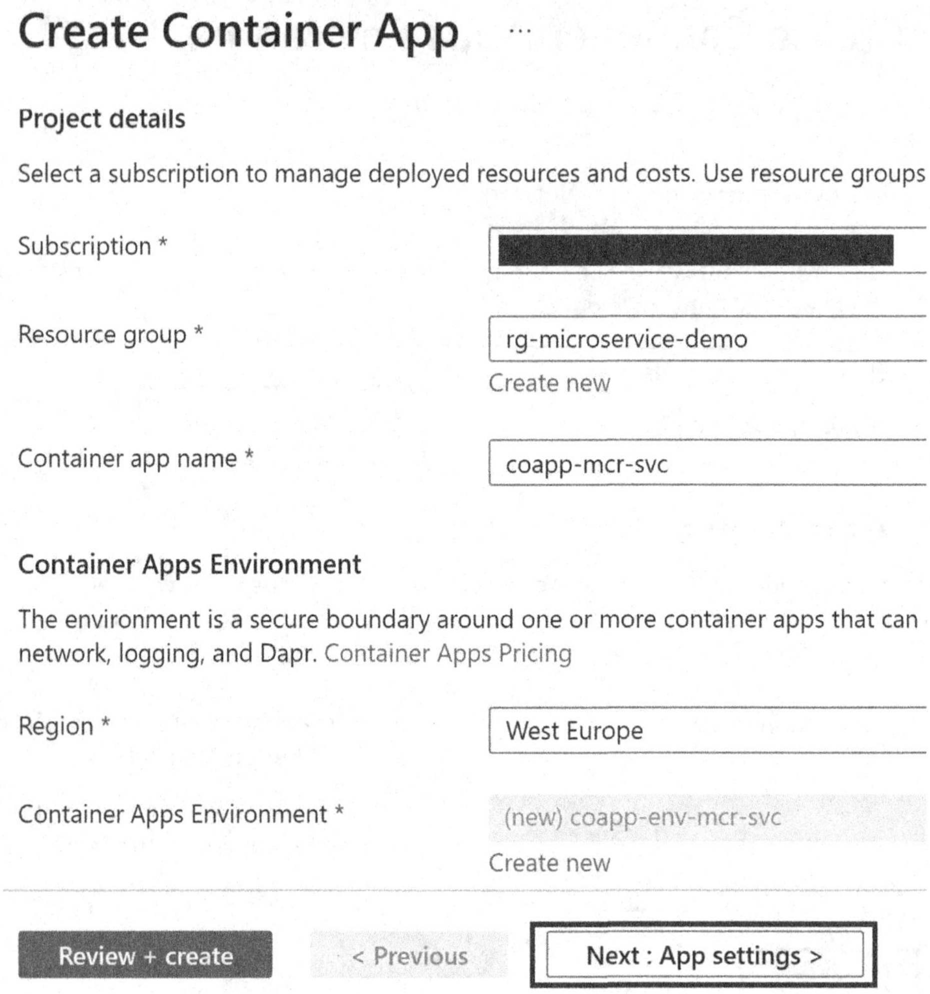

Create Container App   ...

Project details

Select a subscription to manage deployed resources and costs. Use resource groups

Subscription *   ██████████████████████████

Resource group *   rg-microservice-demo

                                 Create new

Container app name *   coapp-mcr-svc

Container Apps Environment

The environment is a secure boundary around one or more container apps that can
network, logging, and Dapr. Container Apps Pricing

Region *   West Europe

Container Apps Environment *   (new) coapp-env-mcr-svc

                                 Create new

| Review + create | < Previous | Next : App settings > |

Figure 6-7. *Click Next : App settings*

Select the Container Registry, container image for the Add API, and the container as
shown in Figure 6-8.

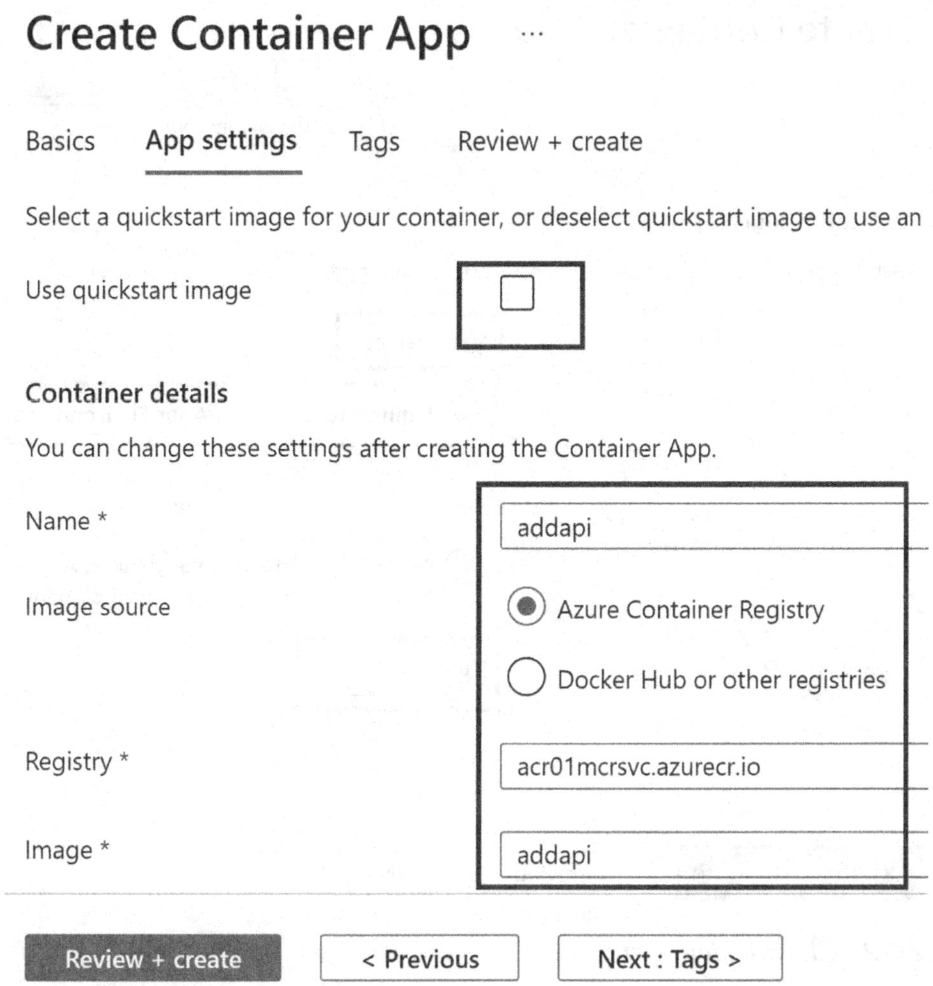

Create Container App ⋯

Basics   **App settings**   Tags   Review + create

Select a quickstart image for your container, or deselect quickstart image to use an

Use quickstart image   ☐

Container details
You can change these settings after creating the Container App.

Name *	addapi
Image source	◉ Azure Container Registry
	○ Docker Hub or other registries
Registry *	acr01mcrsvc.azurecr.io
Image *	addapi

[Review + create]   [< Previous]   [Next : Tags >]

Figure 6-8. *Provide image details*

Enable HTTP Ingress and limit it to the Container Apps Environment as shown in Figure 6-9. Click **Review + create**.

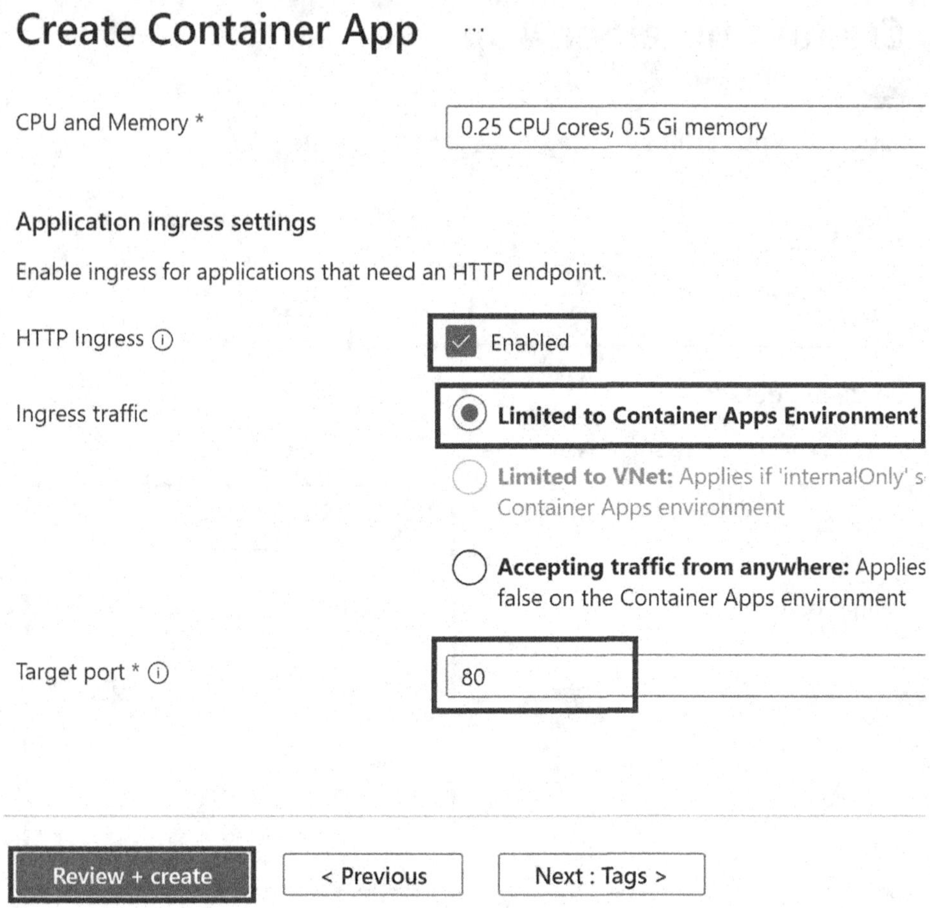

Create Container App   ...

CPU and Memory *

| 0.25 CPU cores, 0.5 Gi memory |

Application ingress settings

Enable ingress for applications that need an HTTP endpoint.

HTTP Ingress ⓘ

☑ Enabled

Ingress traffic

⦿ **Limited to Container Apps Environment**

○ **Limited to VNet:** Applies if 'internalOnly' s·
Container Apps environment

○ **Accepting traffic from anywhere:** Applies
false on the Container Apps environment

Target port * ⓘ

| 80 |

| Review + create | | < Previous | | Next : Tags > |

Figure 6-9. *Click Review + create*

Click **Create** as shown in Figure 6-10 to spin up the Container Apps Environment along with the Add API container app.

140

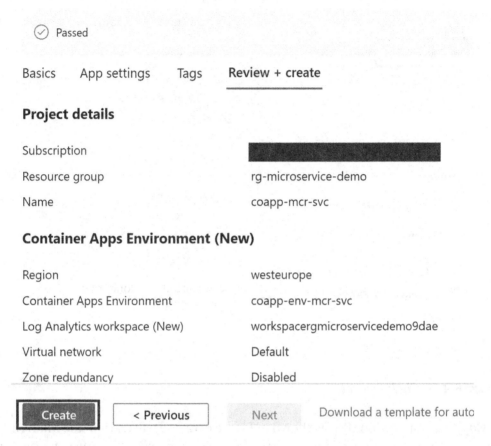

Create Container App   ···

○ Passed

Basics   App settings   Tags   **Review + create**

Project details

Subscription

Resource group   rg-microservice-demo

Name   coapp-mcr-svc

Container Apps Environment (New)

Region   westeurope

Container Apps Environment   coapp-env-mcr-svc

Log Analytics workspace (New)   workspacergmicroservicedemo9dae

Virtual network   Default

Zone redundancy   Disabled

[Create]   [< Previous]   [Next]   Download a template for auto

Figure 6-10. *Click Create*

Once the container app gets created, navigate to the container app in the portal. Go to the **Overview** tab as shown in Figure 6-11.

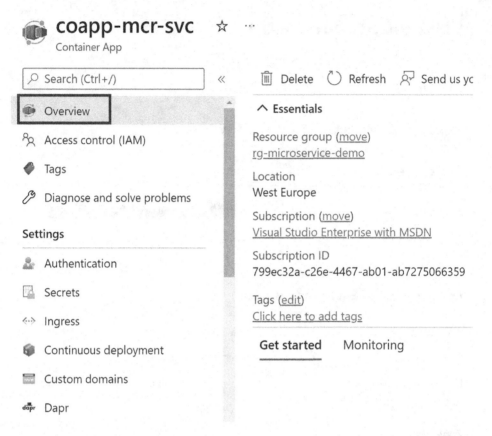

Figure 6-11. *Click Overview*

Copy the Application URL as shown in Figure 6-12. We will use it in the Math API code to access the Add API service running inside the container app. Click the Container Apps Environment for the container app as shown in Figure 6-12.

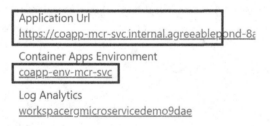

Figure 6-12. *Copy Application URL*

In the Container Apps Environment, click **Apps** and then click **Create** as shown in Figure 6-13. We need to create another container app for the Subtract API in that environment.

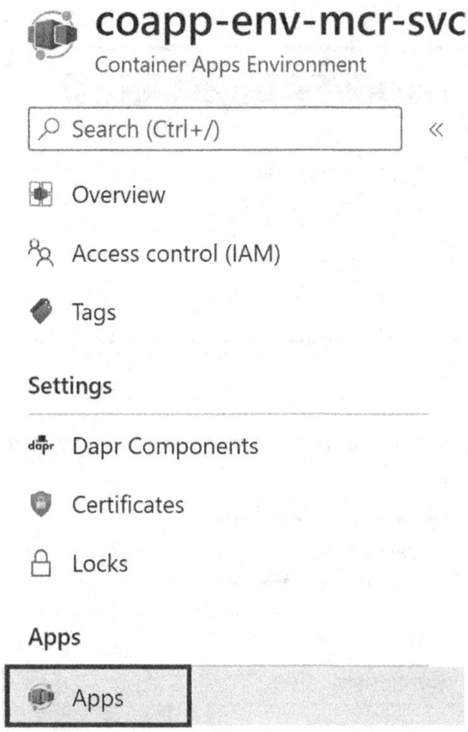

Figure 6-13. *Click Apps*

Provide the subscription details, resource group, container app name, and the location where you want to create the container app, as shown in Figure 6-14. Select the Container Apps Environment. We need to select the Subtract API container image that we have in the Azure container registry. Click **Next : App Settings** as shown in Figure 6-14 to select the container image.

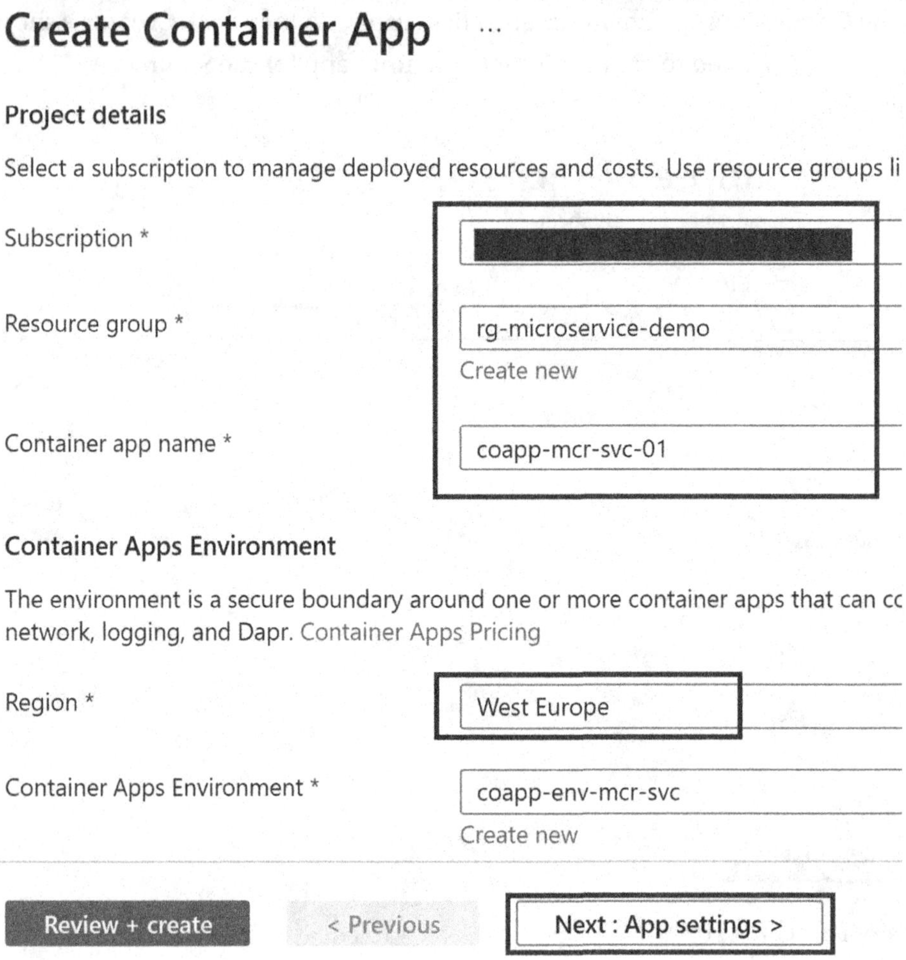

Create Container App ...

Project details

Select a subscription to manage deployed resources and costs. Use resource groups li

Subscription *

▮▮▮▮▮▮▮▮▮▮▮▮▮▮▮▮

Resource group *

rg-microservice-demo

Create new

Container app name *

coapp-mcr-svc-01

Container Apps Environment

The environment is a secure boundary around one or more container apps that can cc network, logging, and Dapr. Container Apps Pricing

Region *

West Europe

Container Apps Environment *

coapp-env-mcr-svc

Create new

| Review + create | < Previous | Next : App settings > |

Figure 6-14. *Click Next : App settings*

Select the Container Registry, container image for the Subtract API, and the container as shown in Figure 6-15.

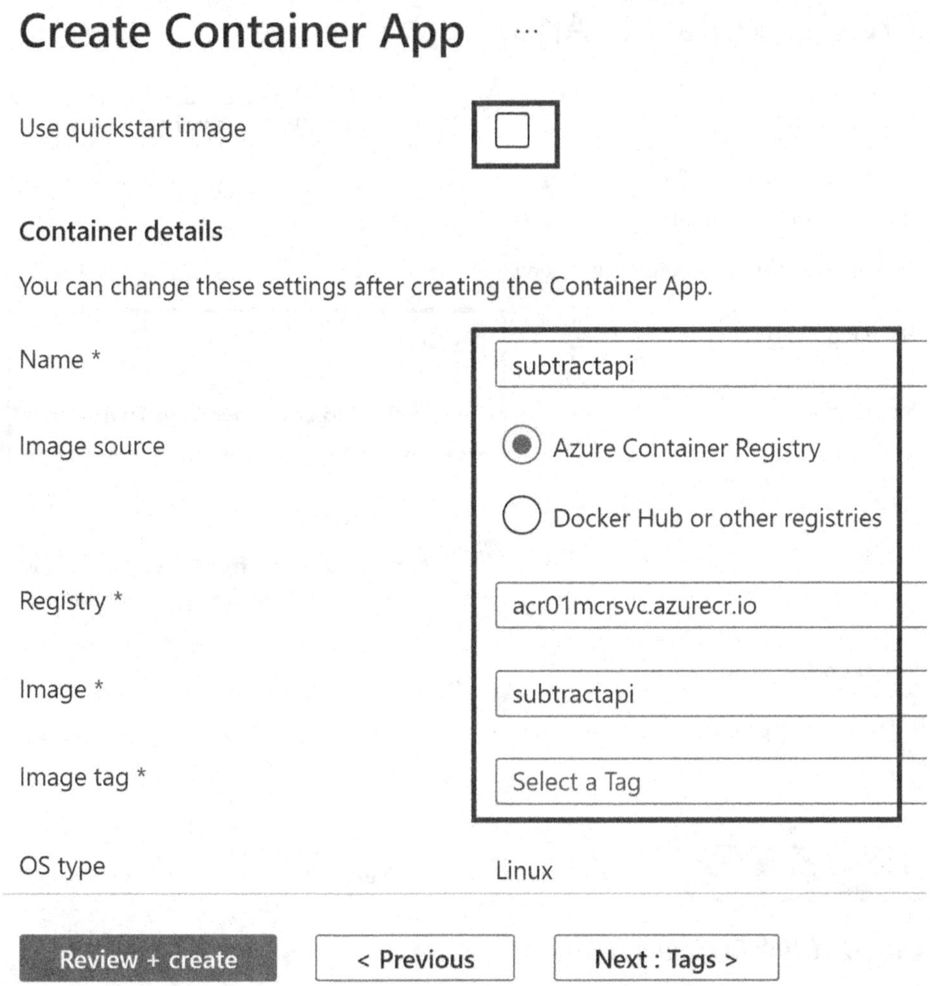

Create Container App   ...

Use quickstart image   ☐

Container details

You can change these settings after creating the Container App.

Name *	subtractapi
Image source	⦿ Azure Container Registry
	◯ Docker Hub or other registries
Registry *	acr01mcrsvc.azurecr.io
Image *	subtractapi
Image tag *	Select a Tag
OS type	Linux

[Review + create]   [< Previous]   [Next : Tags >]

Figure 6-15. *Provide image details*

Enable HTTP Ingress and limit it to the Container Apps Environment as shown in Figure 6-16. Click **Review + create**.

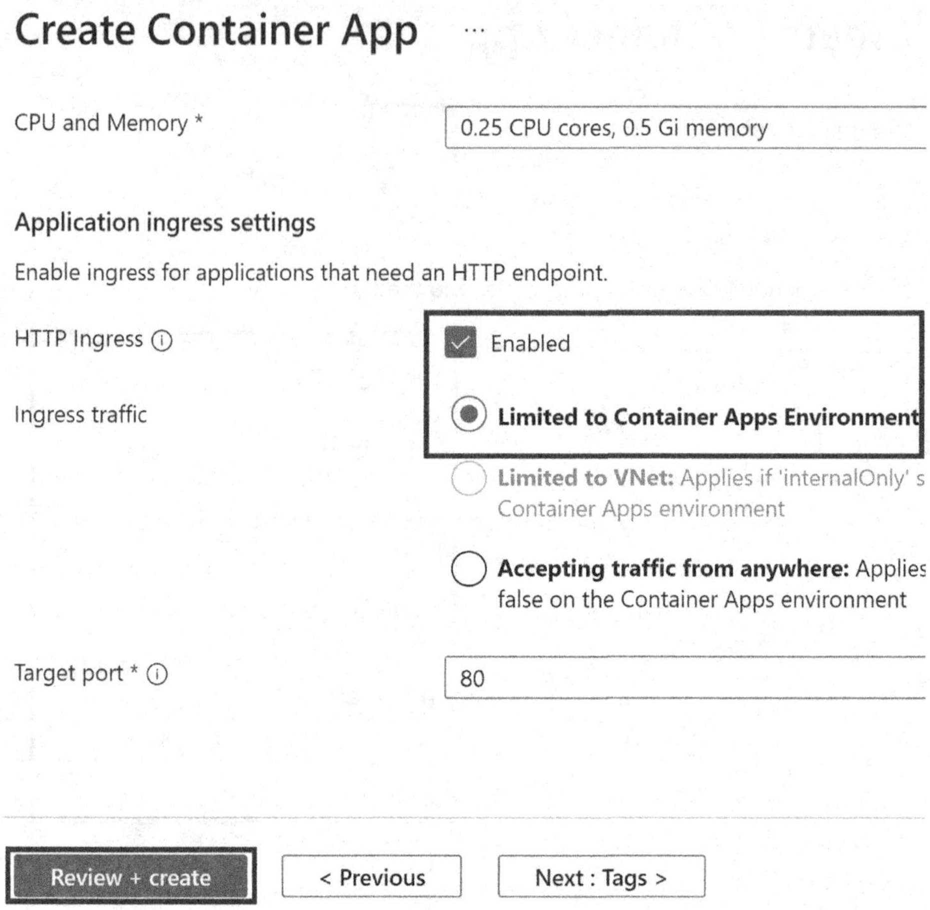

Create Container App ···

CPU and Memory *	0.25 CPU cores, 0.5 Gi memory

Application ingress settings

Enable ingress for applications that need an HTTP endpoint.

HTTP Ingress ⓘ   ☑ Enabled

Ingress traffic   ⦿ **Limited to Container Apps Environment**

⦾ **Limited to VNet:** Applies if 'internalOnly' s
Container Apps environment

⦾ **Accepting traffic from anywhere:** Applies
false on the Container Apps environment

Target port * ⓘ	80

[Review + create]   [< Previous]   [Next : Tags >]

Figure 6-16. *Click Review + create*

Click **Create** to spin up the Subtract API container app inside the Container Apps Environment. Once the container app gets created, go to the **Overview** tab and copy the Application URL as shown in Figure 6-17. We will use this URL in the Math API code to invoke the Subtract API.

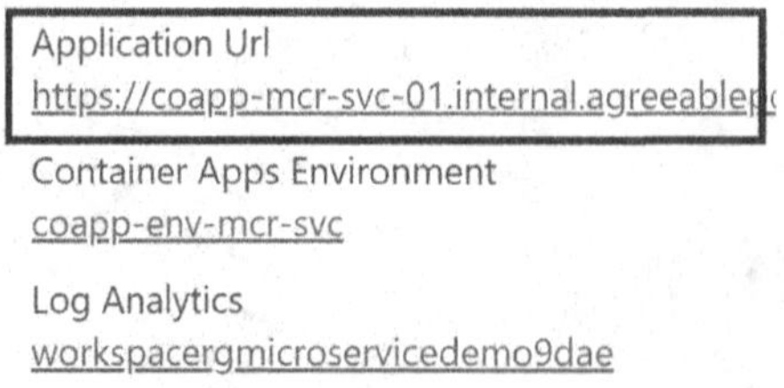

Application Url
https://coapp-mcr-svc-01.internal.agreeable

Container Apps Environment
coapp-env-mcr-svc

Log Analytics
workspacergmicroservicedemo9dae

Figure 6-17. *Copy Application URL*

Modify Math API and Push It to Azure Container Registry

Now let's modify the Math API and add the Container App application URL for the Add API and Subtract API as shown in Listing 6-1.

Listing 6-1. MathController.cs

```
using Microsoft.AspNetCore.Authorization;
using Microsoft.AspNetCore.Mvc;
using System.Net;
using System.Net.Http.Headers;
using System.Text;

namespace MathAPI.Controllers
{
    [Authorize]
    [ApiController]
    [Route("[controller]")]
    public class MathController : Controller
    {
        [HttpGet("Test")]
        public string Test()
        {
            return "Success";
        }
        [HttpGet("Get")]
        public string Get(string ops, int a,int b)
        {
            string result = "";
            string url = "";
            string queryStr = "?a=" + a + "&b=" + b;

            if (ops == "add")
            {
                url = "[Add API Container App URL]/Add" + queryStr;
            }
```

```
            else
            {
                url = "[Subtract API Container App URL]/subtract" +
                queryStr;
            }
            HttpWebRequest request = (HttpWebRequest)WebRequest.
            Create(url);
            WebResponse response = request.GetResponse();
            using (Stream responseStream = response.GetResponseStream())
            {
                StreamReader reader = new StreamReader(responseStream,
                Encoding.UTF8);
                result = reader.ReadToEnd();
            }
            return result;
        }
    }
}
```

Containerize the application and push it to Azure Container Registry as demonstrated in Chapter 4.

Deploy Math API to Azure Container Apps Environment

Now let's the Math API container image in the Azure Container App running in the Container Apps Environment. Go to the **Overview** section of one of the container apps you created earlier and click the Container Apps Environment. In the Container Apps Environment, click the **Apps** section and then click **Create** as shown in Figure 6-18.

coapp-env-mcr-svc | Apps ...

Container Apps Environment

Search (Ctrl+/)	«

+ Create

Overview

Access control (IAM)

Tags

Filter by name

Name ↑↓

coapp-mcr-svc

Settings

coapp-mcr-svc-01

dapr Dapr Components

Certificates

Locks

Apps

Apps

Figure 6-18. Click Apps

Provide the subscription details, resource group, container app name, and the location where you want to create the container app, as shown in Figure 6-19. Select the Container Apps Environment. We need to select the Math API container image that we have in the Azure container registry. Click **Next : App Settings** as shown in Figure 6-19 to select the container image.

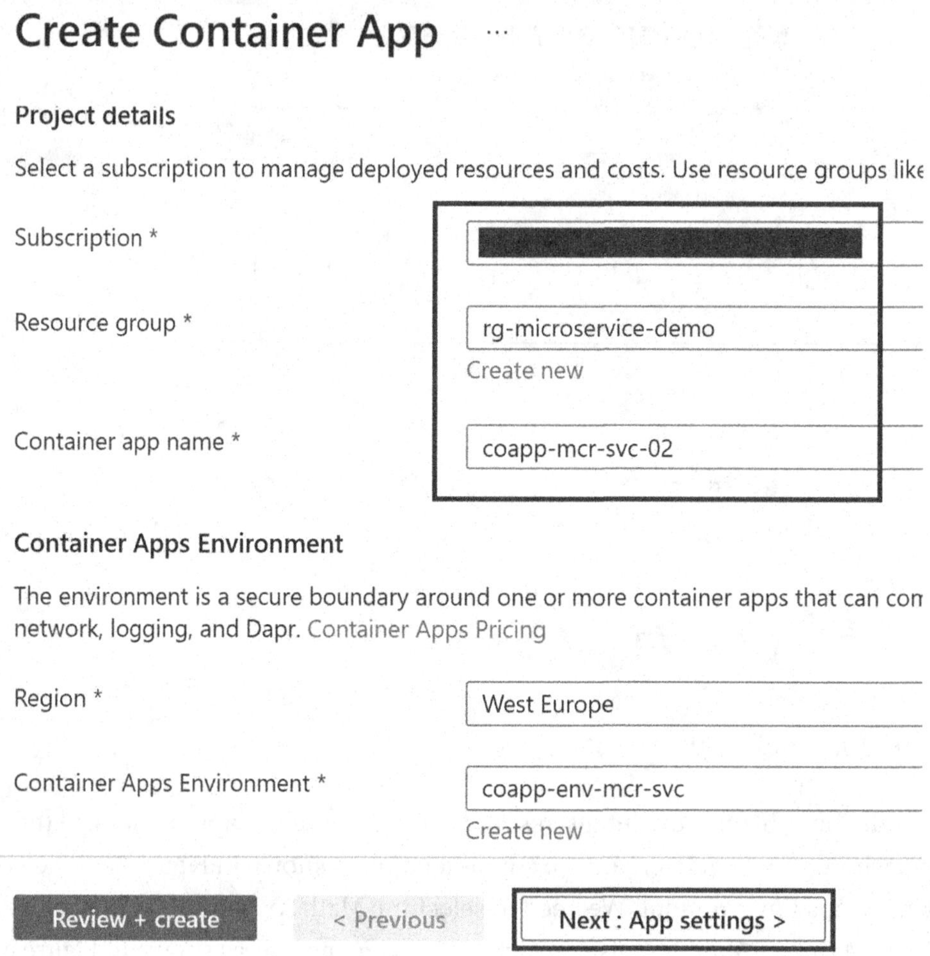

Create Container App   ···

Project details

Select a subscription to manage deployed resources and costs. Use resource groups like

Subscription *

Resource group *   rg-microservice-demo

Create new

Container app name *   coapp-mcr-svc-02

Container Apps Environment

The environment is a secure boundary around one or more container apps that can con
network, logging, and Dapr. Container Apps Pricing

Region *   West Europe

Container Apps Environment *   coapp-env-mcr-svc

Create new

| Review + create | < Previous | Next : App settings > |

Figure 6-19. *Click Next : App settings*

Select the Container Registry, container image for the Subtract API, and the
container as shown in Figure 6-20.

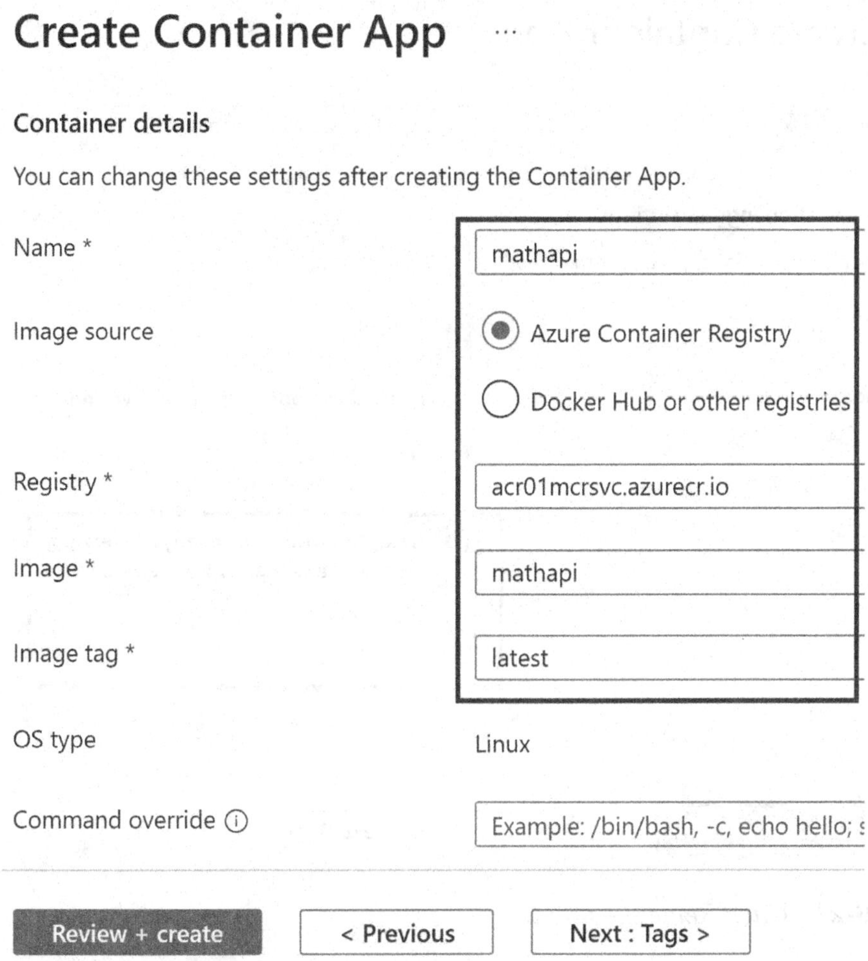

Create Container App ...

Container details

You can change these settings after creating the Container App.

Name *	mathapi
Image source	● Azure Container Registry
	○ Docker Hub or other registries
Registry *	acr01mcrsvc.azurecr.io
Image *	mathapi
Image tag *	latest
OS type	Linux
Command override ⓘ	Example: /bin/bash, -c, echo hello;

[Review + create]   [< Previous]   [Next : Tags >]

Figure 6-20. *Provide image details*

Enable HTTP Ingress and expose it outside the Container Apps Environment as shown in Figure 6-21 so that it can be accessed over the Internet. Click **Review + create**.

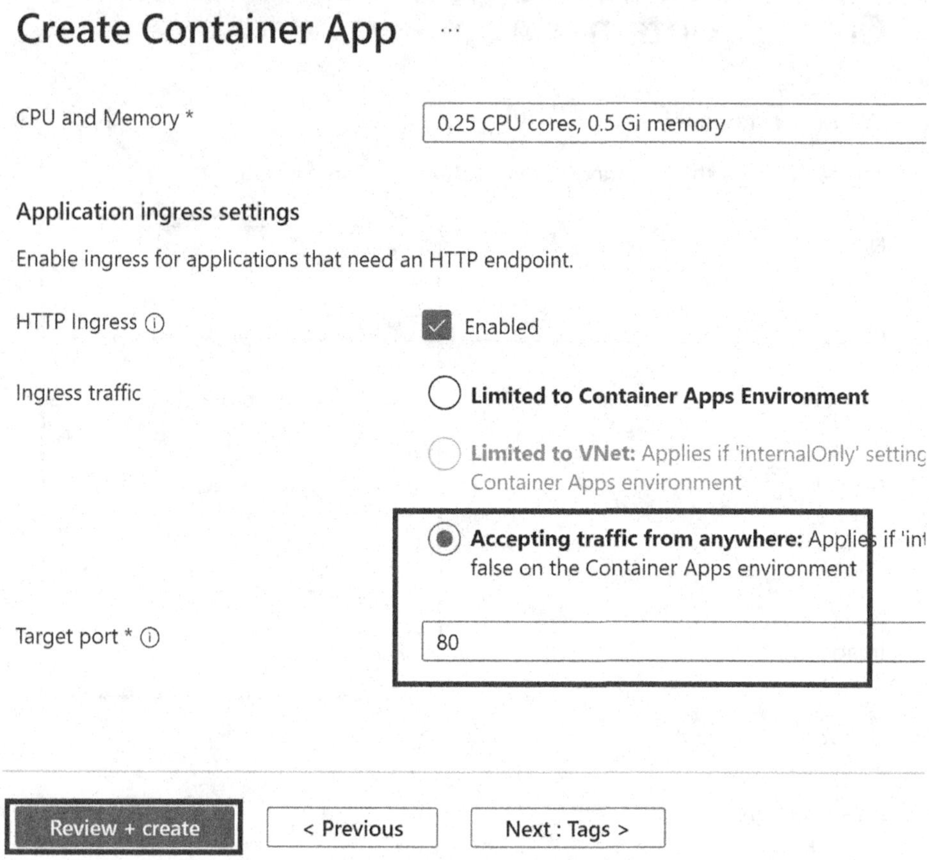

Create Container App   ...

CPU and Memory * | 0.25 CPU cores, 0.5 Gi memory |

Application ingress settings

Enable ingress for applications that need an HTTP endpoint.

HTTP Ingress ⓘ   ☑ Enabled

Ingress traffic   ⚪ **Limited to Container Apps Environment**

                                    ⚪ **Limited to VNet:** Applies if 'internalOnly' setting
                                       Container Apps environment

                                    ⦿ **Accepting traffic from anywhere:** Applies if 'int
                                       false on the Container Apps environment

Target port * ⓘ | 80 |

[Review + create]   [< Previous]   [Next : Tags >]

Figure 6-21. *Click Review + create*

Click **Create** as shown in Figure 6-22 to spin up the container app.

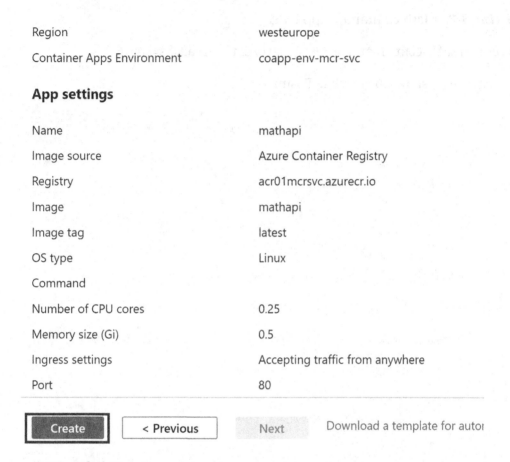

Create Container App   ⋯

Region	westeurope
Container Apps Environment	coapp-env-mcr-svc

App settings

Name	mathapi
Image source	Azure Container Registry
Registry	acr01mcrsvc.azurecr.io
Image	mathapi
Image tag	latest
OS type	Linux
Command	
Number of CPU cores	0.25
Memory size (Gi)	0.5
Ingress settings	Accepting traffic from anywhere
Port	80

Create   < **Previous**   Next   Download a template for autor

Figure 6-22. *Click Create*

Once the container app gets created, go to the **Overview** tab and copy the Application URL as shown in Figure 6-23. We will use this URL to invoke the Math API in Postman.

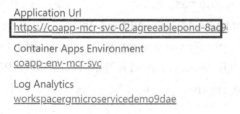

Application Url
https://coapp-mcr-svc-02.agreeablepond-8ac

Container Apps Environment
coapp-env-mcr-svc

Log Analytics
workspacergmicroservicedemo9dae

Figure 6-23. *Copy Application URL*

Go to Postman and invoke the URL for the Math API as shown in Listing 6-2.

Listing 6-2. Math Container App URL

```
https://[Math Container App URL]/Math/Get?ops=add&a=4&b=6
```

Figure 6-24 shows the result in Postman.

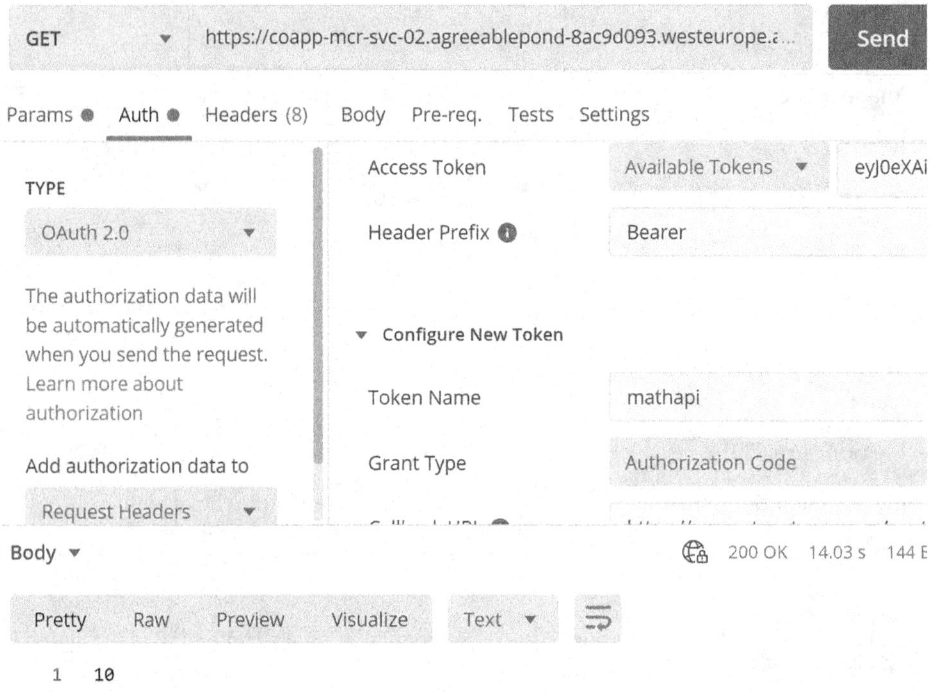

Figure 6-24. *Postman results*

Summary

In this chapter, you learned the basic concepts of Azure Container Apps. We created the Add container app for the Add API and the Subtract container app for the Subtract API inside the Container Apps Environment. We then modified the Math API service to invoke the container app URLs for the Add API and Subtract API. We containerized the Math API and pushed it to Azure Container Registry and then hosted it inside the Math container app.

In the next chapter, you will learn how to implement logging and monitoring for the microservices running inside AKS.

CHAPTER 7

Implement Logging and Monitoring for Microservices Running on AKS

Microservices running on Azure Kubernetes Service can have performance issues and failures. Some of the services may fail at runtime in the production environment, in which case you need to analyze the application logs to debug the failures. The services can get sluggish, in which case you may have to look at the performance metrics to figure out the performance issues. You may have to send an alert using an email or log a ticket in an ITSM tool whenever there is a failure or any anomalies in the services running in the Kubernetes cluster. You can use Azure Monitor and Application Insights to capture logs and metrics for the services running in the AKS cluster.

In this chapter we will configure Azure Monitor and Application Insights for the Math microservices application running in the AKS cluster.

Structure

In this chapter, we will explore the following topics related to monitoring and debugging services running in an AKS cluster:

- Introduction to Azure Monitor and Application Insights
- Create Application Insights

© Ashirwad Satapathi and Abhishek Mishra 2023
A. Satapathi and A. Mishra, *Developing Cloud-Native Solutions with Microsoft Azure and .NET*,
https://doi.org/10.1007/978-1-4842-9004-0_7

- Configure logging for the Math microservices application

- Create a logging-enabled AKS cluster

- Monitor metrics and logs for the microservices application

Objectives

After studying this chapter, you should be able to

- Understand the fundamentals of Application Monitor, Application Insights, and Log Analytics Workspace

- Configure logging and monitoring for .NET-based microservices

Introduction to Azure Monitor and Application Insights

You can ingest performance metrics and logs for your applications and infrastructure to Azure Monitor. Azure Monitor collects the metrics and logs from applications and infrastructure on Azure, on-premises, or on any other cloud. As depicted in Figure 7-1, Azure Monitor can ingest logs from a variety of data sources, including Azure services, Azure subscriptions, operating systems, Azure tenants, and many more sources. Azure Monitor enables you to do the following:

- Collect application logs and metrics using Application Insights

- Collect AKS container logs and metrics using Container Insights

- Collect logs and metrics for virtual machines using Virtual Machine Insights

- Collect insights for network and storage

The ingested logs can be analyzed using Log Analytics, which collects the logs and metrics. You can run Kusto Query Language (KQL) queries to work with the ingested data in Log Analytics and derive insights from it. You can build dashboards to represent the ingested metrics and logs visually and create alerts on anomalies detected from the logs and metrics.

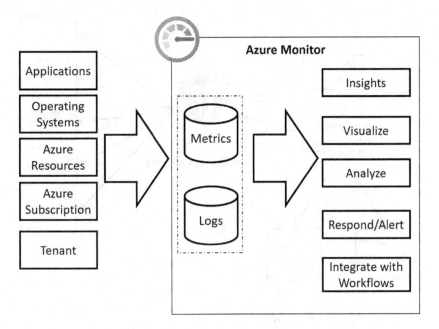

Figure 7-1. *Azure Monitor*

You can collect application logs and metrics using Application Insights. An application can have user interface, backend business and data services, and many other components, as depicted in Figure 7-2. You can enable Application Insights to capture logs from all the application components. You can capture logs from on-premises applications and applications running on Azure and other clouds. Application Insights supports log ingestion from a wide range of programming languages and frameworks like .NET, Java, PHP, Python, and many more.

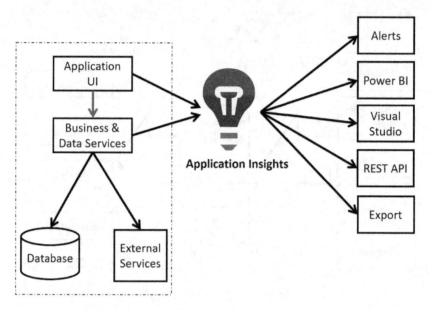

Figure 7-2. *Azure Application Insights*

Create Application Insights

Let's create an Application Insights where the APIs in the Math solution can ingest the logs into the Application Insights. Go to the Azure portal and click **Create a resource** as shown in Figure 7-3.

Figure 7-3. *Create a resource*

You will be navigated to the Azure Marketplace. Search for **Application Insights** as shown in Figure 7-4.

Create a resource
Get Started
Recently created
Categories
AI + Machine Learning
Analytics
Blockchain
Compute
Containers
application insights
Popular Azure services
Virtual machine
Create | Learn more
Kubernetes Service
Create | Docs | MS Learn
Azure Cosmos DB
Create | Docs | MS Learn

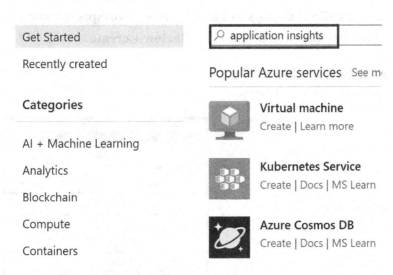

***Figure 7-4.** Search for Application Insights*

Click **Create** as shown in Figure 7-5. This will navigate you to the screen where you can provide details for the Application Insights.

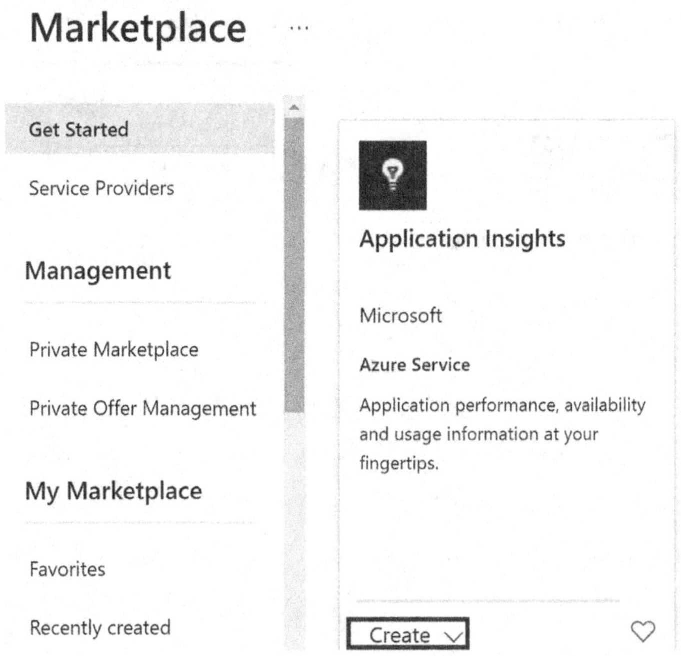

Marketplace
Get Started
Service Providers
Management
Private Marketplace
Private Offer Management
My Marketplace
Favorites
Recently created
Application Insights
Microsoft
Azure Service
Application performance, availability and usage information at your fingertips.
Create

***Figure 7-5.** Click Create*

Provide the basic details like subscription, resource group, and application insights name as shown in Figure 7-6. Choose the Resource Mode as **Workspace-based**. This will ensure that you redirect the logs to a Log Analytics Workspace. You can choose an existing workspace or create a new one. Click **Review + create**.

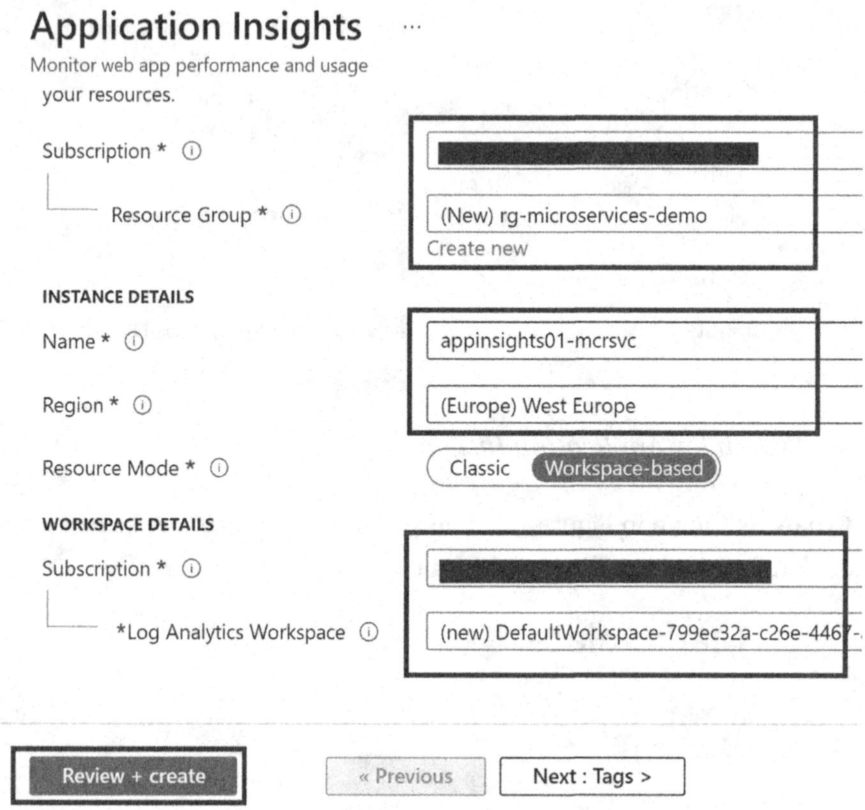

Figure 7-6. *Provide basic details*

Click **Create** as shown in Figure 7-7. This will create an Application Insights for you.

Figure 7-7. Click Create

Configure Logging for the Math Microservices Application

Open the Math microservices application in Visual Studio. We will enable logging for the Add API, Subtract API, and Math API services. Let's enable Application Insights for the Add API first. Right-click the **AddAPI** project and click **Configure Application Insights** as shown in Figure 7-8.

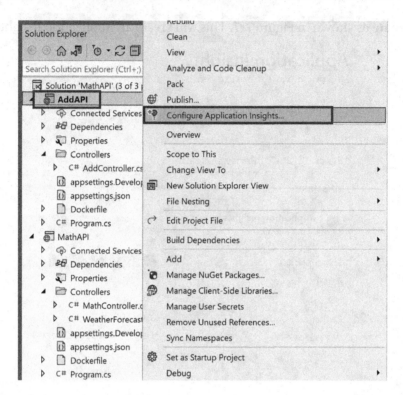

Figure 7-8. *Click Configure Application Insights*

Select Azure Application Insights and then click **Next** as shown in Figure 7-9.

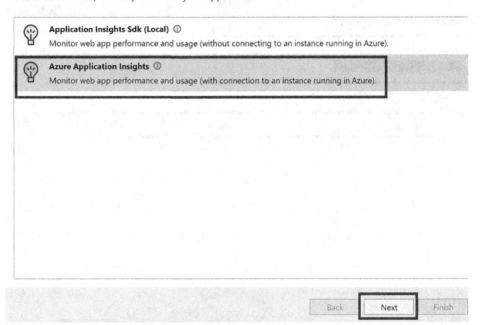

Figure 7-9. *Select Azure Application Insights*

Select the Application Insights we created earlier and then click **Next** as shown in Figure 7-10.

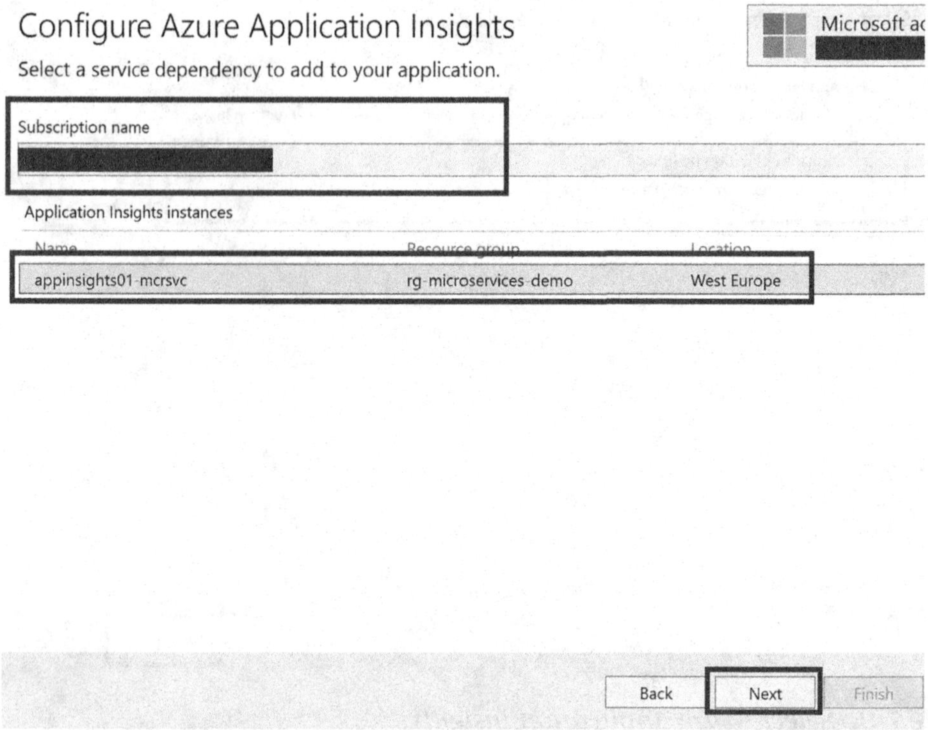

Figure 7-10. Select Application Insights created earlier

Click **Finish** as shown in Figure 7-11 to configure Application Insights for the Add API.

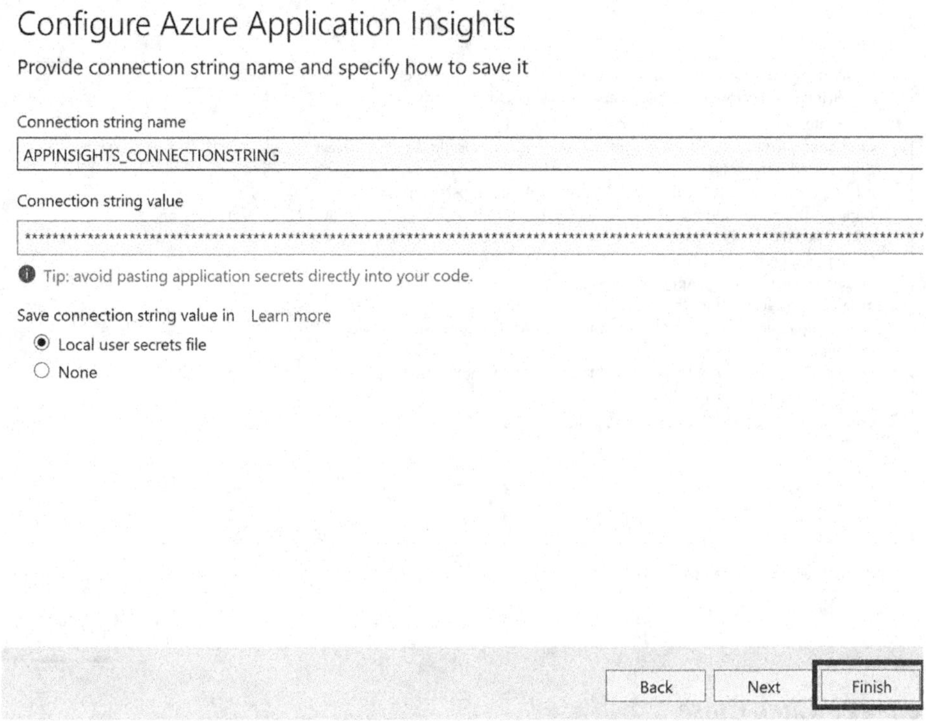

Configure Azure Application Insights

Provide connection string name and specify how to save it

Connection string name

APPINSIGHTS_CONNECTIONSTRING

Connection string value

**/

🛈 Tip: avoid pasting application secrets directly into your code.

Save connection string value in   Learn more
- ⦿ Local user secrets file
- ○ None

Back	Next	**Finish**

Figure 7-11. *Click Finish*

Click **Close** as shown in Figure 7-12 once the configuration completes successfully.

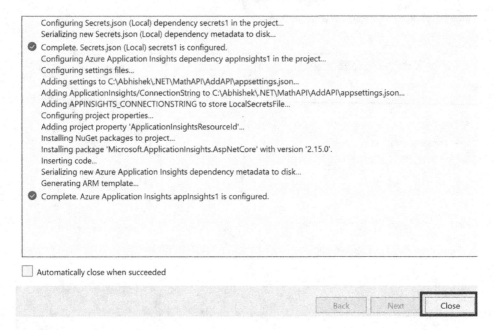

Dependency configuration progress

Configuring Secrets.json (Local) dependency secrets1 in the project...
Serializing new Secrets.json (Local) dependency metadata to disk...
Complete. Secrets.json (Local) secrets1 is configured.
Configuring Azure Application Insights dependency appInsights1 in the project...
Configuring settings files...
Adding settings to C:\Abhishek\.NET\MathAPI\AddAPI\appsettings.json...
Adding ApplicationInsights/ConnectionString to C:\Abhishek\.NET\MathAPI\AddAPI\appsettings.json...
Adding APPINSIGHTS_CONNECTIONSTRING to store LocalSecretsFile...
Configuring project properties...
Adding project property 'ApplicationInsightsResourceId'...
Installing NuGet packages to project...
Installing package 'Microsoft.ApplicationInsights.AspNetCore' with version '2.15.0'.
Inserting code...
Serializing new Azure Application Insights dependency metadata to disk...
Generating ARM template...
Complete. Azure Application Insights appInsights1 is configured.

Automatically close when succeeded

Back   Next   Close

Figure 7-12. *Click Close*

The package `Microsoft.ApplicationInsights.AspNetCore` gets added to the project. The connection string for the Application Insights gets added to the `appsettings.json` file as shown in Listing 7-1.

Listing 7-1. appsettings.json

```json
{
  "Logging": {
    "LogLevel": {
      "Default": "Information",
      "Microsoft.AspNetCore": "Information"
    }
  },
  "AllowedHosts": "*",
  "ApplicationInsights": {
```

```
"ConnectionString": "InstrumentationKey=b6591e30-e2a9-44cc-a541-b1f87f
b65f94;IngestionEndpoint=https://westeurope-5.in.applicationinsights.
azure.com/;LiveEndpoint=https://westeurope.livediagnostics.monitor.
azure.com/"
    }
}
```

Application Insights service gets added to the services collection in `Program.cs` as shown in Listing 7-2.

Listing 7-2. Program.cs

```
var builder = WebApplication.CreateBuilder(args);

// Add services to the container.

builder.Services.AddControllers();
// Learn more about configuring Swagger/OpenAPI at https://aka.ms/
aspnetcore/swashbuckle
builder.Services.AddEndpointsApiExplorer();
builder.Services.AddSwaggerGen();
builder.Services.AddApplicationInsightsTelemetry(builder.
Configuration["APPINSIGHTS_CONNECTIONSTRING"]);

var app = builder.Build();

// Configure the HTTP request pipeline.
if (app.Environment.IsDevelopment())
{
    app.UseSwagger();
    app.UseSwaggerUI();
}

app.UseHttpsRedirection();

app.UseAuthorization();

app.MapControllers();

app.Run();
```

We can add the code to ingest logs into the Application Insights for the Add Controller as shown in Listing 7-3.

Listing 7-3. AddController.cs

```
using Microsoft.AspNetCore.Mvc;

namespace AddAPI.Controllers
{
    [ApiController]
    [Route("[controller]")]
    public class AddController : Controller
    {
        private readonly ILogger<AddController> _logger;

        public AddController(ILogger<AddController> logger)
        {
            _logger = logger;
        }

        [HttpGet]
        public int Add(int a, int b)
        {
            _logger.LogInformation("Adding Two Numbers "+ a + " and "+b);
            return a + b;
        }
    }
}
```

Containerize the Add API and push it to the Azure container registry using the steps illustrated in the earlier chapters.

Now we'll enable Application Insights for the Subtract API. Right-click the
SubtractAPI project and click **Configure Application Insights** as shown in Figure 7-13.

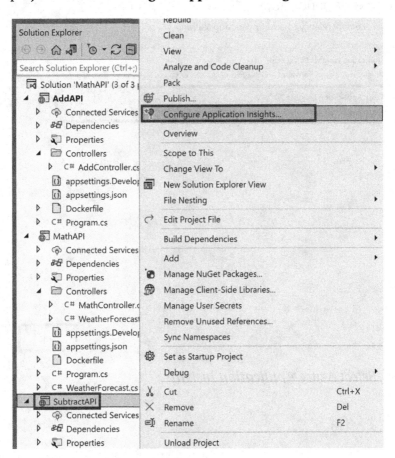

Figure 7-13. *Configure Application Insights*

Select Azure Application Insights and then click **Next** as shown in Figure 7-14.

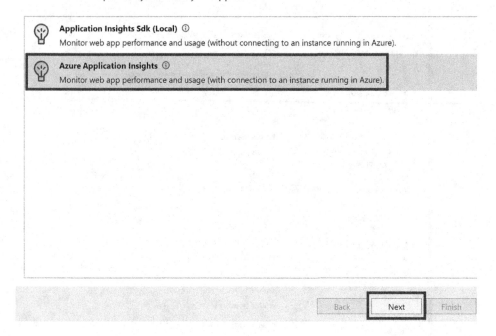

Figure 7-14. *Select Azure Application Insights*

Select the Application Insights we created earlier and then click **Next** as shown in Figure 7-15.

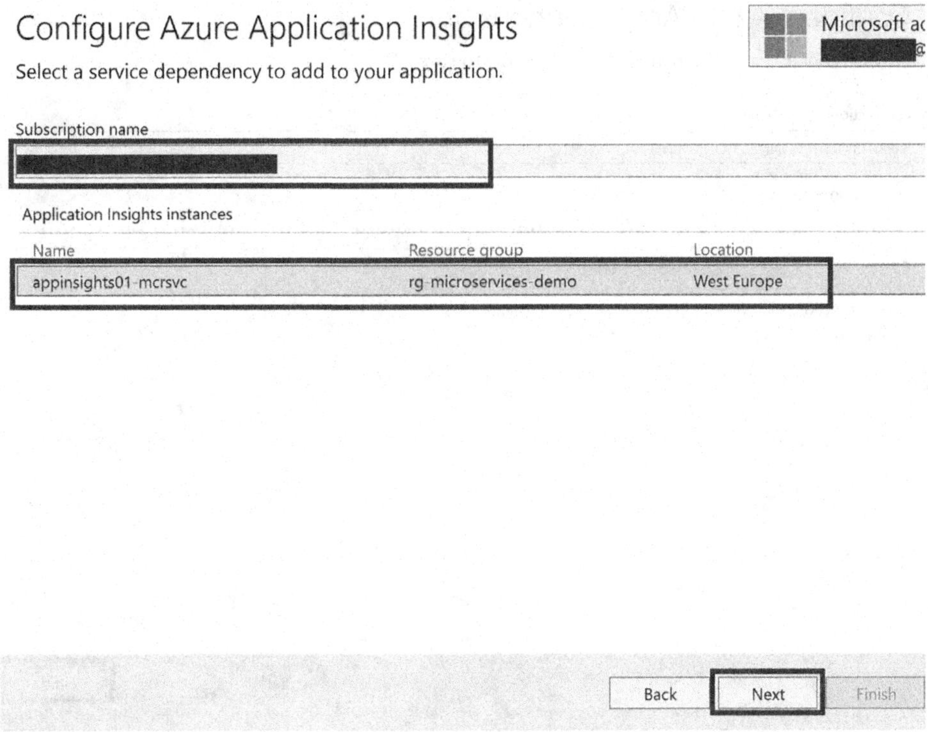

Figure 7-15. *Select Application Insights created earlier*

Click **Finish** as shown in Figure 7-16 to configure Application Insights for the Subtract API.

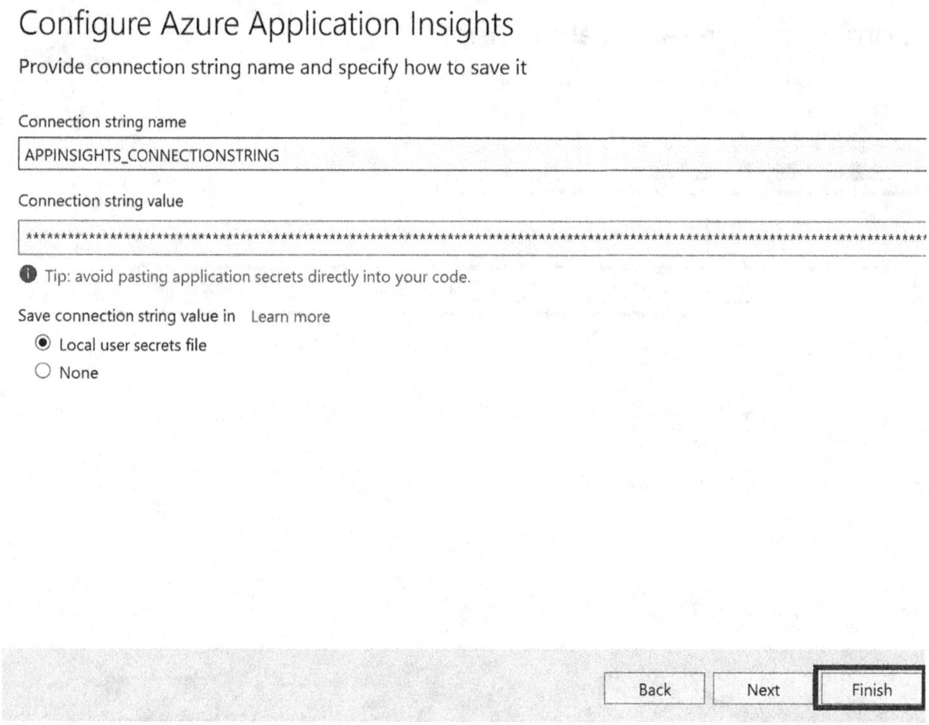

Configure Azure Application Insights

Provide connection string name and specify how to save it

Connection string name

APPINSIGHTS_CONNECTIONSTRING

Connection string value

****

ⓘ Tip: avoid pasting application secrets directly into your code.

Save connection string value in   Learn more
   ⊙ Local user secrets file
   ○ None

Back	Next	**Finish**

Figure 7-16. *Click Finish*

Click **Close** as shown in Figure 7-17 once the configuration completes successfully.

Dependency configuration progress

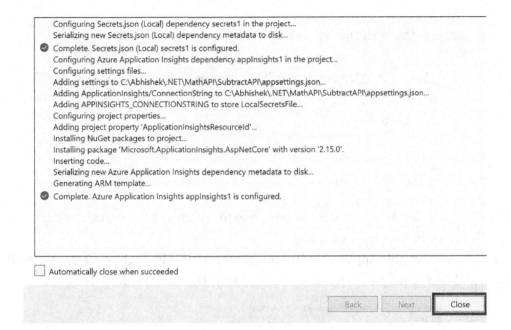

Figure 7-17. *Click Close*

We can add the code to ingest logs into the Application Insights for the Subtract Controller as shown in Listing 7-4.

Listing 7-4. SubtractController.cs

```
using Microsoft.AspNetCore.Mvc;

namespace SubtractAPI.Controllers
{
    [ApiController]
    [Route("[controller]")]
    public class SubtractController : Controller
    {
        private readonly ILogger<SubtractController> _logger;

        public SubtractController(ILogger<SubtractController> logger)
```

```
    {
        _logger = logger;
    }

    [HttpGet]
    public int Add(int a, int b)
    {
        _logger.LogInformation("Subtracting Two Numbers " + a + "
        and " + b);
        return a - b;
    }
  }
}
```

Containerize the Subtract API and push it to the Azure container registry using the steps illustrated in the earlier chapters.

Finally, we'll enable Application Insights for the Math API. Right-click the **MathAPI** project and click **Configure Application Insights** as shown in Figure 7-18.

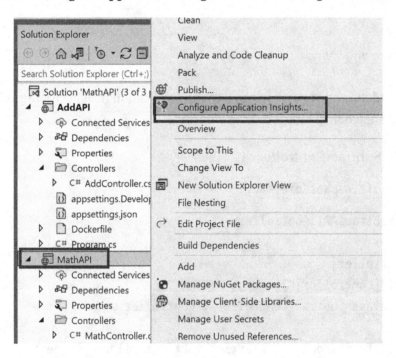

Figure 7-18.   *Configure Application Insights*

Select Azure Application Insights and then click **Next** as shown in Figure 7-19.

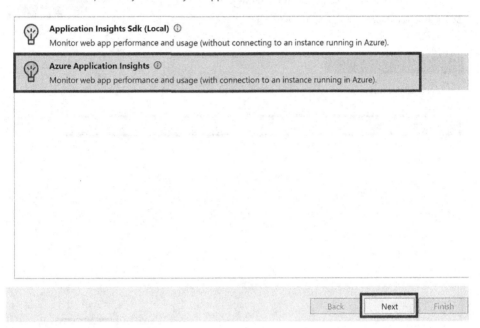

Figure 7-19. *Select Azure Application Insights*

Select the Application Insights we created earlier and then click **Next** as shown in Figure 7-20.

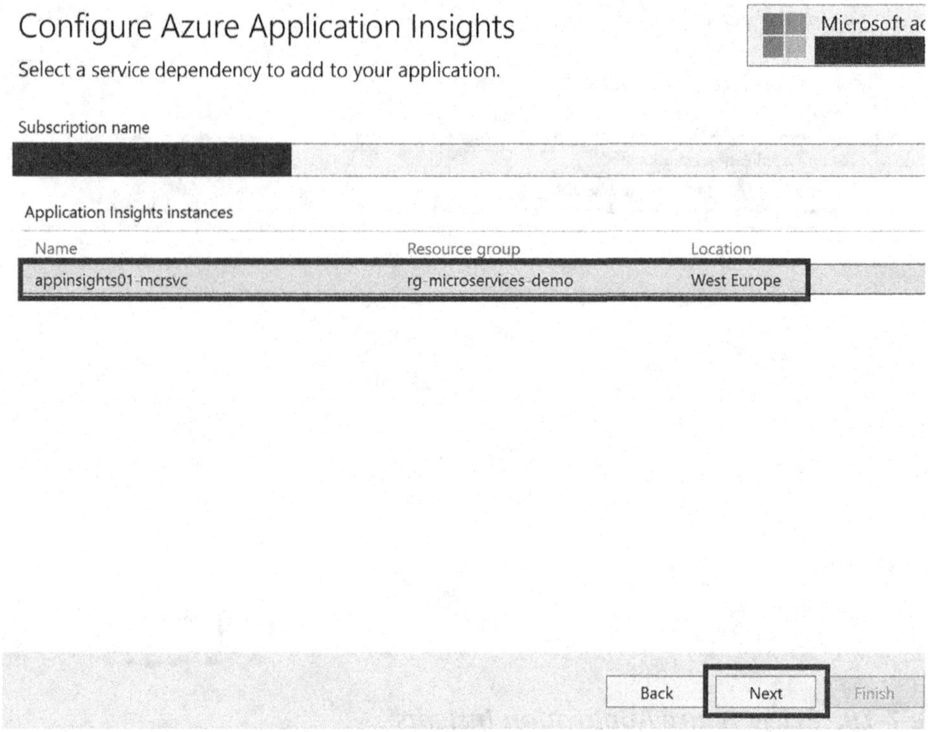

Figure 7-20. *Click Application Insights created earlier*

Click **Finish** as shown in Figure 7-21 to configure Application Insights for the Math API.

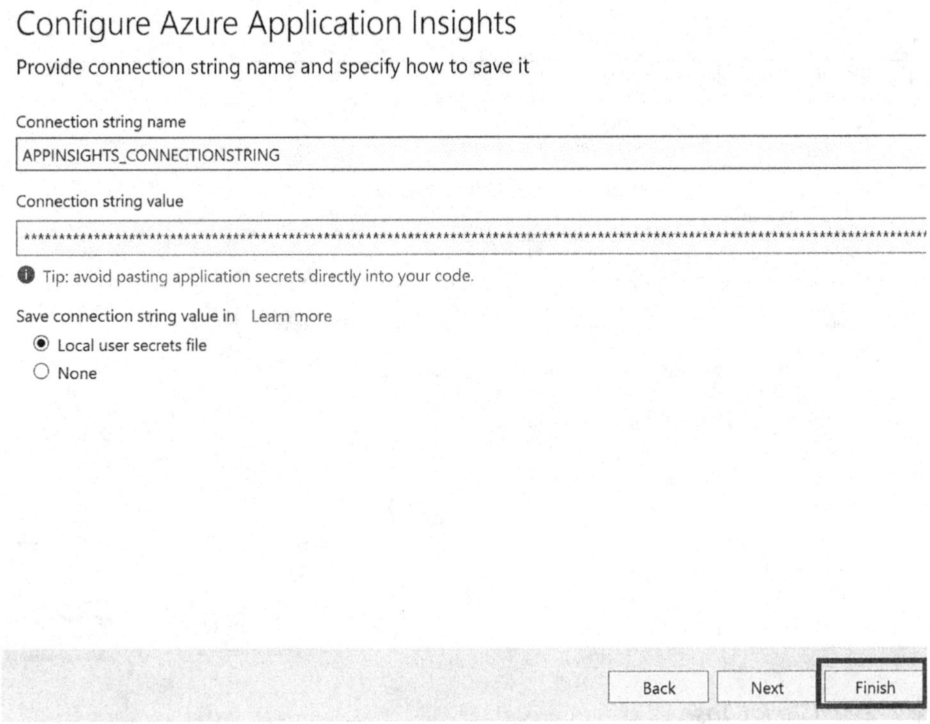

Configure Azure Application Insights

Provide connection string name and specify how to save it

Connection string name

APPINSIGHTS_CONNECTIONSTRING

Connection string value

****

ⓘ Tip: avoid pasting application secrets directly into your code.

Save connection string value in   Learn more

⦿ Local user secrets file

○ None

Back	Next	Finish

Figure 7-21. *Click Finish*

Click **Close** as shown in Figure 7-22 once the configuration completes successfully.

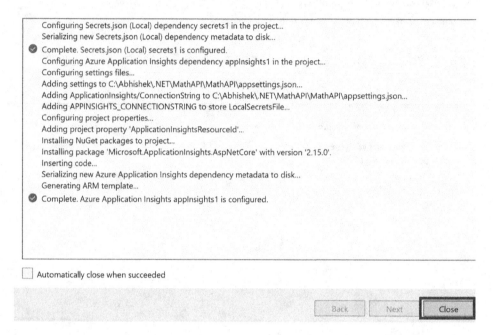

Dependency configuration progress

```
Configuring Secrets.json (Local) dependency secrets1 in the project...
Serializing new Secrets.json (Local) dependency metadata to disk...
✓ Complete. Secrets.json (Local) secrets1 is configured.
Configuring Azure Application Insights dependency appInsights1 in the project...
Configuring settings files...
Adding settings to C:\Abhishek\.NET\MathAPI\MathAPI\appsettings.json...
Adding ApplicationInsights/ConnectionString to C:\Abhishek\.NET\MathAPI\MathAPI\appsettings.json...
Adding APPINSIGHTS_CONNECTIONSTRING to store LocalSecretsFile...
Configuring project properties...
Adding project property 'ApplicationInsightsResourceId'...
Installing NuGet packages to project...
Installing package 'Microsoft.ApplicationInsights.AspNetCore' with version '2.15.0'.
Inserting code...
Serializing new Azure Application Insights dependency metadata to disk...
Generating ARM template...
✓ Complete. Azure Application Insights appInsights1 is configured.
```

☐ Automatically close when succeeded

Back   Next   Close

***Figure 7-22.** Click Close*

We can add the code to ingest logs into the Application Insights for the Math Controller as shown in Listing 7-5. Also make sure that you provide the Cluster IP address for the Add API and Subtract API in the Math Controller code.

***Listing 7-5.** MathController.cs*

```
using Microsoft.AspNetCore.Authorization;
using Microsoft.AspNetCore.Mvc;
using System.Net;
using System.Net.Http.Headers;
using System.Text;

namespace MathAPI.Controllers
{
    [Authorize]
    [ApiController]
```

```
[Route("[controller]")]
public class MathController : Controller
{
    private readonly ILogger<MathController> _logger;

    public MathController(ILogger<MathController> logger)
    {
        _logger = logger;
    }

    [HttpGet("Test")]
    public string Test()
    {
        return "Success";
    }
    [HttpGet("Get")]
    public string Get(string ops, int a,int b)
    {
        _logger.LogInformation("Operation "+ops+" selected for numbers
        "+a+" and "+ b);

        string result = "";
        string url = "";
        string queryStr = "?a=" + a + "&b=" + b;

        if (ops == "add")
        {
            url = "http://[Cluster IP]/Add" + queryStr;
        }
        else
        {
            url = "http://[Cluster IP]/subtract" + queryStr; ;
        }
        HttpWebRequest request = (HttpWebRequest)WebRequest.
        Create(url);
        WebResponse response = request.GetResponse();
        using (Stream responseStream = response.GetResponseStream())
```

```
        {
            StreamReader reader = new StreamReader(responseStream,
            Encoding.UTF8);
            result = reader.ReadToEnd();
        }
        return result;
    }
  }
}
```

Containerize the Math API and push it to the Azure container registry using the steps illustrated in the earlier chapters.

Create a Logging-Enabled AKS Cluster

Now let's create a logging-enabled AKS cluster. We will deploy the Math API microservices application to this cluster. Go to the Azure portal and click **Create a resource** as shown in Figure 7-23.

Figure 7-23. *Create a resource*

You will be navigated to the Azure Marketplace. Click **Containers** and then click
Kubernetes Service as shown in Figure 7-24.

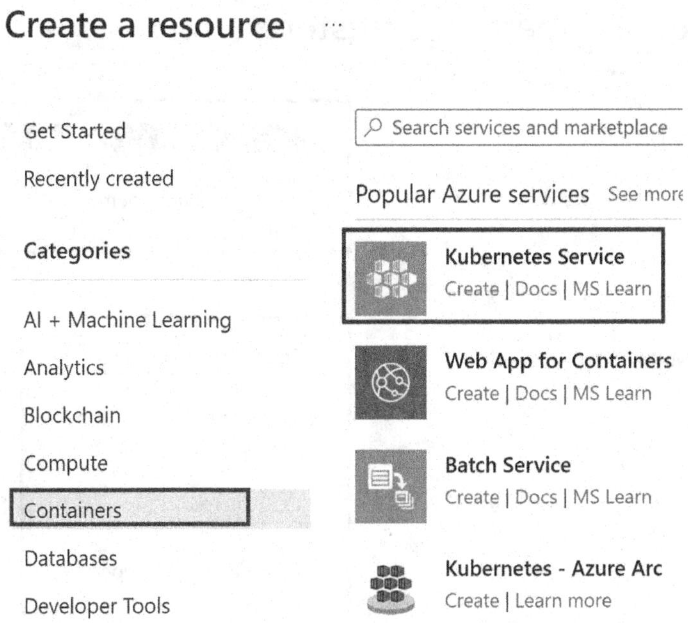

Figure 7-24. *Click Containers*

Provide the basic details like resource group, subscription, region, and other necessary details for the Kubernetes cluster as shown in Figure 7-25.

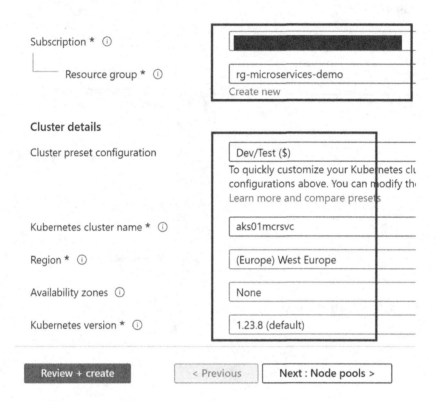

Create Kubernetes cluster ···

Subscription * ⓘ

└──── Resource group * ⓘ

rg-microservices-demo

Create new

Cluster details

Cluster preset configuration

Dev/Test ($)

To quickly customize your Kubernetes clu
configurations above. You can modify th·
Learn more and compare presets

Kubernetes cluster name * ⓘ

aks01mcrsvc

Region * ⓘ

(Europe) West Europe

Availability zones ⓘ

None

Kubernetes version * ⓘ

1.23.8 (default)

Review + create   < Previous   Next : Node pools >

Figure 7-25. *Provide basic details*

Go to the **Integrations** tab and select your Azure container registry as shown in Figure 7-26. Enable container monitoring and select a Log Analytics Workspace. You may use the same Log Analytics Workspace that you created for Application Insights. Click **Review + create**.

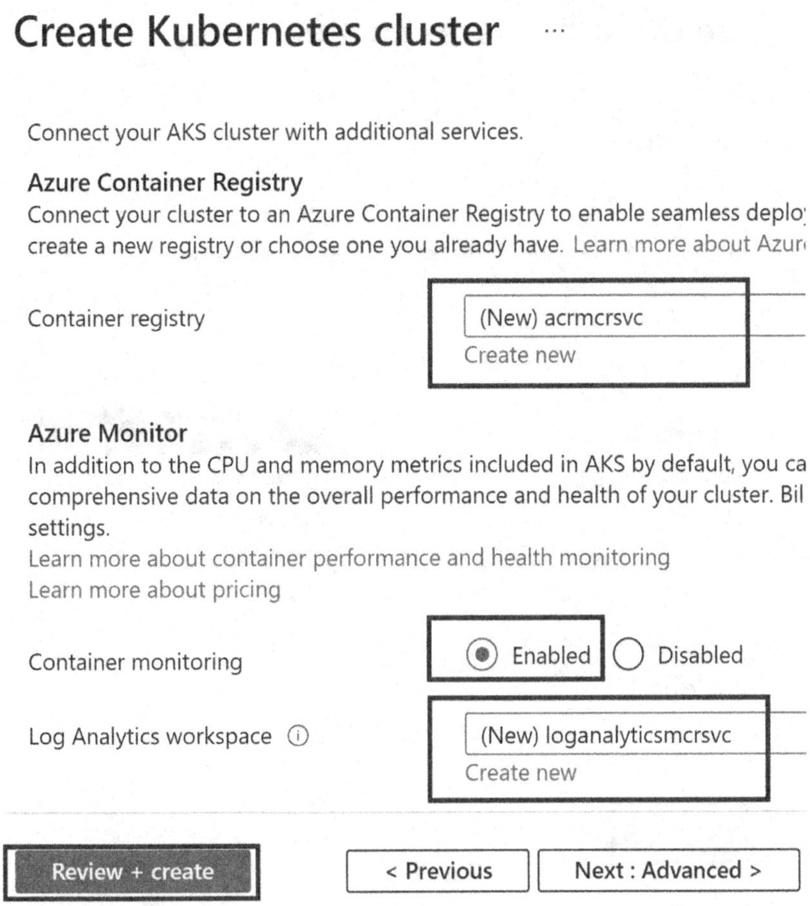

Create Kubernetes cluster   ...

Connect your AKS cluster with additional services.

Azure Container Registry

Connect your cluster to an Azure Container Registry to enable seamless deplo:
create a new registry or choose one you already have. Learn more about Azur

Container registry

> (New) acrmcrsvc
> Create new

Azure Monitor

In addition to the CPU and memory metrics included in AKS by default, you ca
comprehensive data on the overall performance and health of your cluster. Bil
settings.
Learn more about container performance and health monitoring
Learn more about pricing

Container monitoring   ◉ Enabled   ◯ Disabled

Log Analytics workspace ⓘ

> (New) loganalyticsmcrsvc
> Create new

[Review + create]   [< Previous]   [Next : Advanced >]

Figure 7-26. *Click Review + create*

Click **Create** as shown in Figure 7-27. The Kubernetes cluster will get created.

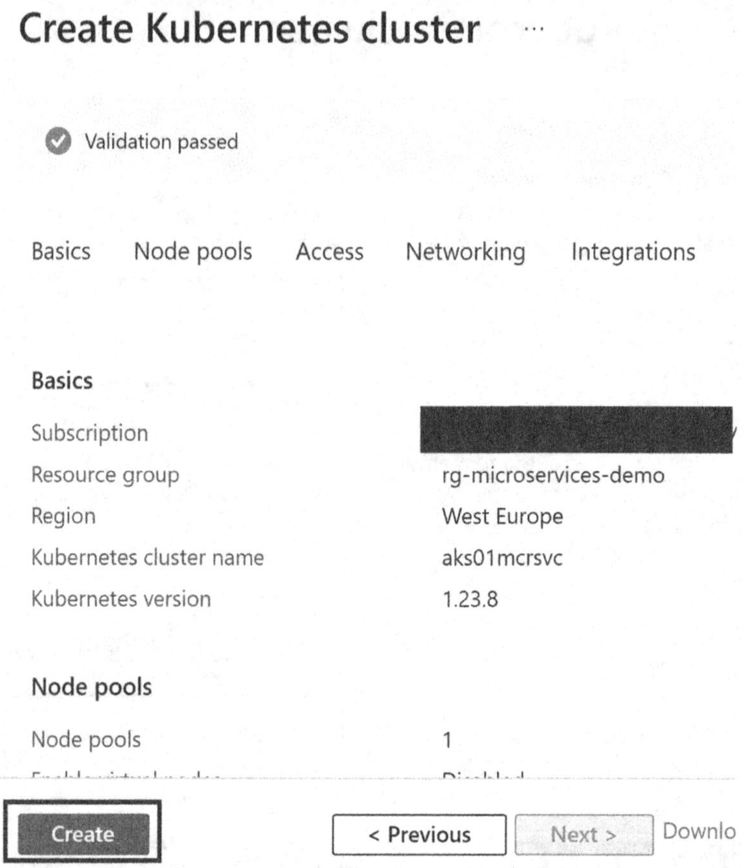

Create Kubernetes cluster   ...

✓ Validation passed

Basics   Node pools   Access   Networking   Integrations

Basics

Subscription	
Resource group	rg-microservices-demo
Region	West Europe
Kubernetes cluster name	aks01mcrsvc
Kubernetes version	1.23.8

Node pools

Node pools	1

[Create]   [< Previous]   [Next >]   Downlo

Figure 7-27. Click Create

Once the cluster gets created, start deploying the Add API and the Subtract API. Get their cluster IP address, modify the Math Controller code to use the Cluster IP address for the Add API and Subtract API, containerize the Math API, push it to the Azure container registry, and then deploy it on Azure Kubernetes Service. You can follow the steps illustrated in the previous chapters.

Monitor Metrics and Logs for the Microservices Application

Once the application is deployed, get the Load Balancer service external IP for the Math API as shown in Figure 7-28. Invoke the API using Postman as demonstrated in the previous chapters. This will generate logs and metrics for the application.

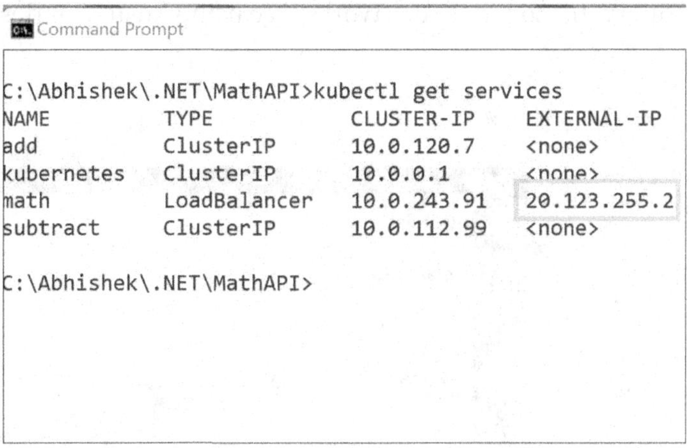

```
🔲 Command Prompt

C:\Abhishek\.NET\MathAPI>kubectl get services
NAME         TYPE           CLUSTER-IP     EXTERNAL-IP
add          ClusterIP      10.0.120.7     <none>
kubernetes   ClusterIP      10.0.0.1       <none>
math         LoadBalancer   10.0.243.91    20.123.255.2
subtract     ClusterIP      10.0.112.99    <none>

C:\Abhishek\.NET\MathAPI>
```

Figure 7-28. *Get External IP*

Go to the Application Insights for Azure Kubernetes Service and click **Transactions search** as shown in Figure 7-29. You can see the logs for the application here.

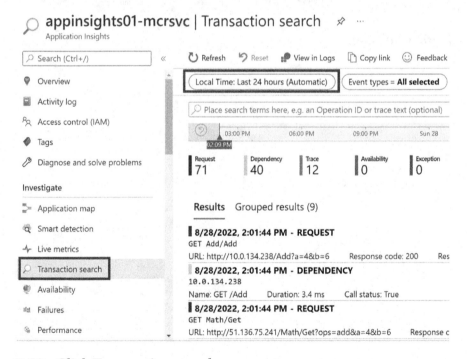

Figure 7-29. *Click Transaction search*

Click **Logs** to query the Log Analytics Workspace using Kusto Queries as shown in Figure 7-30.

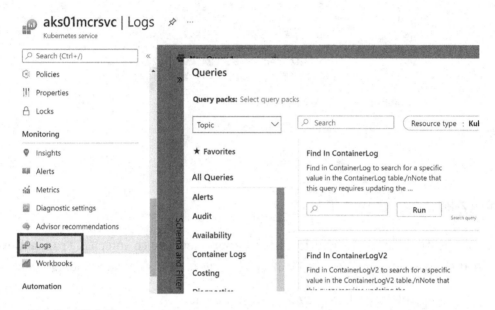

Figure 7-30. *Click Logs*

Run the Kusto Query shown in Figure 7-31 to search for logs that have *Operation* in the log text. We have *Operation* in the Math API logs. Click **Run**.

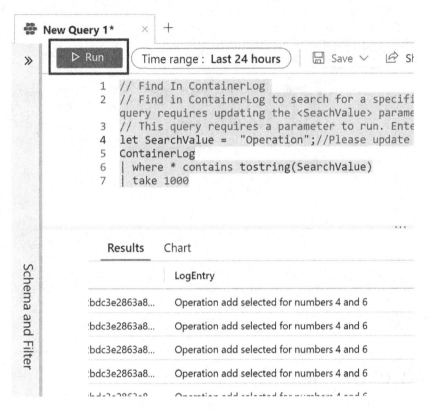

Figure 7-31. *Query Log Analytics Workspace*

Run the Kusto Query shown in Figure 7-32 to search for logs that have *Adding Two Numbers* in the log text. We have this text in the Add API logs. Click **Run**.

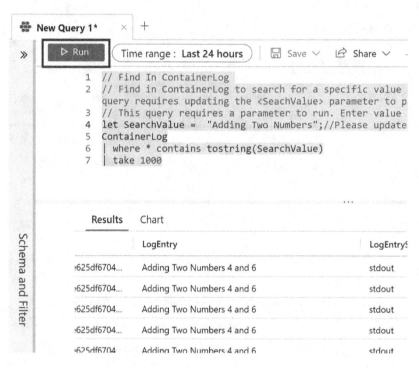

Figure 7-32. *Query Log Analytics Workspace*

Now let's investigate metrics for the cluster. Click **Insights**. In the Cluster tab you can see the compute metrics such as Node CPU Utilization %, as shown in Figure 7-33, and Node Memory Utilization %, as shown in Figure 7-34.

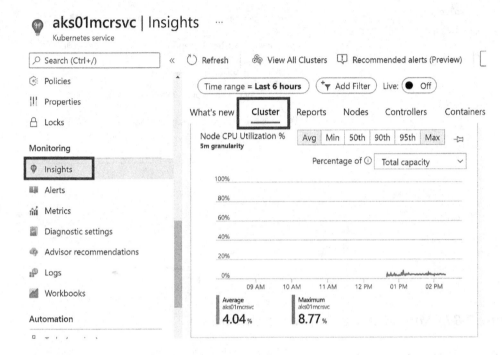

Figure 7-33. *Node CPU Utilization % metrics*

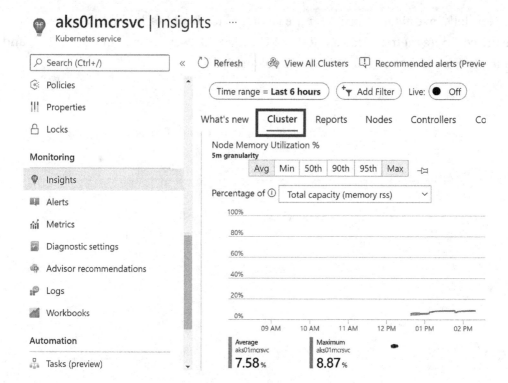

Figure 7-34. *Node Memory Utilization % metrics*

You can check for other compute metrics in the Cluster tab.

Click the **Nodes** tab to get insights like compute utilization for the nodes in the cluster, as shown in Figure 7-35. You can drill down and view other essentials like processes running in the nodes and many more.

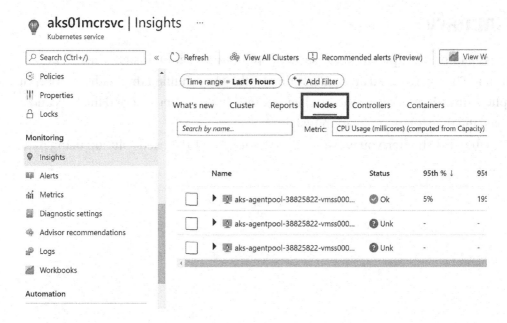

Figure 7-35. *Nodes tab of Application Insights*

Click the Containers tab to get insights for the containers running in the nodes, as shown in Figure 7-36.

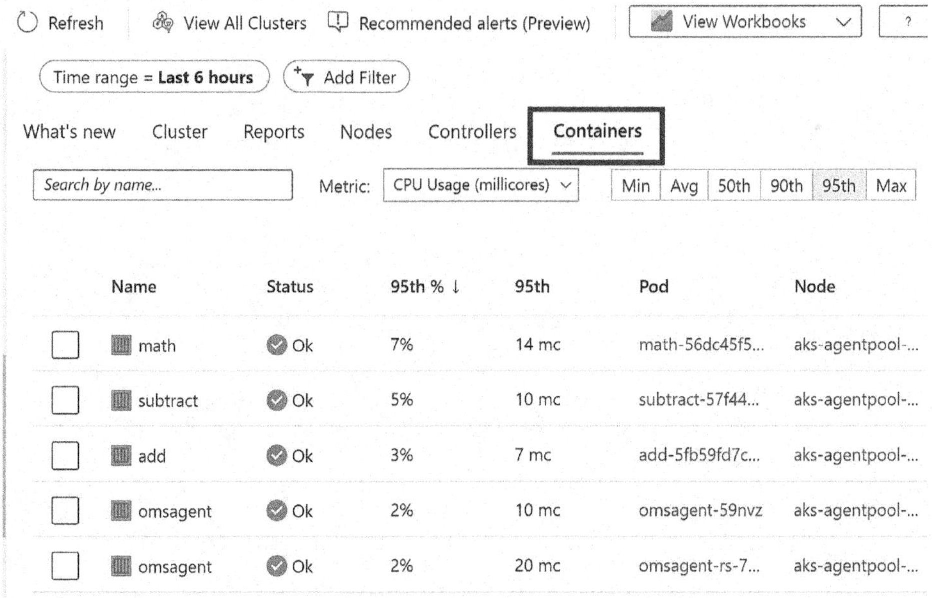

Figure 7-36. *Containers tab of Application Insights*

Summary

In this chapter, we explored the basic concepts of Application Insights and Azure Monitor. Then we created an Application Insight and modified the Math microservices application to ingest logs to the Application Insights. We then queried the logs and viewed the metrics in Application Insights.

In the next chapter, you will learn how to build an IoT-based solution using Azure and .NET.

CHAPTER 8

Build an IoT Solution with Azure IoT Hub, Azure Functions, and Azure Cosmos DB

With the rapid development in technology, we are living in a world full of smart devices. Starting from our smartphones to refrigerators, electronics good have been getting smart each passing day. Almost all devices have the capability to generate information and transmit the same over the Internet directly or via channels of communication. This capability enables us to gather information and insights that were unthinkable a few decades back. With all this progress, the Internet of Things (IoT) market is growing like never before. The impact of IoT in different industries is huge, and many organizations have been investing heavily over the past few years to build IoT solutions for various use cases such as smart manufacturing, smart power grids, and connected vehicles.

The focus of this chapter is to demonstrate how to build an IoT solution using different Azure services. We will explore ways to tap into the power of Azure IoT Hub to register IoT devices and process incoming events from it using Azure Functions by building a real-time health monitoring system. Later in the chapter we'll see how to persist the data coming from the IoT hub in Azure Cosmos DB. This chapter will give you the skills required to get started on your IoT journey.

© Ashirwad Satapathi and Abhishek Mishra 2023
A. Satapathi and A. Mishra, *Developing Cloud-Native Solutions with Microsoft Azure and .NET*,
https://doi.org/10.1007/978-1-4842-9004-0_8

Structure

In this chapter, we will explore the following topics:

- Introduction to IoT
- What is Azure IoT Hub?
- What is Azure Cosmos DB?
- Provision an IoT hub and a Cosmos DB instance
- Develop a solution using IoT Hub, Azure Function, and Cosmos DB

Objectives

After studying this chapter, you should be able to:

- Understand the fundamentals of Azure IoT Hub
- Develop an IoT solution leveraging the power of Microsoft Azure

Introduction to IoT

The Internet of Things refers to a network of devices ("things") that consist of sensors, software, and/or hardware to connect and share information with other devices or a system over the Internet. Over the past decade, IoT has become one of the most popular and impactful technologies in the 21st century. Its impact can be felt everywhere in the world, as many devices that we use in our day-to-day activities are smart devices. These devices can be anything ranging from a smartphone to a smartwatch. According to a report by IoT Analytics, the number of active IoT devices as of 2021 is around 12.2 billion and is expected to grow to approximately 27 billion by 2025 (`https://iot-analytics.com/number-connected-iot-devices/`).

What Is Azure IoT?

To build IoT solutions, Microsoft Azure provides a suite of managed cloud services. We can leverage these services to build highly scalable, mission-critical solutions. Some of the key services provided by the Azure IoT suite are Azure IoT Hub, Azure IoT Central, Azure IoT Edge. We can use this set of services to build solutions that are able to gather telemetry data from devices, process that data, and generate insights. This describes the bare minimum that we can do with these services. We can perform a plethora of operations using this set of services. For example, with services like Azure IoT Edge, we can process data at the device level and send alerts, if necessary, without sending the data to the cloud. If we provision devices at scale, we can do it with ease by using services like Azure DPS.

A typical IoT solution consists of three components:

- *Things*: Any device that is able to send data to the cloud. Things can be industrial equipment, sensors, home appliances, and a range of other devices.

- *Insights*: Refers to the processing of the data collected by IoT devices over time to generate actionable insights by using artificial intelligence (AI).

- *Actions*: Refers to steps taken by the system or applications once they get the insights after processing the data generated by the IoT devices. Actions can be anything ranging from sending alerts to initiating a workflow to perform a chain of steps.

For the purpose of this chapter, we are going to use a managed Azure IoT service i.e., Azure IoT hub, Azure Functions, and Azure Cosmos DB. Let's discuss Azure IoT Hub, Azure Functions, and Cosmos DB briefly in the following sections.

What Is Azure IoT Hub?

Azure IoT Hub is a fully managed cloud service offered by Microsoft Azure to build IoT solutions. It provides various features like device registration, event routing, send device to cloud, and cloud-to-device commands. Azure IoT Hub acts as a message gateway and stores telemetry data generated by the IoT devices until a listener or consumer of these events starts consuming them. Azure IoT Hub has first-class integration support for different Azure services like Azure Stream Analytics, Azure Functions, Azure Logic Apps, Azure Event Grid, and so on. Azure IoT Hub provides a secure mechanism for devices to connect to it by use shared access signature (SAS) tokens or certificates. Azure IoT Hub supports multiple communication protocols like Advanced Message Queuing Protocol (AMQP), MQTT, and HTTPS. Apart from that, IoT Hub provides a rich set of client libraries for different languages to manage devices and services.

In this chapter, we explore ways to provision an IoT Hub instance in the Azure portal and register a device in it.

What Is Azure Functions?

Azure Functions is a part of the Function-as-a-Service (FaaS), serverless offering of Microsoft Azure. With Azure Functions, we can build a variety of applications, ranging from serverless Web APIs to event-driven solutions. Azure Functions provides us with a mechanism to deploy our code as functions that scale on demand. We don't need to worry about configuring the scaling configurations for our functions because it is handled by the service itself. It is handled internally by a scale controller that looks at the amount of traffic coming to the functions and scales it out as needed. When the number of requests decreases, the scale controller automatically scales down the function instances. If we want to limit the number of instances our functions scale out to, we can also do that.

Azure Functions comes with a rich set of triggers and bindings. *Triggers* in Azure Functions are simply events that initiate function execution. Some examples of triggers are the HTTP trigger, ServiceBus trigger, and IoT Hub trigger. Bindings provide a way to declaratively connect with other resources. There are two classifications of bindings in Azure Functions: input and output. *Input bindings* let you read data from resources, while *output bindings* let you write data into the resources or persist them. Azure Cosmos DB and Azure Blob Storage are a few resources for which input and output bindings are currently available. For the purpose of this chapter, we will be developing an IoT Hub Triggered Azure Function that will use the Cosmos DB output binding.

What Is Azure Cosmos DB?

Azure Cosmos DB is the flagship NoSQL offering of Microsoft Azure. It is a fully managed NoSQL database of Azure. It is the successor of DocumentDB. Cosmos DB provides single-digit millisecond response time, offers enterprise-grade security, and has SLA-backed availability. Since the service is fully managed by Microsoft Azure, we need not worry about the scaling in and scaling out of the services. Cosmos DB also provides a mechanism to take automatic backups periodically.

Cosmos DB provides various APIs such as Core SQL API, MongoDB API, Gremlin API, Cassandra API, and Table API. This allows developers with previous experience with any NoSQL database to leverage their previous experience to work with Cosmos DB. For any green field project, Core SQL API is the recommended API to use for the Cosmos DB instances. Core SQL API enables us to perform query operations using SQL syntaxes. Cosmos DB also offers various client libraries in different languages. It is ideal for any web, mobile, or IoT workloads that need a NoSQL backend along with massive scalability.

With that introduction to Cosmos DB and IoT Hub, let's have a look at the problem statement that we are trying to solve in this chapter.

Problem Statement

You are working for a fictional company that is working toward building an IoT solution to gather healthcare information from patients and store it in a persistent form of storage. The IoT device is going to collect information like pulse rate and body temperature. This data needs to be collected and stored in persistent storage every second. The leadership team of your company wants to develop a proof of concept (PoC) to build the capability. Since you had previously shown interest in the area of IoT, your manager has asked you to come up with a solution and PoC to solve this problem. Your manager has requested that you design the solution using Azure IoT services (as management is keen to continue their cloud journey with Microsoft Azure) and to build a simulator to send telemetry data for the PoC because the team lacks sufficient budget right now.

Proposed Solution

Now that you have a brief understanding of the problem to solve, we will be working as a team toward designing and developing a solution to complete the requirements of our fictional company. After careful consideration, we have come up with a solution to solve the problem. We plan to use Azure IoT Hub to receive telemetry data and manage our IoT devices. Once the telemetry events (i.e., data) are sent from the IoT devices, they lie

197

dormant in the IoT hub. We need to have a way to process these events. We have decided to use Azure Function for processing these events from Azure IoT Hub. This Azure Function is going to process the events and store the data in a Cosmos DB instance.

Since we don't have an IoT device with us, we have decided to build a console application that is going to acts as a virtual IoT device.

Before we start building the solution, we need a couple of things in place. The following are the prerequisites to start development activities:

1. Create an Azure IoT Hub instance

2. Register an IoT device in the Azure IoT hub

3. Create a Cosmos DB instance

Once we have the prerequisites in place, we will start building our solution using Visual Studio 2022.

Create an Azure IoT Hub in Azure Portal

Go to the Azure portal and search for **IoT Hub**. Click **IoT Hub** in the results as shown in Figure 8-1.

Figure 8-1. *Search for IoT Hub*

Click **Create** to create an Azure IoT hub, as shown in Figure 8-2.

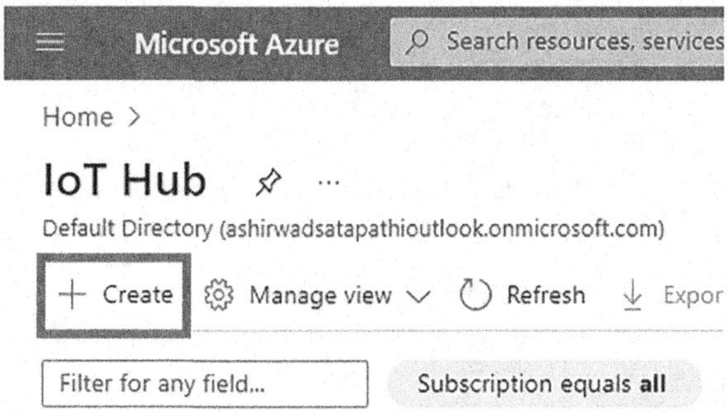

Figure 8-2. *Click Create*

Provide the resource group, subscription, IoT hub name, and region in the corresponding fields, as shown in Figure 8-3, and then click **Next: Networking**. The IoT hub name needs to be globally unique.

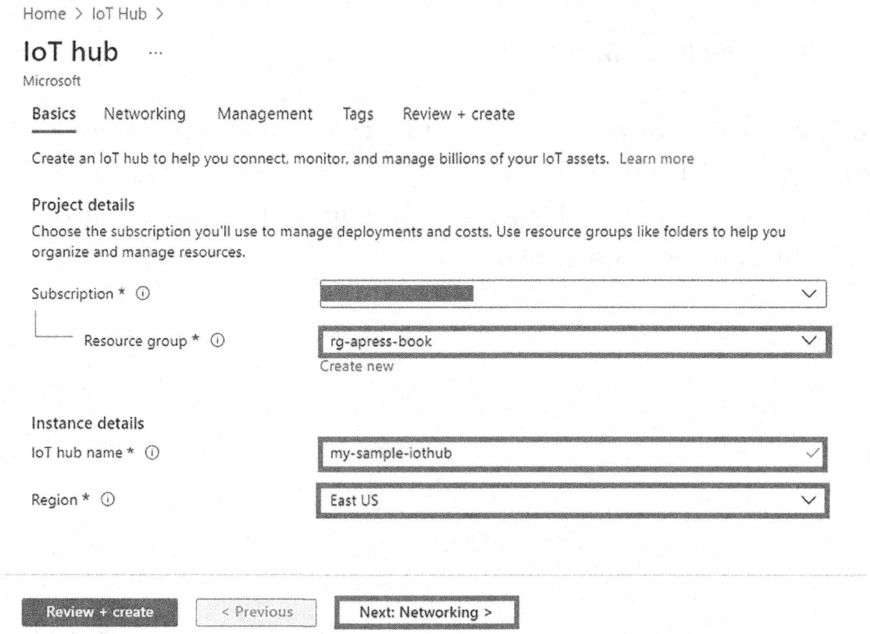

Figure 8-3. *Click Next: Networking*

Select **Public access** as the connectivity configuration and click **Next: Management** as shown in Figure 8-4.

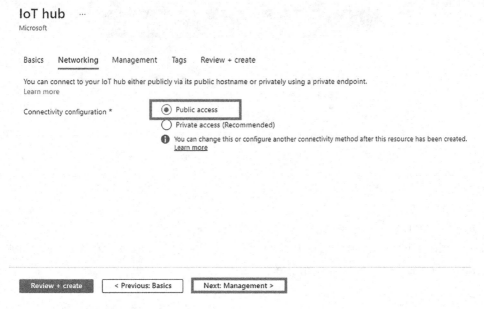

Figure 8-4. *Click on Next: Management*

In the **Pricing and scale tier** field, select **F1: Free tier** and click **Review + create** as shown in Figure 8-5. For the purpose of this chapter, we used the F1 tier, but for a production workload, choosing a higher tier is recommended. And we can only have one IoT hub with the F1 tier in a subscription.

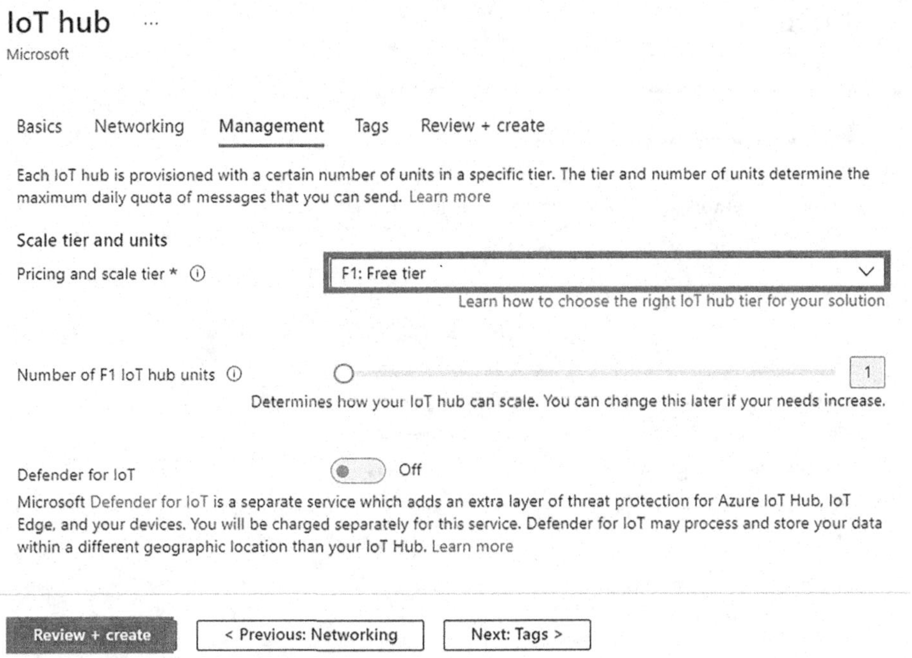

IoT hub ···

Microsoft

Basics   Networking   **Management**   Tags   Review + create

Each IoT hub is provisioned with a certain number of units in a specific tier. The tier and number of units determine the maximum daily quota of messages that you can send. Learn more

Scale tier and units

Pricing and scale tier * ⓘ

| F1: Free tier | ⌄ |

Learn how to choose the right IoT hub tier for your solution

Number of F1 IoT hub units ⓘ   ◯ | 1 |

Determines how your IoT hub can scale. You can change this later if your needs increase.

Defender for IoT   (●) Off

Microsoft Defender for IoT is a separate service which adds an extra layer of threat protection for Azure IoT Hub, IoT Edge, and your devices. You will be charged separately for this service. Defender for IoT may process and store your data within a different geographic location than your IoT Hub. Learn more

| Review + create | | < Previous: Networking | | Next: Tags > |

Figure 8-5. *Click Review + create*

Figure 8-6 shows a summary of all the configuration details entered in the previous screen. A validation will be done for the same. Once the validation is successful, click **Create**.

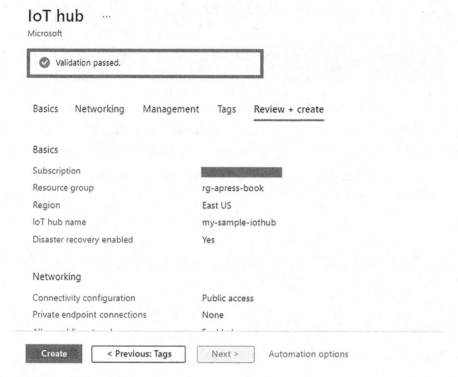

Figure 8-6. *Click Create*

Once the resource is provisioned, click **Go to resource** as shown in Figure 8-7.

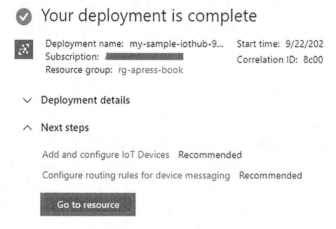

Figure 8-7. *Click Go to resource*

Now, we need to get the endpoint and Event Hub–compatible name of the provisioned IoT hub. This information will be required by our Azure Function to subscribe for messages coming to the IoT hub. You might be confused about why we are talking about getting the Event Hub–compatible name while we are dealing with the IoT hub in our scenario. The reason is that the IoT hub is built on top of Event Hub. To get the required information, click the **Built-in endpoints** option in the Hub setting section of our IoT hub resource, as shown in Figure 8-8. From there, we need to take the **event hub-compatible name** and **event hub-compatible endpoint**.

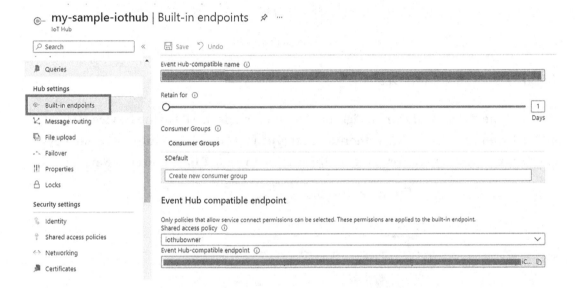

Figure 8-8. *Click Built-in endpoints*

Now that we have provisioned the IoT hub and copied the necessary details, we will explore ways to register a device in IoT Hub.

Register an IoT Device to IoT Hub in Azure Portal

For any device to be able send telemetry data or events to an IoT hub, it needs to be registered with that IoT hub. Unless your device is registered with the IoT hub, it can't send or receive any events or commands to or from the IoT hub. To register a device with the IoT hub, go to the **Devices** options present under the Device management section of the IoT hub and click + **Add Device** as shown in Figure 8-9.

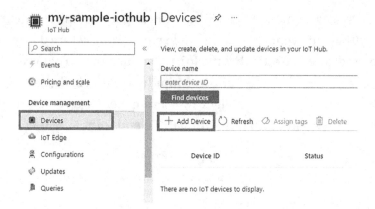

Figure 8-9. *Click +Add Device*

In the next screen, shown in Figure 8-10, enter the device ID in the **Device ID** field, select **Symmetric key** in the **Authentication type** field, check the **Auto-generate keys** check box , select **Enable** for **Connect this device to an IoT hub**, and click **Save**.

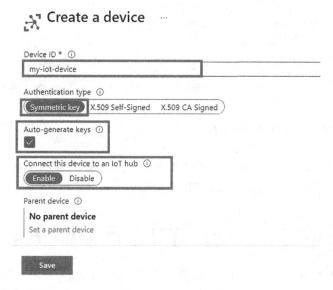

Figure 8-10. *Click Save*

Now this device is going to get registered with our IoT hub, as shown in Figure 8-11. As we have registered the device, we need to collect the connection string for the device to use it in our console application, which will work as our virtual IoT device. To get this connection string, click the newly created device under Device ID.

Figure 8-11. *Click the device*

We need to get the primary connection string for this page for later use in the chapter, so copy the value in the **Primary Connection String** field as shown in Figure 8-12.

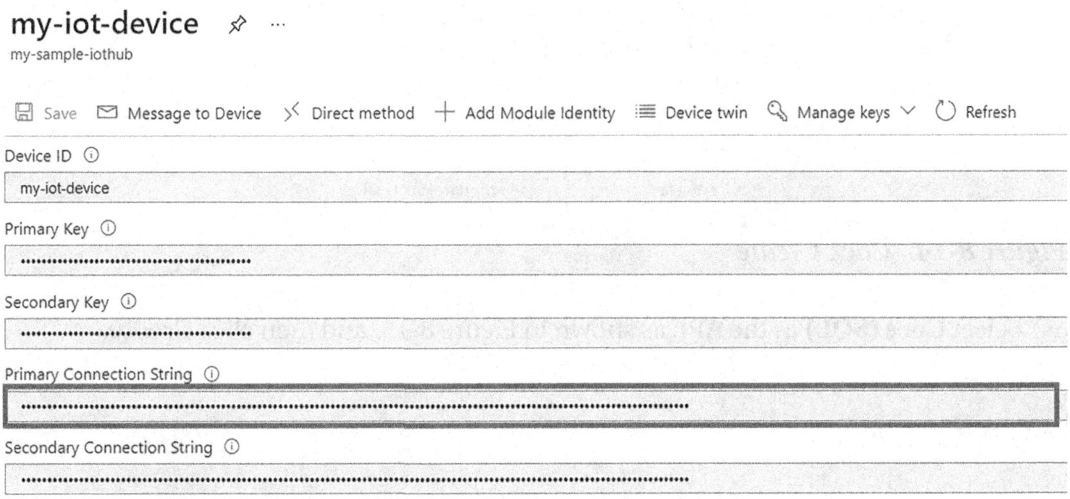

Figure 8-12. *Get the primary connection string*

We will use this primary connection string in our console event to send telemetry events to the IoT hub. In the next section, we are going to look into ways to provision a Cosmos DB instance.

Create an Azure Cosmos DB Instance in Azure Portal

Go to the Azure portal and search for **Azure Cosmos DB**. Click **Azure Cosmos DB** in the search results as shown in Figure 8-13.

Figure 8-13. *Click Azure Cosmos DB*

Click Create to create an Azure Cosmos DB instance, as shown in Figure 8-14.

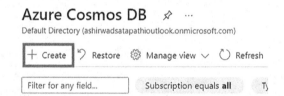

Figure 8-14. *Click Create*

Select **Core (SQL)** as the API, as shown in Figure 8-15, and then click **Create**.

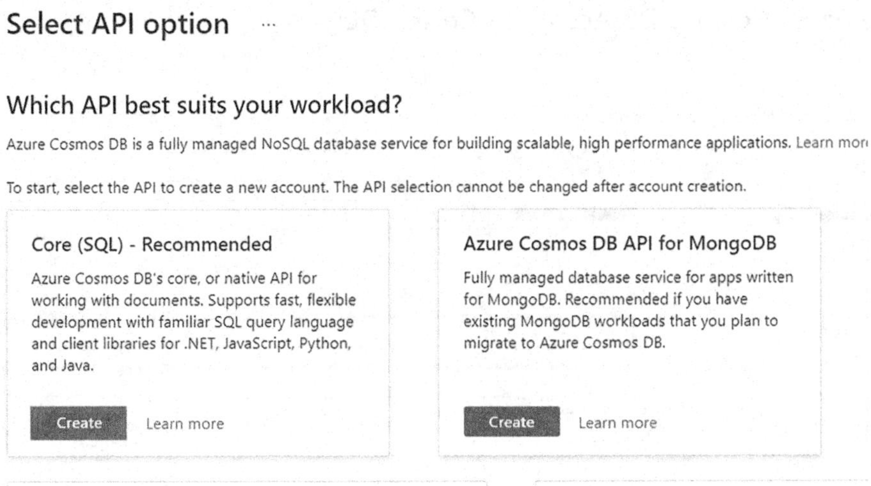

Select API option   ⋯

Which API best suits your workload?

Azure Cosmos DB is a fully managed NoSQL database service for building scalable, high performance applications. Learn more

To start, select the API to create a new account. The API selection cannot be changed after account creation.

Core (SQL) - Recommended	Azure Cosmos DB API for MongoDB
Azure Cosmos DB's core, or native API for working with documents. Supports fast, flexible development with familiar SQL query language and client libraries for .NET, JavaScript, Python, and Java.	Fully managed database service for apps written for MongoDB. Recommended if you have existing MongoDB workloads that you plan to migrate to Azure Cosmos DB.
[Create] Learn more	[Create] Learn more

Figure 8-15. *Select Core (SQL) API*

We need to select the Subscription and Resource Group and then provide the account name, location and capacity mode in the corresponding fields as shown in Figure 8-16. Go ahead with the default options here. Once you have entered the required information, click **Review + create**.

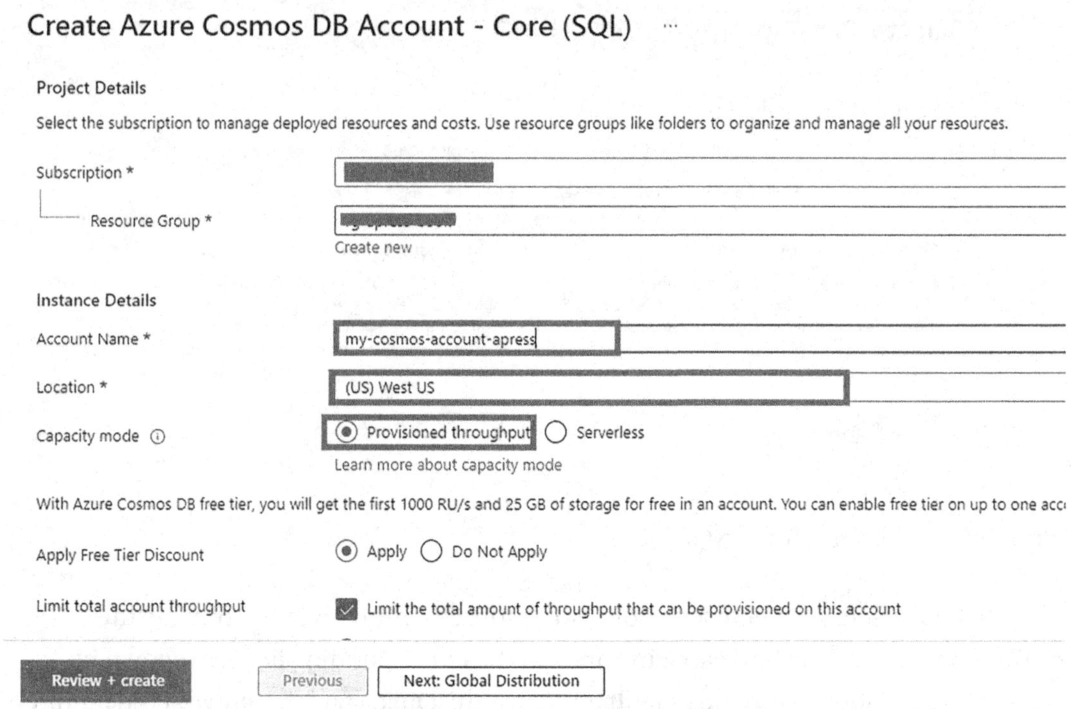

Create Azure Cosmos DB Account - Core (SQL)   ...

Project Details

Select the subscription to manage deployed resources and costs. Use resource groups like folders to organize and manage all your resources.

Subscription *

Resource Group *

Create new

Instance Details

Account Name *   my-cosmos-account-apress

Location *   (US) West US

Capacity mode ⓘ   ◉ Provisioned throughput   ○ Serverless

Learn more about capacity mode

With Azure Cosmos DB free tier, you will get the first 1000 RU/s and 25 GB of storage for free in an account. You can enable free tier on up to one acc

Apply Free Tier Discount   ◉ Apply   ○ Do Not Apply

Limit total account throughput   ☑ Limit the total amount of throughput that can be provisioned on this account

| Review + create | Previous | Next: Global Distribution |

Figure 8-16. *Click on Review + create*

Figure 8-17 shows a summary of all the configuration selected for this resource in the previous screen. A validation will be done. Once the validation is successful, click **Create**.

Create Azure Cosmos DB Account - Core (SQL) ···

✓ Validation Success

Basics   Global Distribution   Networking   Backup Policy   Encryption   Tags   **Review + create**

Creation Time

Estimated Account Creation Time (in minutes)   2

ⓘ   The estimated creation time is calculated based on the location you have selected

Basics

Subscription

Resource Group   rg-apress-book

Location   West US

Account Name   (new) my-cosmos-account-apress

API   Core (SQL)

Capacity mode   Provisioned throughput

Geo-Redundancy   Disable

[Create]   [Previous]   [Next]   Download a template for automation

Figure 8-17. *Click Create*

Once the resource has been provisioned, click **Go to resource** as shown in Figure 8-18.

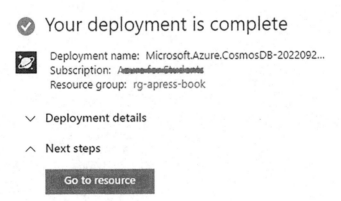

✓ **Your deployment is complete**

Deployment name: Microsoft.Azure.CosmosDB-2022092...
Subscription: Azure for Students
Resource group: rg-apress-book

⌄ Deployment details

⌃ Next steps

[Go to resource]

Figure 8-18. *Click Go to resource*

Now that we have provisioned our Cosmos DB instance, we have to create a Cosmos database and Cosmos container to store the data generated by our IoT device. A container is equivalent to a table in a relational database management system (RDMS). To create a container, click **Data Explorer** and then click **New Container** as shown in Figure 8-19.

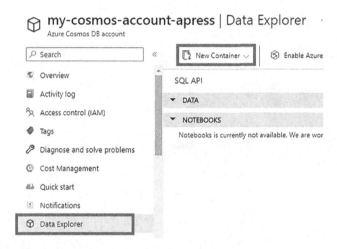

Figure 8-19. *Click Data Explorer*

Next, provide the database name, database throughput, database max RU, container name, and partition key (see Figure 8-20). Once provided, click **OK** to provision your container.

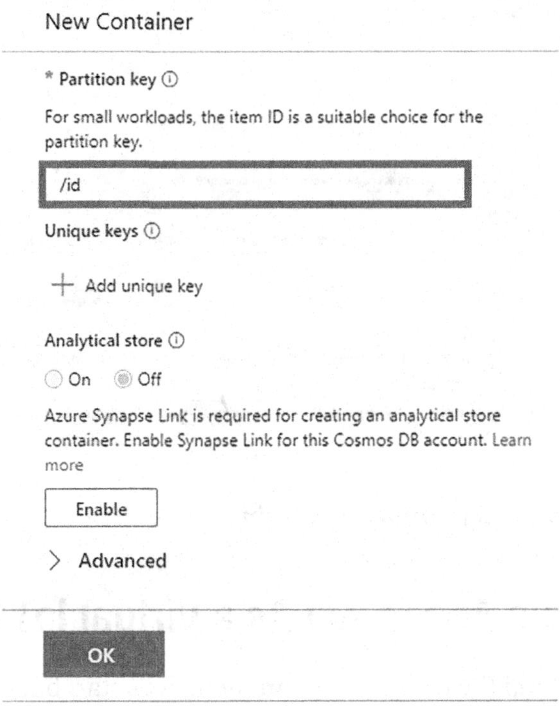

New Container

* Partition key ⓘ

For small workloads, the item ID is a suitable choice for the
partition key.

    /id

Unique keys ⓘ

    + Add unique key

Analytical store ⓘ

○ On   ◉ Off

Azure Synapse Link is required for creating an analytical store
container. Enable Synapse Link for this Cosmos DB account. Learn
more

    Enable

⟩ Advanced

    OK

Figure 8-20. *Click OK*

We can view the newly created container in the Data Explorer as shown in
Figure 8-21.

Figure 8-21. *Container was created*

Now that we have created all the resources, we have to collect the connection string
of our cosmos db to interact with it. To do so, go to the Keys section of the cosmos db
resource, as shown in Figure 8-22, and copy the primary connection string.

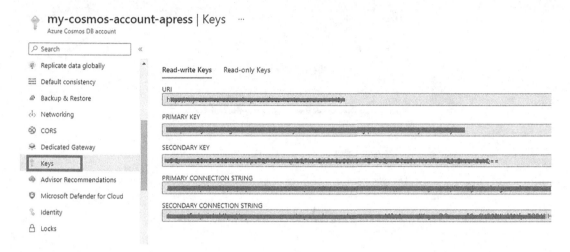

Figure 8-22. *Copy primary connection string*

Create a Console App to Act As a Virtual IoT Device

Now that we have covered the business requirement, let's start building our virtual IoT device by using the Console App Template. Open Visual Studio 2022 and click **Create a new project**. Select the **Console App** template and click **Next**.

In the **Configure your new project** window, enter the project name, location, and solution name in the corresponding fields and then click **Next**.

In the **Additional information** window, choose your target framework and select the **Do not use top level-statements** check box. Once you have provided all the information, click **Create**. Visual Studio creates a console app with the configuration that you entered.

The first thing that we have to do here is install the Device SDK of Azure IoT hub and Netwonsoft.Json NuGet package. To do this, open the Package Manager Console and type the following:

```
Install-Package Microsoft.Azure.Devices.Client -Version 1.41.2
Install-Package Newtonsoft.Json
```

Next, create a new class called `HealthModel.cs` and enter the following code. This class is going to represent the telemetry data that will be sent by our device to the IoT hub.

```
public class HealthModel
{
```

```
        public string Id { get; set; }
        public int PluseRate { get; set; }
        public int Temprature { get; set; }
        public DateTime RecordedAt { get; set; }
}
```

Now replace the program.cs class with the following code. This code
generates a randomly generated pulse rate and temperature values using the
GetRandomNumberInRange method and uses it construct the HealthModel object. This
model is then serialized and sent to the IoT hub using the SendEventAsync method of
the DeviceClient instance. The DeviceClient is created using the connection string
that we had previously collected for the registered device.

```
public class Program
{
    private static DeviceClient deviceClient;
    private readonly static string connectionString = "<enter your device
    connection string>";
    static void Main(string[] args)
    {
        Console.WriteLine("Sending Messages");
        Task.Delay(10000).Wait();
        deviceClient = DeviceClient.CreateFromConnectionString(connectionSt
        ring, TransportType.Mqtt);
        int i = 0;
        bool result;
        //sends sensor data from the device simulator every second for
        10 minutes
        while (i < 1)
        {
            Task.Delay(6000).Wait();
            result = SendMessages(deviceClient);
            if (result)
            {
                Console.WriteLine($"Message {i} delivered");
            }
```

```csharp
        else
        {
            Console.WriteLine("Message failed");
        }
        i++;
    }
}

/// <summary>
/// Method to send data from the device simulator to IoT Hub
/// </summary>
/// <param name="deviceClient"></param>
/// <returns></returns>
public static bool SendMessages(DeviceClient deviceClient)
{
    var sensorData = new HealthModel()
    {
        Id = Guid.NewGuid().ToString(),
        PluseRate = GetRandomNumberInRange(90, 110),
        RecordedAt = DateTime.UtcNow,
        Temprature = GetRandomNumberInRange(90, 110)
    };
    var jsonData = JsonConvert.SerializeObject(sensorData);

    try
    {
        var data = new Message(Encoding.ASCII.GetBytes(jsonData));
        deviceClient.SendEventAsync(data).GetAwaiter().GetResult();
        //Console.WriteLine("Message Sent");
        return true;
    }
    catch (Exception ex)
    {
        Console.WriteLine($"Error Info - {ex.Message}");
        return false;
    }
```

```
    }

    /// <summary>
    /// Method to generate random value to mock the Soil Moisture
    level values
    /// </summary>
    /// <param name="minNumber"></param>
    /// <param name="maxNumber"></param>
    /// <returns></returns>
    public static int GetRandomNumberInRange(int minNumber, int maxNumber)
    {
        return new Random().Next(minNumber,maxNumber);
    }
}
```

Now we will have to run our program and it will send one message to the IoT hub. Once the message is sent, you can view that the field with the number of messages used today will have changed in the usage section of the overview page of your IoT hub. You can find the source code for our virtual IoT device at `https://github.com/AshirwadSatapathi/MyVirtualIoTDevice`.

Create an IoT Hub Triggered Azure Function to Store Data in Cosmos DB

Now that we have our virtual IoT device up and running, it is capable of sending messages to the IoT hub. Next, we need to build the function that is going to process the message and store it in Cosmos DB.

Before we start creating our function project, make sure that you have installed the Azure development workload for your workload. If you have not done so, you can open Visual Studio Installer and install it.

Now, Open Visual Studio 2022 and click **Create a new project**. Select the **Azure Function** template and click **Next**.

In the **Configure your new project** window, enter your project name, location, and solution name and then click **Next**.

In the **Additional information** section, select the Function worker as **.NET 6 LTS**, select the Function type as **IoT Hub trigger**, enter the connection string setting name as the key name where you will store the IoT hub endpoint that we have gathered earlier, and provide the path. The path is the Event Hub–compatible name. Once you have entered all the information, click **Next**. This will generate an IoT hub triggered function out of the box.

Now open the Package Manager Console and type the following command to install the NuGet package for the Cosmos DB extension and Newtonsoft.Json. We need to install the Cosmos DB extension because we want to use cosmos db output binding for azure function.

```
Install-Package Microsoft.Azure.WebJobs.Extensions.CosmosDB
Install-Package Newtonsoft.Json
```

Open the local.settings.json file and add the IoT hub connection string and the Cosmos DB connection for the keys iotHubConn and dbConn, respectively. While storing the IoT hub connection string, make sure that you remove the entity path section from the Event Hub–compatible endpoint.

Next, create the HealthModel class that we had created for our Virtual IoT device earlier.

Replace the Function1 class with the following code. This function listens to the messages coming to the Azure IoT hub and consumes them, thanks to the IoT hub trigger, and later gets the deserializes the message to the HealthModel type. Finally, it uses the cosmos Db output binding to write the data to our cosmos db container that we had provisioned earlier.

```
public class Function1
{
    private static HttpClient client = new HttpClient();

    [FunctionName("IoTHubEventProcessor")]
    public void Run(
        [IoTHubTrigger("<event hub compatible name>", Connection =
        "iotHubConn")]string message,
        [CosmosDB(
            databaseName:"<database name>",
            collectionName:"<container name>",
```

```
        ConnectionStringSetting ="dbConn"
    )] IAsyncCollector<dynamic> documentsOut,
    ILogger log)
{

    log.LogInformation($"C# IoT Hub trigger function processed a
    message: {message}");

    HealthModel data = JsonConvert.DeserializeObject<HealthModel>
    (message);

    documentsOut.AddAsync(
        new
        {
            id = data.Id,
            pulseRate = data.PluseRate,
            temprature = data.Temprature,
            recordedAt = data.RecordedAt
        }
    ).Wait();

}
}
```

As Figure 8-23 shows, our function was able to process the messages sent by our virtual IoT device to the IoT hub.

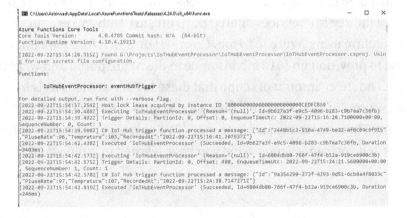

Figure 8-23. *IoTHubEventProcessor process the events*

We can now go to the cosmos db container to check if the data was written there or not. As can be confirmed from Figure 8-24, our function was able to write the data in cosmos db.

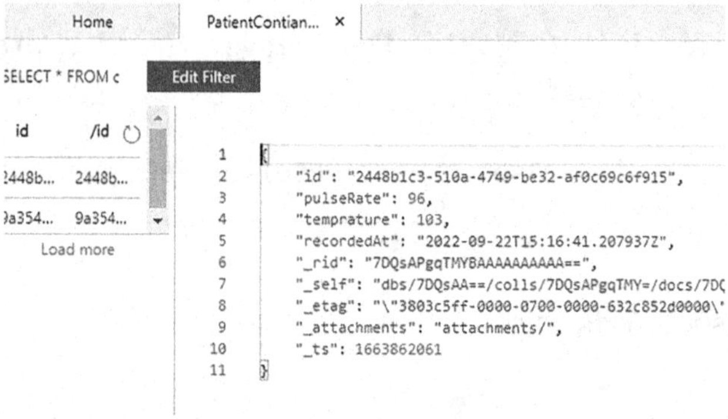

Figure 8-24. *View the data in cosmos db container*

You might observe there are few additional keys present in the record. These are auto-generated by Cosmos DB for each document and we should not be worried about it. And with this, we have built our proof of concept for the IoT solutions. You can find the source code at `https://github.com/AshirwadSatapathi/IoTHubEventProcessor`.

Summary

The world of IoT is an interesting and is rapidly evolving. To enable customers to tap into the full potential of IoT, Microsoft Azure provides a suite of IoT services. We have briefly explored one of the key IoT services offered by Azure, IoT Hub. We examined ways to build an IoT solution using Azure IoT Hub, Cosmos DB, and Azure Functions. While also explored ways to provision an IoT Hub instance in the Azure portal and ways to register an IoT device. The sheer amount of scope that these IoT service let's us is immense. As one example, we could build solutions focused on agriculture, a potential use case being smart irrigation. There are many such use cases. We only touched the tip of the iceberg in this chapter, but you can leverage what you have learned to build wonderful solutions.

CHAPTER 9

Build a Desktop Application for Speech-to-Text Conversation Using Azure Cognitive Services

Modern applications using artificial intelligence (AI). For example, you can build a healthcare application that can help medical practitioners and doctors dictate the drugs prescription for the patient and the AI-based application will convert the doctor's verbal dictation into a text-based prescription that the patient can use to procure drugs for the treatment. Building an AI-based application from scratch can be challenging. You need to develop your AI model on top of a huge amount of data. However, public cloud providers provide Platform-as-a-Service (PaaS)-based AI services that you can consume to build modern AI-based applications. The cloud providers take care of the data and model. You simply need to pay for the data you use.

In this chapter we will explore Azure Cognitive Services and how to use its Speech service to convert speech to text.

Structure

In this chapter, we will explore the following topics related to Azure Cognitive Services:

- Introduction to Azure Cognitive Services

- Provision the Speech service

- Build a .NET-based desktop application to convert speech to text

© Ashirwad Satapathi and Abhishek Mishra 2023
A. Satapathi and A. Mishra, *Developing Cloud-Native Solutions with Microsoft Azure and .NET*,
https://doi.org/10.1007/978-1-4842-9004-0_9

Objectives

After studying this chapter, you should be able to

- Understand the fundamentals of Azure Cognitive Services

- Work with the Speech service

Introduction to Azure Cognitive Services

Azure Cognitive Services provides PaaS-based artificial intelligence capability for developing AI-based applications. You need not arrange any dataset nor train any model. You simply need to consume these services for your AI use cases. Under the hood, Azure has done the heavy lifting in training the models and exposing these trained models as services that you can consume without concern for the underlying infrastructure. All these services are exposed as REST APIs that you can consume or use SDKs available in popular languages and platforms like .NET, Java, and Python.

The following are the offerings from Azure Cognitive Services:

- Vision

- Speech

- Language

- Decision

Vision

Vision comprises the following services:

- Computer Vision service helps you with capability to process and extract insights from videos and images.

- Custom Vision helps you build your own custom image classifiers and deploy them on Azure. You can apply labels to the images based on specific characteristics of the images.

- Face service helps you in performing face recognition.

Speech

Speech service helps you build intelligent applications that can convert speech audio to text and vice versa.

Language

Language comprises the following services:

- Language Understanding Intelligent Service (LUIS) helps you perform natural language processing and helps the applications understand human natural language.

- Translator translates machine-based text from one language to another.

- Language Service helps you analyze text and derive insights like sentiments and key phrases from the text.

- QnA Maker helps you build a question-and-answer database from your semi-structured data.

Decision

The following are the services offered by Decision APIs:

- Anomaly Detector helps you infer anomalies in any time-series data.

- Content Moderator helps you build applications that can moderate data that can be offensive or risky.

- Personalizer helps you capture real-time user personal preferences that will help you understand user behaviors.

Provision Speech Service

Let's spin up a Speech service that we can use in a .NET application to convert speech to text. Go to the Azure portal and click **Create a resource** as shown in Figure 9-1.

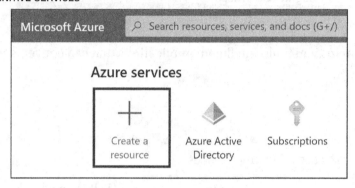

Figure 9-1. *Click Create a resource*

You will be navigated to the Azure Marketplace. Click **AI + Machine Learning** and
then click **Speech** as shown in Figure 9-2.

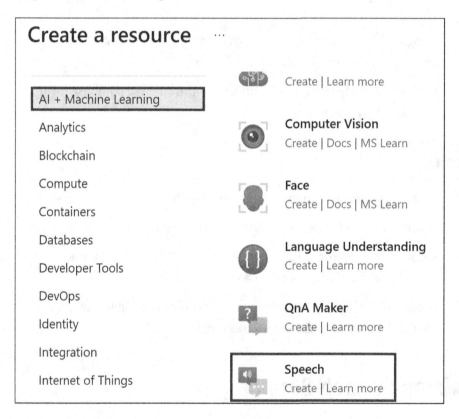

Figure 9-2. *Click Speech*

Provide the basic details like name, subscription, resource group, pricing tier, and region for the Speech service, as shown in Figure 9-3, and then click **Create + review**.

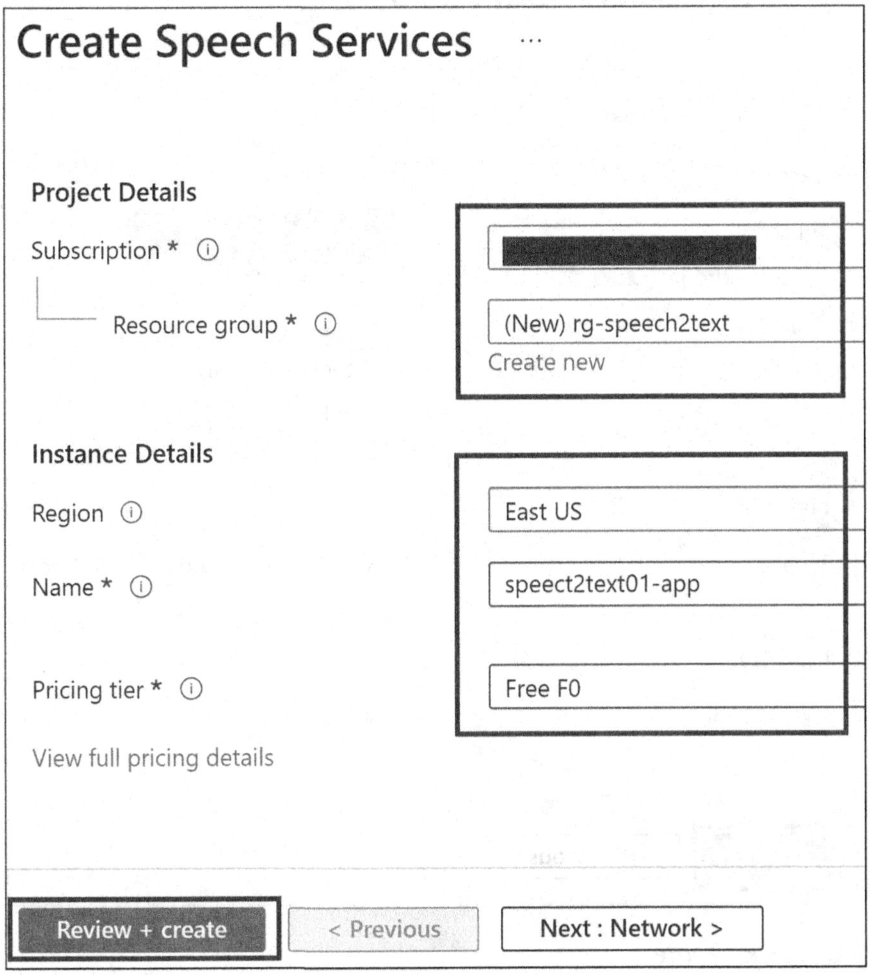

Create Speech Services   ...

Project Details

Subscription * ⓘ

⌐
└── Resource group * ⓘ

| |
| |
| ▇▇▇▇▇▇▇▇▇▇▇ |
| (New) rg-speech2text |
| Create new |

Instance Details

Region ⓘ

Name * ⓘ

Pricing tier * ⓘ

View full pricing details

| |
| East US |
| speect2text01-app |
| Free F0 |

| Review + create | < Previous | Next : Network > |

Figure 9-3. *Click Review + create*

223

Click **Create** as shown in Figure 9-4. This will spin up the Speech service.

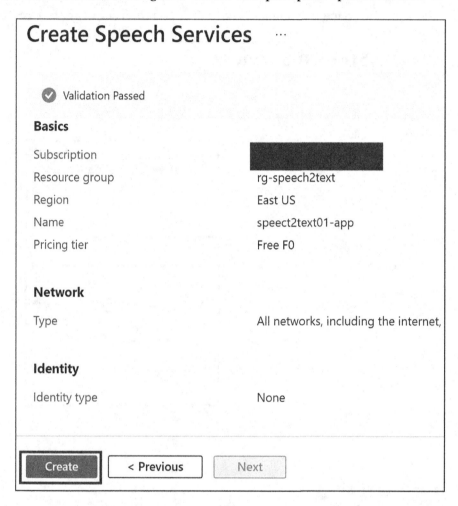

Figure 9-4. *Click Create*

Once the Speech service gets created, go to the **Keys and Endpoints** section and click **Show Keys** as shown in Figure 9-5. Copy the value in the **KEY 1** *field*. We will use this key while consuming the service from the .NET desktop application.

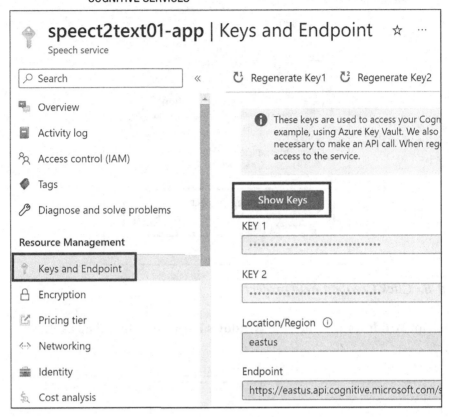

Figure 9-5.   Copy the key in KEY 1 field

Build a .NET-Based Desktop Application to Convert Speech to Text

Let's build a .NET-based desktop application that will convert speech to text using the Speech service we created earlier. Open Visual Studio and click **Create a new project** as shown in Figure 9-6.

Figure 9-6. *Click Create a new project*

Search for **Windows** and click the **Windows Forms App** template as shown in
Figure 9-7.

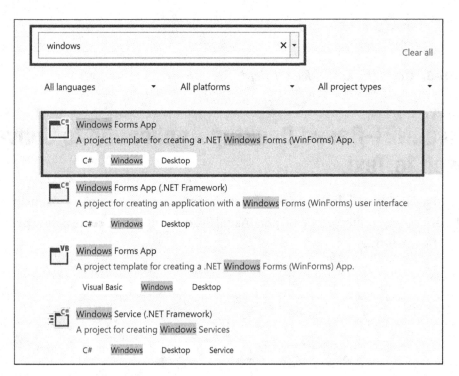

Figure 9-7. *Select the first Windows Forms App template*

Provide the details for the project as shown in Figure 9-8 and click **Next**.

Figure 9-8. *Provide project details*

Select the .NET framework version as shown in Figure 9-9 and click **Create**. This will create the Windows Forms application project.

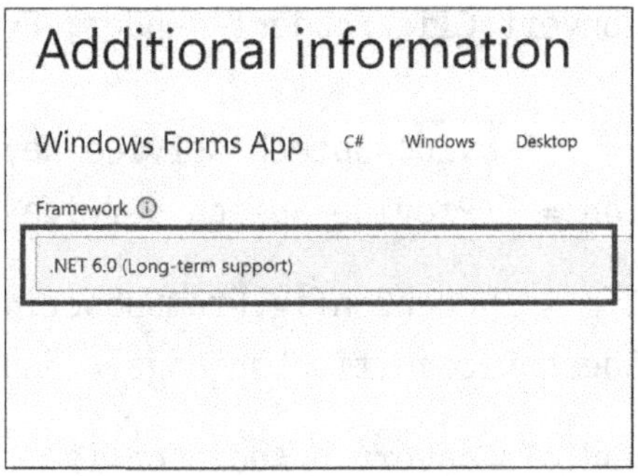

Figure 9-9. *Select .NET version*

Design a form that will take the full path along with the name of the video file. It should have a button to invoke the Speech service and convert the audio speech into text. It should also have a label to display text for the converted speech. Figure 9-10 represents the form design.

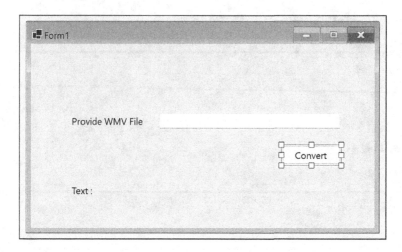

Figure 9-10. *Form design*

Go to the Form1.cs file and add the code shown in Listing 9-1 for the button click event. You invoke the Speech service to convert a wav format file to text. You display the text in the label you have added.

Listing 9-1. Form1.cs

```
private async void btnConvert_Click(object sender, EventArgs e)
        {
            string key = "[Provide Speech service Key]";
            string region = "[Provide Speech service location]";

            var speechCfg = SpeechConfig.FromSubscription(key, region);
            speechCfg.SpeechRecognitionLanguage = "en-US";

            using var audioToConvert = AudioConfig.
FromWavFileInput(txtWMVFile.Text);
            using var speechCoversionOutput = new
SpeechRecognizer(speechCfg, audioToConvert);
            var speechConversionResult = await speechCoversionOutput.
RecognizeOnceAsync();
```

228

```
        lblOutput.Text = lblOutput.Text + " " +
speechConversionResult.Text;
    }
```

Run the code. Provide the wav file along with the fully qualified path and click **Convert** as shown in Figure 9-11.

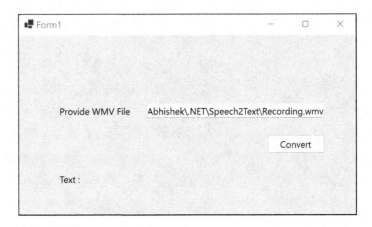

Figure 9-11. *Provide wav file to convert*

The converted text from the speech will get displayed as shown in Figure 9-12.

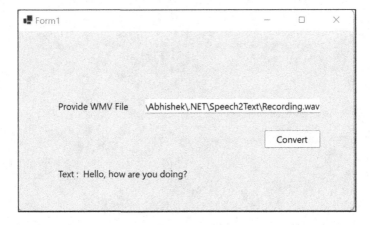

Figure 9-12. *Converted output*

Summary

In this chapter, we explored the basic concepts of Azure Cognitive Services. Then we created a speech service and invoked the Speech service from a .NET-based desktop application to convert a wav audio file speech to text. In the next chapter, you will learn how to build a multilanguage text translator using Azure Cognitive Services and .NET.

CHAPTER 10

Build a Multilanguage Text Translator Using Azure Cognitive Services

The world around us has been embracing AI to build intelligent solutions like never before. Many applications coming to the market these days include intelligent features out of the box. Some common examples of such features include auto-completion of texts in chat-based apps and the use of facial recognition to unlock our smartphones. Often, these features aren't easy to build and involve complex algorithms. Most of the time, these complex algorithms require vast amounts of data, extensive research, and a huge amount computational resources to train, process, and build AI models. Many companies may not even have the required resources to build their own AI models for a particular use case. To overcome this, developers tend to use services or pretrained AI models offered by other companies.

In this chapter, we explore ways to integrate AI into our applications by leveraging the power of Azure Cognitive Services, a set services that allows us to use state-of-the-art algorithms and AI models developed by Microsoft to perform operations ranging from speech recognition to image classification. By the end of this chapter, we will build a web API that is capable of translating text from one language to another.

Structure

In this chapter, we will explore the following topics related to Azure Cognitive Services:

- Introduction to Azure Cognitive Services

© Ashirwad Satapathi and Abhishek Mishra 2023
A. Satapathi and A. Mishra, *Developing Cloud-Native Solutions with Microsoft Azure and .NET*,
https://doi.org/10.1007/978-1-4842-9004-0_10

- Provision a Translator Service in the Azure portal

- Build a multilanguage text translator app

Objectives

After studying this chapter, you should be able to

- Understand the fundamentals of Azure Cognitive Services

- Integrate the prowess of translator service in your application

Azure Cognitive Services

Microsoft provides a suite of cloud-based AI services to add intelligence to applications by leveraging state-of-the-art AI models built and designed over time through extensive research. Microsoft calls this suite of cloud-based AI service Azure Cognitive Services. These services help developers add cognitive capabilities to their applications with prior knowledge of machine learning or AI. These services provide a set of REST APIs and client libraries that we can leverage to integrate the prowess of these cognitive services into our applications to make them smart. We can securely connect with these services using different methods of authentication. The following are the ways we can authenticate our requests to Azure Cognitive Services:

- Subscription key

- Token

- Azure Active Directory (Azure AD)

A word of caution here that not all services that are part of the suite of Azure Cognitive Services support all the of the preceding methods of authentications. For example, the Speech services and text translation service currently support token-based authentication, but that is not the case with other services that are part of the suite. The number of services that support token-based authentication is expanding, though, and may change by the time this book gets published.

Apart from providing different mechanisms to authenticate your support, Azure Cognitive Services also has support for virtual networks. This enables you to control access to your resources from allowed IP addresses.

Cognitive Services in Azure are broadly classified into four categories:

- *Vision*: Vision services comprise the Computer Vision, Custom Vision, and Face services. As the name suggests, the set of services falling under this category assists our application to work with image-based data and make intelligent decisions. Use cases where the Vision services can come in handy are facial recognition and character recognition.

- *Speech*: Speech services comprise the text-to-speech, speech-to-text, speaker recognition, and speech translation services. This set of services assists us in integrating speech capabilities in our applications. We can use these services to build solutions that can help us texts in our meetings or calls. Voice assistants are a popular use case for which these services are of great help.

- *Language*: Language services is a collection of various NLP features along with services like Translator, LUIS, and QnA Maker. These services assist us by integrating the ability to process and analyze unstructured texts in our applications. We can leverage these services to perform complex operations like sentiment analysis, opinion mining, and language detection, to name a few. Sentiment classification is a popular use of the Language services.

- *Decision*: Decision services is a collection of services that include Anomaly Detector, Content Moderator, and Personalizer. These services assist us by integrating the ability to provide recommendation to take informed decision in our application. We can leverage these services to detect potential abnormalities in a time series data or to provide monitoring for censored or abusive content.

With that review of Azure Cognitive Services and its use cases in mind, we will now explore the translator service to solve the problem of our fictional company.

Problem Statement

You are working for a fictional company named Aztec Corp. that wants to add a text translation feature to one of its flagship products. You are part of the team that will be working on this feature. Your product owner and management have decided to go ahead with Azure Translation service to perform text translation. You are assigned with the task to perform a proof of concept (PoC) to translate any given text from language A to language B. Once done, your team members can incrementally work on your PoC to build the feature by using your PoC as a base for further development.

Proposed Solution

After going through the initial set of requirements, you have distilled the problem statement into two phases:

- Develop an interface that takes text as input, language to be translated in and returns the translated text to the user.

- Integrate the Azure text analytics service to our interface to perform the text translation.

You have decided the interface is going to be an ASP.NET Core Web API that will take the source language, text to be translated, and target language in the request body and output the translated text.

Before we start building the web API, we need a couple of things in place. The following are the prerequisites to start development activities:

1. Create an Azure Translator Resource

2. Get the key and endpoint of the Translator Resource

Once we have these two things in place, we will start building our web API using Visual Studio 2022. Before we start provisioning our Translator resource, let's look at what Azure Translator is and what capabilities it has.

What Is Azure Translator?

Azure Translator is a cloud-based AI service that enables developers to integrate text translation capabilities into their applications. It is part of the Azure Cognitive Services suite of Microsoft. Azure Translator supports text translation from over 100+ languages. It leverages the neural machine translator technology to process the texts and generate the desired outcome Apart from text translation, Azure Translator enables us to perform operations such as language detection and transliteration of text, to name a few. It also comes with an offering called Custom Translator that enables you to build your own customized neural machine translation system. We will be leveraging Azure Translator to complete our PoC in the upcoming sections.

Create an Azure Translator Instance in Azure Portal

To create an Azure Translator instance, go to the Azure portal and type **Translators** in the search box. Click the **Translators** in the search results as shown in Figure 10-1.

Figure 10-1. *Search for Translator*

Click **Create** to provision a new Azure Translator instance, as shown in Figure 10-2.

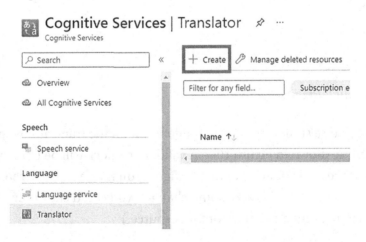

Figure 10-2. *Click Create*

Next, select the subscription and resource group. If you don't have a subscription, you can create a new one in this screen. After that, select the region and pricing tier and enter the name of tour resource, as shown in Figure 10-3. The name of the resource needs to be globally unique. For the purpose of this chapter, we will be going ahead with the free tier, **Free F0**. This tier provides us with the capability to translate 2 million characters every month. If you wanted to use this resource for production workloads, you would need to have a higher tier that satisfies your requirement. Once you have entered all the details, click **Review + create**.

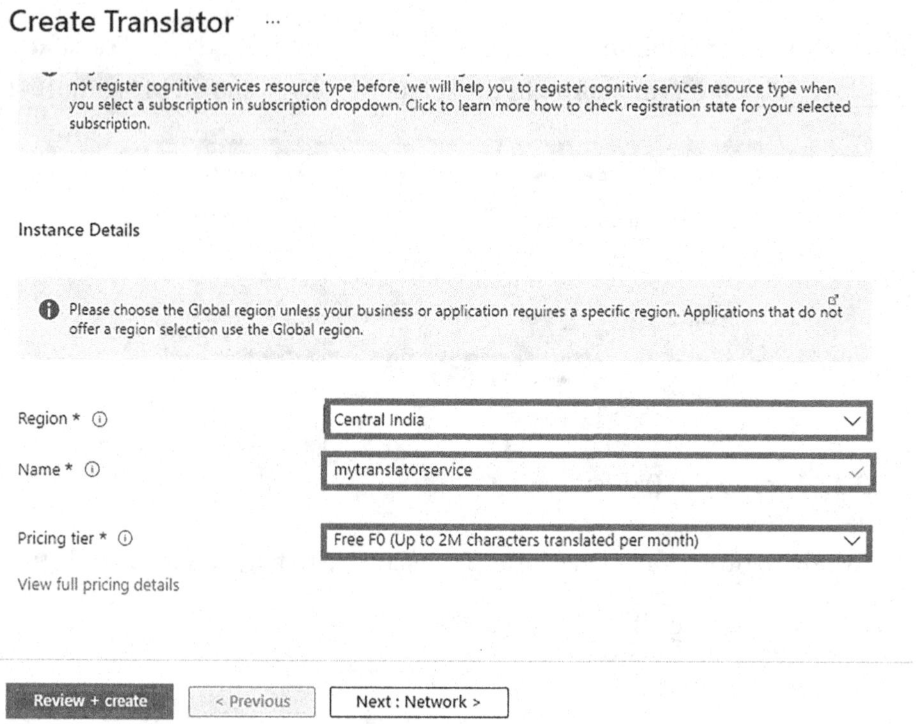

Figure 10-3. *Click Review + create*

Next you will see a summary of the configuration for the translator resource from the previous screen, as shown in Figure 10-4. A validation check will be performed on the configuration. Once the validation of the configuration is done, click **Create** to provision our resource. (If you wanted to make some changes, you could click Previous and make the necessary configuration changes for the resource.)

Create Translator ···

✅ Validation Passed

Basics

Subscription	▇▇▇▇▇▇▇▇▇
Resource group	rg-apress-book
Region	Central India
Name	mytranslatorservice
Pricing tier	Free F0 (Up to 2M characters translated per month)

Network

Type	All networks, including the internet, can access this resource.

Identity

Identity type	None

[Create]   [< Previous]   [Next]

Figure 10-4. *Click Create*

Once the resource has been successfully provisioned, you will see the message **Your deployment is complete**, as shown in Figure 10-5. Once you see that message, click **Go to resource** to go to the newly provisioned translator resource.

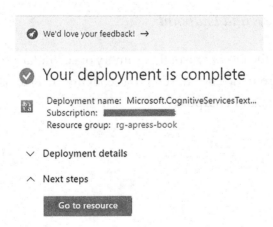

Figure 10-5. *Click Go to resource*

Having provisioned the translator resource in Azure, now we need to access it to integrate it with our application. To access or interact with Azure Translator service from our application, we would need to authenticate our application's request to the translator resource. This can be done in different ways, such as using Azure Active Directory–based authentication or key-based authentication. For the purpose of this demonstration, we will be using key-based authentication. For enterprise applications, it is recommended to use Azure AD–based authentication or managed identity if the applications are deployed inside Azure in an Azure Function or App Service by providing necessary RBAC permissions to the Azure Translator instance.

Click the **Keys and Endpoint** section, as shown in Figure 10-6, to fetch the key, endpoint, and region details for our translator resource.

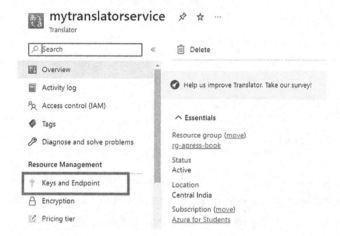

Figure 10-6. *Click Keys and Endpoint*

We will have to get the either one of the primary or secondary key, the resource endpoint, and region from the current screen (see Figure 10-7) to use later in our application for authentication purposes.

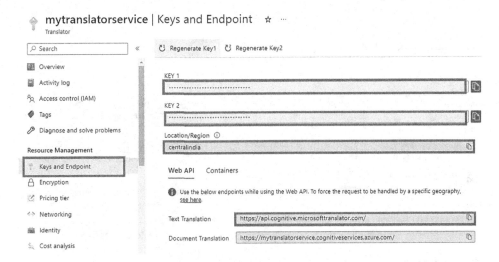

Figure 10-7. *Get the key, endpoint, and region*

Now that we have provisioned the resource and have the required information to authenticate our request to the translator service, we can start building the application to translate languages from one language to the other in the next section.

Create a Multilanguage Text Translator Using ASP. NET Core

In this section, we're going to complete the proof of concept for our fictional company to build a feature for its flagship product, as briefly discussed in the "Proposed Solution" section.

As we have already covered the business requirement and provisioned the required resources, let's start building our web API using the ASP.NET Core Web API template. Open Visual Studio 2022 and click **Create a new project** as shown in Figure 10-8.

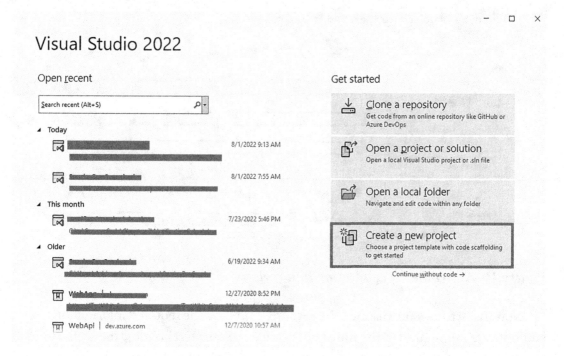

Figure 10-8. *Click Create a new project*

Select the **ASP.NET Core Web API** project template as shown in Figure 10-9 and click **Next**.

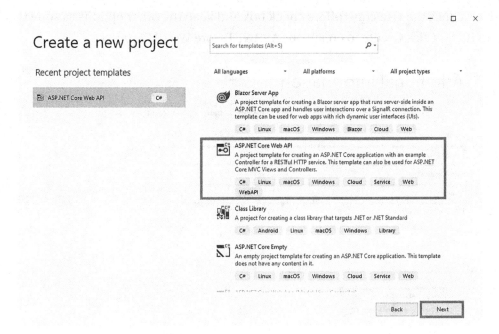

Figure 10-9. *Click Next*

Enter the project name, location, and solution name in the corresponding fields, as shown in Figure 10-10, and click **Next**.

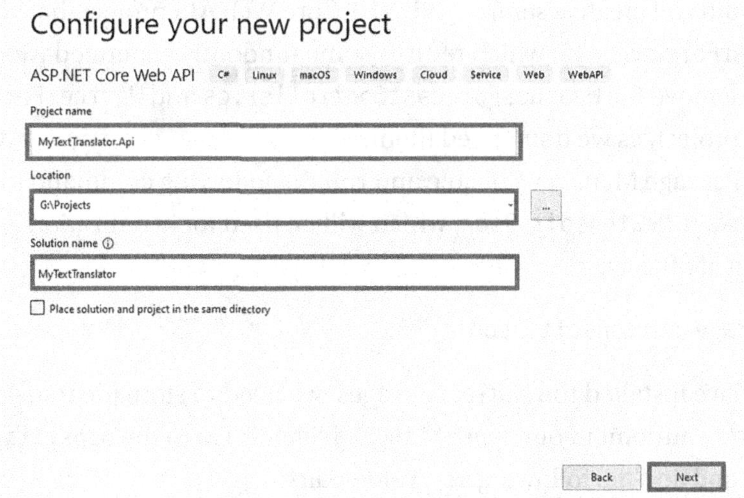

Configure your new project

ASP.NET Core Web API   C#   Linux   macOS   Windows   Cloud   Service   Web   WebAPI

Project name

```
MyTextTranslator.Api
```

Location

```
G:\Projects
```

Solution name ⓘ

```
MyTextTranslator
```

☐ Place solution and project in the same directory

Back   Next

Figure 10-10. *Enter the project name, location, and solution name*

Now check the **Use controllers** check box and keep the other options as shown in Figure 10-11. Click **Create** to create our ASP.NET Core Web API project.

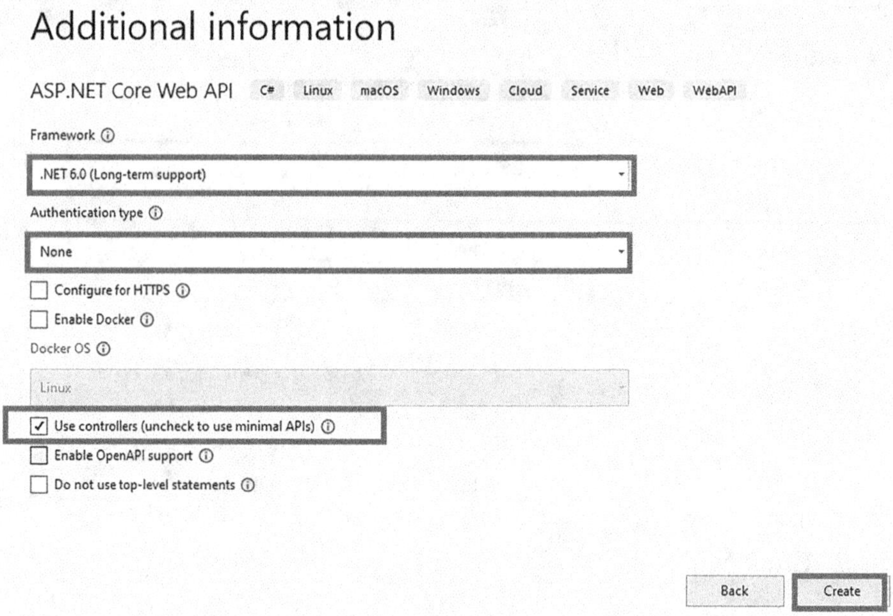

Additional information

ASP.NET Core Web API   C#   Linux   macOS   Windows   Cloud   Service   Web   WebAPI

Framework ⓘ

.NET 6.0 (Long-term support)   ▾

Authentication type ⓘ

None   ▾

☐ Configure for HTTPS ⓘ
☐ Enable Docker ⓘ
Docker OS ⓘ

Linux   ▾

☑ Use controllers (uncheck to use minimal APIs) ⓘ
☐ Enable OpenAPI support ⓘ
☐ Do not use top-level statements ⓘ

Back   Create

Figure 10-11. Click Create

Visual Studio will create a sample ASP.NET Core Web API project that contains a simple WeatherForecast API, which returns some randomly generated weather forecast information. Remove the WeatherForecastController.cs and WeatherForecast.cs files from our project, as we don't need them.

Open the Package Manager Console and run the following command to install the NuGet package Newtonsoft.Json, which will be used for serialization and deserialization of objects:

```
Install-Package Newtonsoft.Json
```

Once we have installed the NuGet packages, we need to store the translator service's key, region, and endpoint in our appsettings.json file. Go to the appsettings.json file of our project and add the following key/value pairs:

```
"key": "<enter your key>",
"endpoint": "<enter your endpoint>",
"location": "<enter the region>"
```

Let's create two folders in our project: Business and Models. The Business folder will contain our interface and the classes implementing them. The Models folder will contain the classes of our data models.

After creating both folders, create a class called TranslatePayload.cs in the Models folder and paste the following code. This class represents the data sent by the client app in the request payload, which would contain the text to be translated along with the source and destination language. We have used data annotations to mark the necessary fields as required.

```
public class TranslatePayload
{
    [Required]
    public string SourceLanguageCode { get; set; }
    [Required]
    public string TargetLanguageCode { get; set; }
    [Required]
    public string TextToBeTranslated { get; set; }
}
```

Now that our model is ready, let's create an interface called ITranslateBusiness. cs in the Business folder and add the following method definition. As shown, our interface contains one method definition, TranslateText, which will be responsible for taking the TranslatePayload data coming from the request payload and returning the translated text in the target language.

```
public interface ITranslateBusiness
{
    Task<string> TranslateText(TranslatePayload translatePayload);
}
```

Now that we know what each of the methods is designed to perform, let's create a class called TranslateBusiness.cs to implement the ITranslateBusiness interface. Before implementing the interface, add the following properties:

```
private string key;
private string endpoint;
private string location;
```

243

Now instantiate the properties by using constructor injection. Replace your constructor with the following code:

```
public TranslateBusiness(IConfiguration configuration)
{
    key = configuration.GetValue<String>("key");
    endpoint = configuration.GetValue<String>("endpoint");
    location = configuration.GetValue<String>("location");
}
```

In the preceding code snippet, we are leveraging an IConfiguration instance to access the values that we had stored with the key name as key, endpoint, and location in our appsetting.json file.

Now we need to implement the TranslateText method of the ITranslateBusiness interface in the class. We will be making calls to the REST endpoints of Translator APIs because there is no available client library for the translator service at the time of writing. The TranslateText method will create an HttpClient instance to interact with the APIs of the Translator Service. We are passing the source and target language in the query string and passing the text to be translated in the request body of our object of type HttpRequestMessage. We specify the key and region in headers of our HttpRequestMessage object and call the SendAsync method of our HttpClient object by passing the HttpRequestMessage object as parameters to make a call to the API of the translator service. Once the request is processed, we will receive the translated text in the response. Add the following code snippet to implement the methods.

```
public async Task<string> TranslateText(TranslatePayload translatePayload)
{
    string route = $"/translate?api-version=3.0&from={translatePayload.
    SourceLanguageCode}&to={translatePayload.TargetLanguageCode}";
    object[] body = new object[] { new { Text = translatePayload.
    TextToBeTranslated } };
    var requestBody = JsonConvert.SerializeObject(body);
    string result = String.Empty;
    using (var client = new HttpClient())
    using (var request = new HttpRequestMessage())
    {
```

```
request.Method = HttpMethod.Post;
request.RequestUri = new Uri(endpoint + route);
request.Content = new StringContent(requestBody, Encoding.UTF8,
"application/json");
request.Headers.Add("Ocp-Apim-Subscription-Key", key);

request.Headers.Add("Ocp-Apim-Subscription-Region", location);

HttpResponseMessage response = await client.SendAsync(request).
ConfigureAwait(false);

result = await response.Content.ReadAsStringAsync();


}
return result;
}
```

With the implementation of the `TranslateText` method in place, let's go to our `program.cs` file and add a singleton service in our DI container as follows:

```
builder.Services.AddSingleton<ITranslateBusiness, TranslateBusiness>();
```

Next, add an empty API controller called `TranslateController.cs` in the `Controllers` folder and then add the following constructor code in the controller to inject the `ITranslateBusiness` object into our `_translateBusiness` property using constructor dependency injection:

```
private readonly ITranslateBusiness _translateBusiness;
public TranslateController(ITranslateBusiness translateBusiness)
{
    _translateBusiness = translateBusiness;
}
```

Let's add our action in our `TranslateController`. We are going to have only one action, `GetTranslatedText`. The purpose of this action is to call the `TranslateText` method of the `TranslateBusiness` class by passing the payload coming from the request body.

- *URL route*: `http://localhost:5185/api/Translate`

- *HTTP verb*: GET

Add the following code snippet to add the GetTranslatedText action in our controller:

```
[HttpGet]
public async Task<IActionResult> GetTranslatedText(TranslatePayload
translatePayload)
{
    var translatedText = await _translateBusiness.TranslateText(translate
    Payload);
    if (String.IsNullOrEmpty(translatedText))
    {
        return BadRequest();
    }
    return Ok(new { result = translatedText});
}
```

And with this our API project to schedule notifications for our fictional dental clinic is complete. Press Ctrl+F5 to build and run our project. You can find the complete source code of this API project at the following GitHub repository: https://github.com/AshirwadSatapathi/MyTextTranslator.

Test Our API Using Postman

Now that we have developed our API and have run it locally, let's perform a sanity test on the functionalities of our API. Open Postman and create a collection for requests. After creating the collection, add a request to test the TranslateText API. Define the request method as GET and define the route as http://localhost:5185/api/Translate and then click the **Body** tab to add the required information, SourceLanguageCode, TargetLanguageCode, and TextToBeTranslated, in the payload as key/value pairs. The SourceLanguageCode and TargetLanguageCode needs to be code for the language. Refer to https://learn.microsoft.com/en-us/azure/cognitive-services/translator/language-support to find the languages for different codes. After you add the preceding information, click **Send** to send a request to our API. The API will now receive a request, process this information, and return the translated text in the target language, as shown in Figure 10-12.

Figure 10-12. *Test the API*

In the last few sections, we have developed a web API to translate text from one language to another, but if we wanted to translate text from one language to multiple languages, we could absolutely do that by adding the language code for the same in the query string of our `HttpRequestMessage uri` property. The source and target language of the text can be any language that is supported by Azure Translator service. If we wanted to automatically detect the source language without having to specify it in our request payload, then we could leverage the language detection feature and detect the source language of the given text and then translate it to the target language.

Summary

Azure Cognitive Services provides a suite of AI services as SaaS offering that enable developers to add cognitive capabilities to their applications. We can perform operations ranging from image classification to text-to-speech detection. These services help developers add cognitive capabilities in their applications without requiring knowledge of the underlying algorithms or any investment of time and resources to train and test such algorithms. As part of this chapter, we explored a particular service of Azure Cognitive Services, Azure Translator, to solve a common problem that people and developers often face while interacting with people from different regions who speak different languages. We built an API that translates text from one source language to a target language. Apart from this, the translator service allows us to perform document translation as well as to create our own custom translator by building a neural machine translation system by leveraging the Azure Translator service.

CHAPTER 11

Deploy an ASP.NET Web Application to an Azure Web App Using GitHub Actions

DevOps is an important aspect for any application development process. The developers can develop the code and check it in to the source control repository. As soon as the code check processing is complete, the DevOps continuous integration pipeline builds the code and keeps the application's deployable package in a centralized location. Then the DevOps continuous deployment pipeline picks up the package and deploys it to the target environment. This entire process repeats every time the developer makes changes to the code base and checks in the code. There are lot of DevOps tool offerings in the industry. A few of the popular ones are Jenkins, Azure DevOps, and GitHub Actions, to name a few.

In this chapter we will explore GitHub Actions and how to deploy a .NET application to an Azure web app using GitHub Actions.

Structure

In this chapter, we will explore the following topics related to Azure Cognitive Service:

- Introduction to GitHub Actions
- Build a .NET application and push it to GitHub
- Provision an Azure web app
- Deploy an application to Azure the web app using GitHub Actions

© Ashirwad Satapathi and Abhishek Mishra 2023
A. Satapathi and A. Mishra, *Developing Cloud-Native Solutions with Microsoft Azure and .NET*,
https://doi.org/10.1007/978-1-4842-9004-0_11

249

Objectives

After studying this chapter, you should be able to

- Understand the fundamentals of GitHub Actions
- Deploy code to an Azure web app using GitHub Actions

Introduction to GitHub Actions

GitHub Actions helps you to build continuous integration (CI) and continuous deployment (CD) workflows in GitHub that can build the application code checked in to GitHub and deploy it on target environments with ease. You can write YAML-based workflows that have multiple steps to perform different DevOps activities. These workflows get triggered whenever an event occurs in GitHub. For example, whenever the developer checks in the code to GitHub, an event occurs and this triggers the GitHub Actions workflow that will build and deploy the checked in code. The workflows run on servers called *runners*. Figure 11-1 depicts the architecture of GitHub Actions.

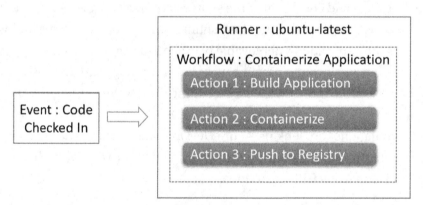

Figure 11-1. *GitHub Actions architecture*

GitHub actions are much more than DevOps tools. You can use GitHub actions to perform automations in the GitHub environment, like adding a label automatically whenever code is checked in to GitHub.

The workflows comprise a set of actions. Each of the actions performs an activity; for example, containerize the application, build the application, or push the container image to a container registry. GitHub provides a wide range of GitHub actions in the GitHub Marketplace. You can use GitHub actions to develop DevOps pipelines meeting your application and business needs.

Build a .NET Application and Push It to GitHub

Let's build a .NET web application and commit it to a GitHub repository. We will then configure a GitHub action to deploy the code to an Azure web app. Open Visual Studio and click **Create a new project** as shown in Figure 11-2.

Figure 11-2. *Click Create a new project*

Select **ASP.NET Core Web App** as shown in Figure 11-3 and then click **Next**.

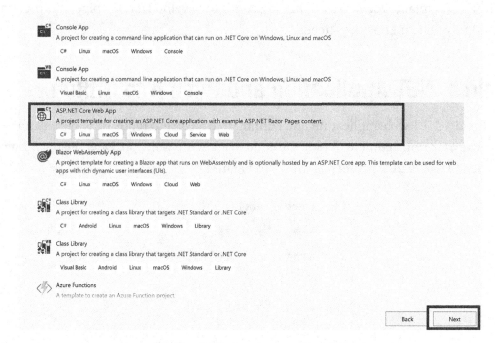

Figure 11-3. *Select ASP.NET Core Web App*

Provide the details for the project as in Figure 11-4 and click **Next**.

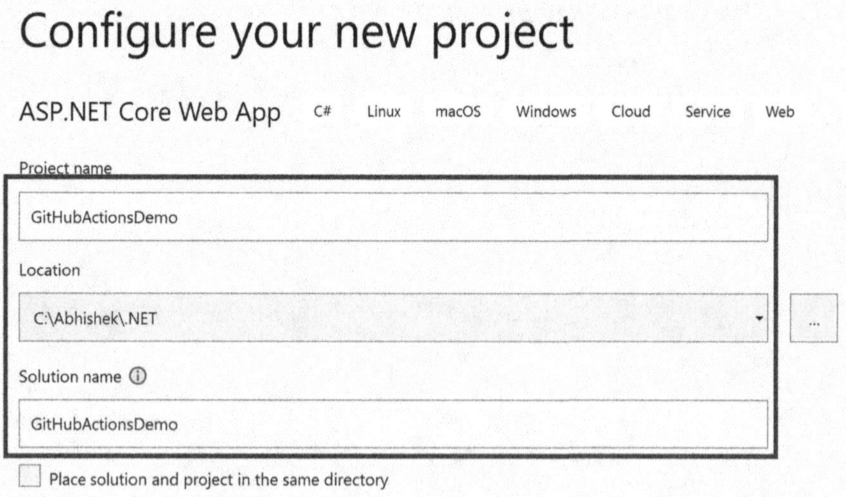

Configure your new project

ASP.NET Core Web App   C#   Linux   macOS   Windows   Cloud   Service   Web

Project name

> GitHubActionsDemo

Location

> C:\Abhishek\.NET

Solution name ⓘ

> GitHubActionsDemo

☐ Place solution and project in the same directory

Figure 11-4. *Provide project details*

Select the framework for .NET that you will use to build the application, as shown in Figure 11-5, and then click **Create**. The default web application code will get generated. We can push this project to the GitHub repository without making any changes.

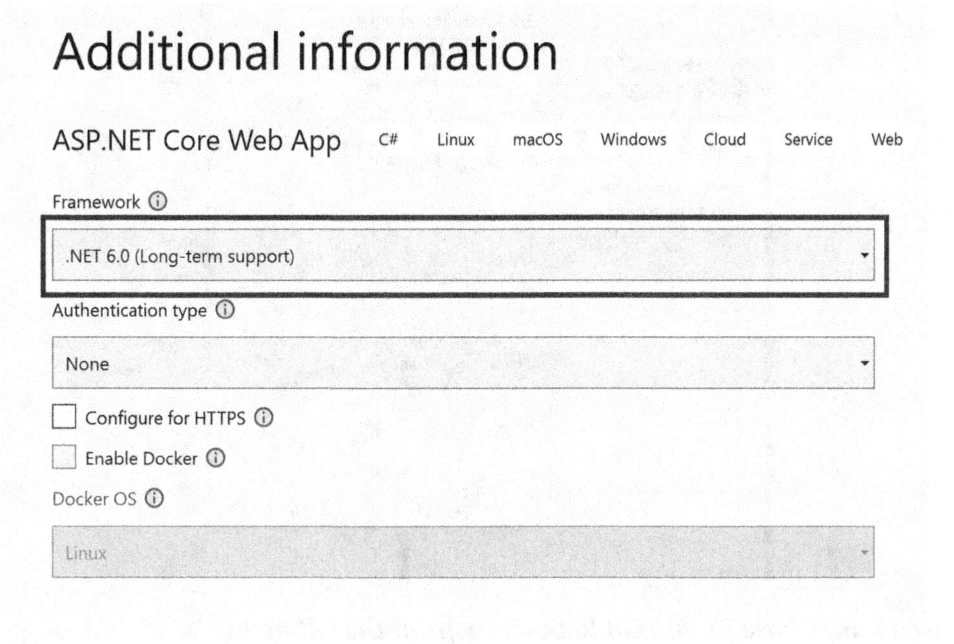

Additional information

ASP.NET Core Web App   C#   Linux   macOS   Windows   Cloud   Service   Web

Framework ⓘ

.NET 6.0 (Long-term support)

Authentication type ⓘ

None

☐ Configure for HTTPS ⓘ

☐ Enable Docker ⓘ

Docker OS ⓘ

Linux

Figure 11-5. *Select .NET version*

Now let's push the code to the GitHub repository. Click the **Git** menu and then click **Create Git Repository** as shown in Figure 11-6.

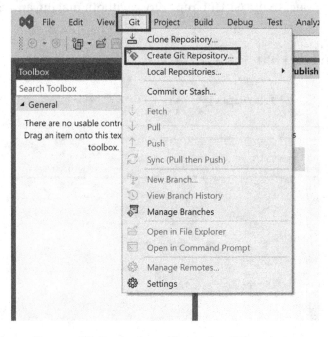

Figure 11-6. *Chose Create Git Repository from the Git menu*

Click the **Account** drop-down arrow and select **GitHub account** as shown in Figure 11-7. You need to sign it and authorize Visual Studio to push the code to the GitHub repository.

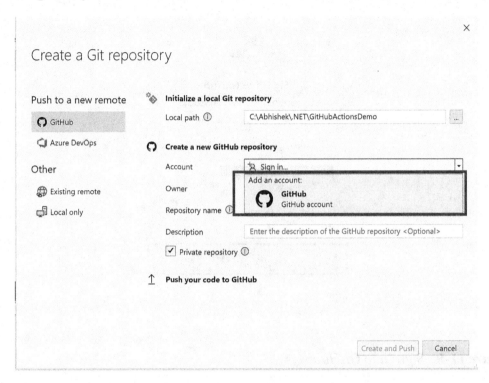

Figure 11-7. *Select GitHub account*

Provide your GitHub credentials when prompted and sign in to GitHub as shown in Figure 11-8.

Figure 11-8. *Sign in to GitHub*

Click **Authorize github** as shown in Figure 11-9 to authorize Visual Studio to push code to the GitHub repository.

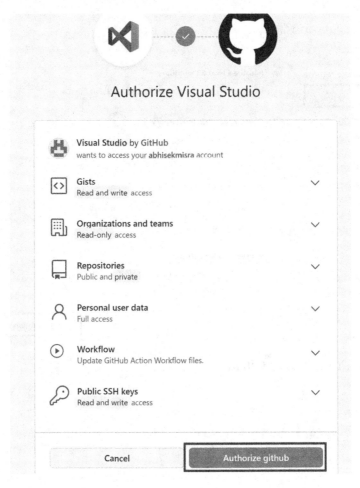

Figure 11-9. *Authorize GitHub*

Select your repository and click **Create and Push** as shown in Figure 11-10.

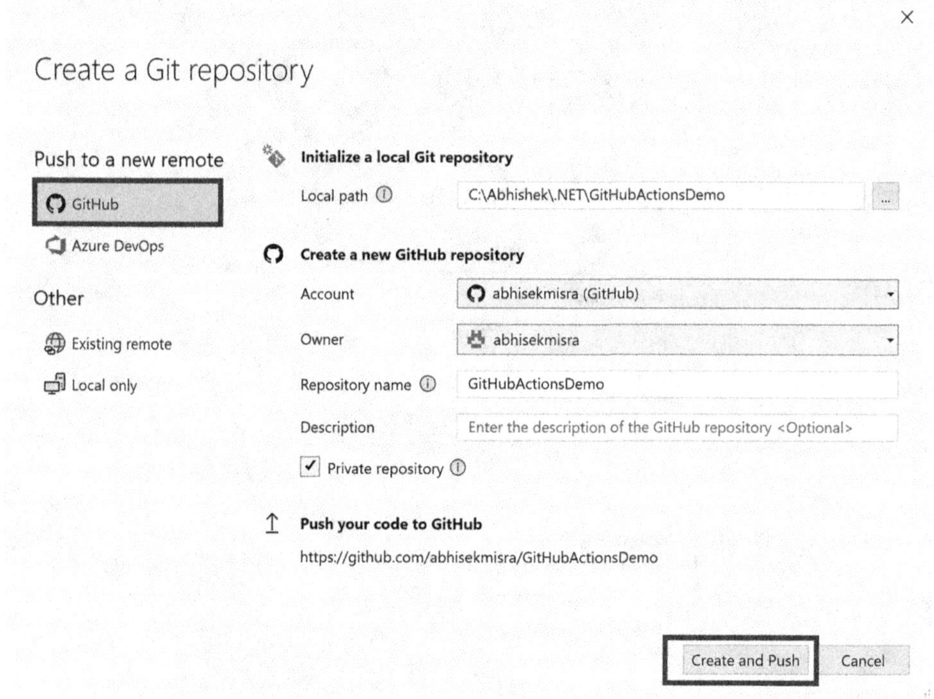

Figure 11-10. *Push code to GitHub*

You can log in to your GitHub account and verify the checked in code, shown in Figure 11-11.

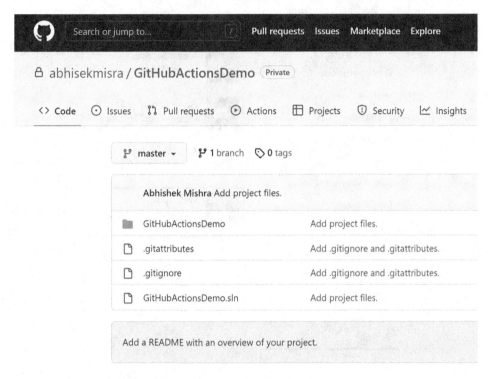

Figure 11-11. *Checked in code in the GitHub repository*

Provision Azure Web App

Now let's provision an Azure web pp. We will deploy the web application checked in to GitHub to this web app using a GitHub action. Go to the Azure portal and click **Create a resource** as shown in Figure 11-12.

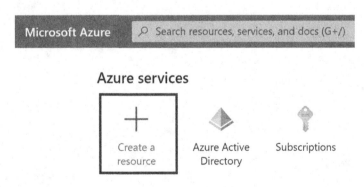

Figure 11-12. *Click Create a resource*

You will be navigated to the Azure Marketplace. Click **Web** and then click **Web App** as shown in Figure 11-13.

Figure 11-13. *Click Web App*

Provide the basic details for the web app as shown in Figure 11-14.

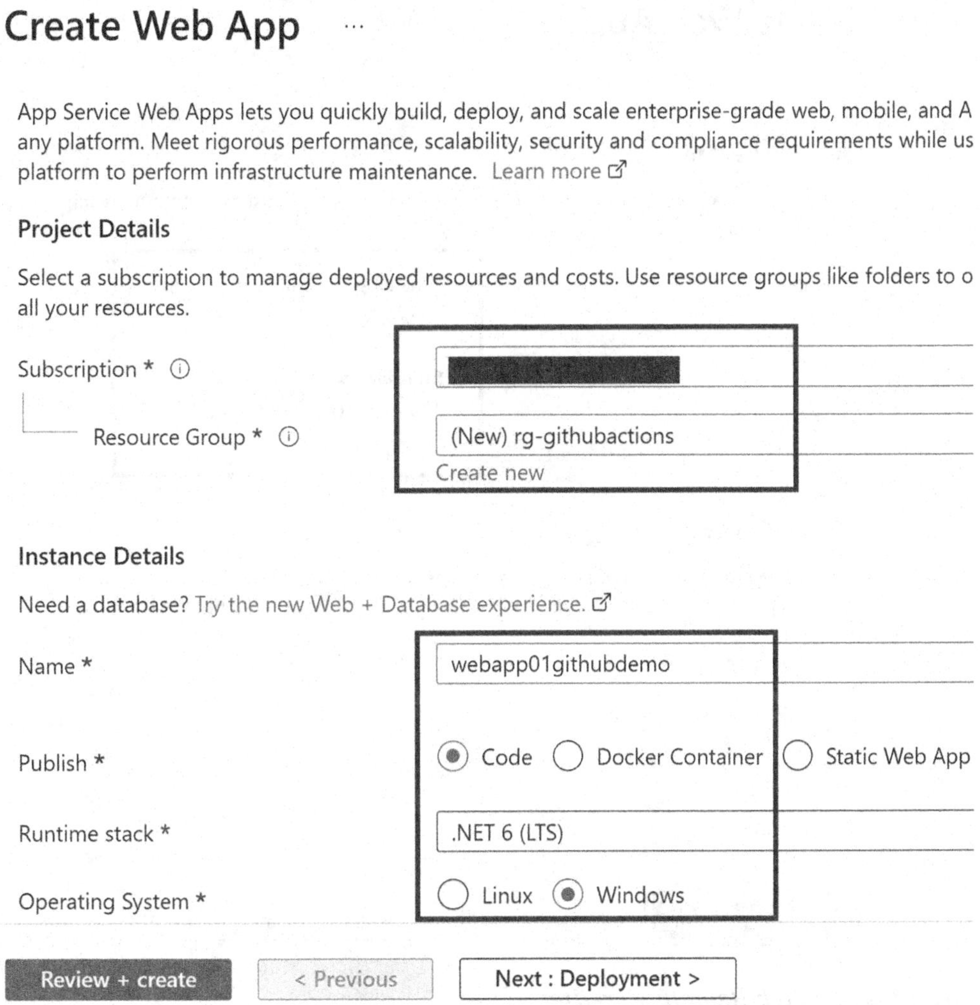

Create Web App   ···

App Service Web Apps lets you quickly build, deploy, and scale enterprise-grade web, mobile, and A any platform. Meet rigorous performance, scalability, security and compliance requirements while us platform to perform infrastructure maintenance. Learn more ☐

Project Details

Select a subscription to manage deployed resources and costs. Use resource groups like folders to o all your resources.

Subscription * ⓘ

Resource Group * ⓘ   (New) rg-githubactions
                            Create new

Instance Details

Need a database? Try the new Web + Database experience. ☐

Name *   webapp01githubdemo

Publish *   ◉ Code   ◯ Docker Container   ◯ Static Web App

Runtime stack *   .NET 6 (LTS)

Operating System *   ◯ Linux   ◉ Windows

[Review + create]   [< Previous]   [Next : Deployment >]

Figure 11-14. *Provide basic details*

Create an App Service plan as shown in Figure 11-15 and then click **Review + create**.

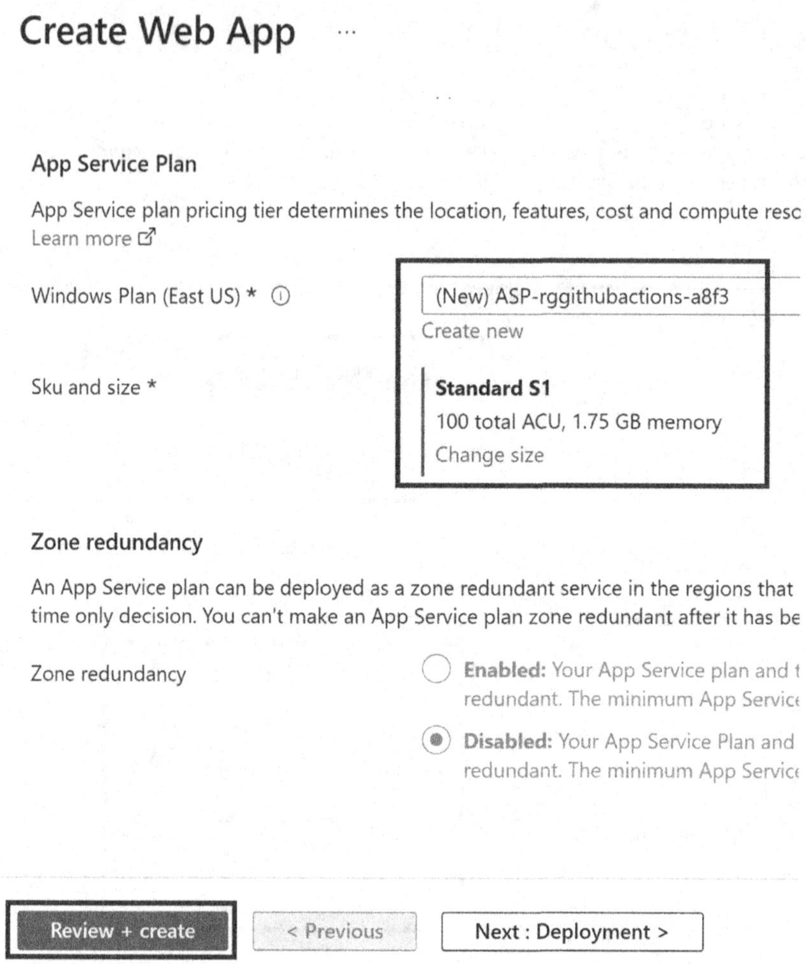

Create Web App   ⋯

App Service Plan

App Service plan pricing tier determines the location, features, cost and compute resc
Learn more ☐

Windows Plan (East US) * ⓘ

> (New) ASP-rggithubactions-a8f3
> Create new
>
> **Standard S1**
> 100 total ACU, 1.75 GB memory
> Change size

Sku and size *

Zone redundancy

An App Service plan can be deployed as a zone redundant service in the regions that
time only decision. You can't make an App Service plan zone redundant after it has be

Zone redundancy

◯ **Enabled:** Your App Service plan and t
   redundant. The minimum App Service

◉ **Disabled:** Your App Service Plan and
   redundant. The minimum App Service

[Review + create]   [< Previous]   [Next : Deployment >]

Figure 11-15. *Click Review + create*

Click **Create** as shown in Figure 11-16 to provision the web app.

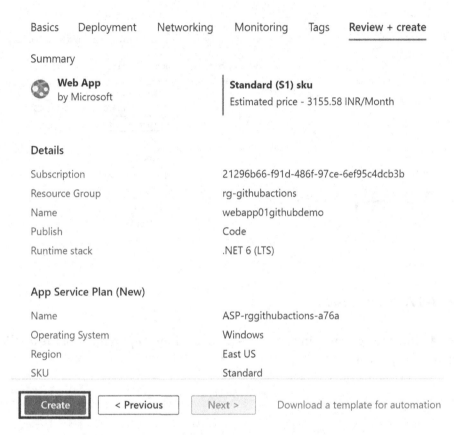

Create Web App   ⋯

| Basics | Deployment | Networking | Monitoring | Tags | **Review + create** |

Summary

Web App
by Microsoft

Standard (S1) sku
Estimated price - 3155.58 INR/Month

Details

Subscription	21296b66-f91d-486f-97ce-6ef95c4dcb3b
Resource Group	rg-githubactions
Name	webapp01githubdemo
Publish	Code
Runtime stack	.NET 6 (LTS)

App Service Plan (New)

Name	ASP-rggithubactions-a76a
Operating System	Windows
Region	East US
SKU	Standard

`Create`   `< Previous`   `Next >`   Download a template for automation

Figure 11-16. *Click Create*

Deploy Application to Azure Web App Using GitHub Actions

Not let's configure GitHub actions for the Azure web app and deploy to the web app the application code checked in to the GitHub repository. Go to the Azure web app you created and click **Deployment Center**. Select **GitHub** as the source as shown in Figure 11-17.

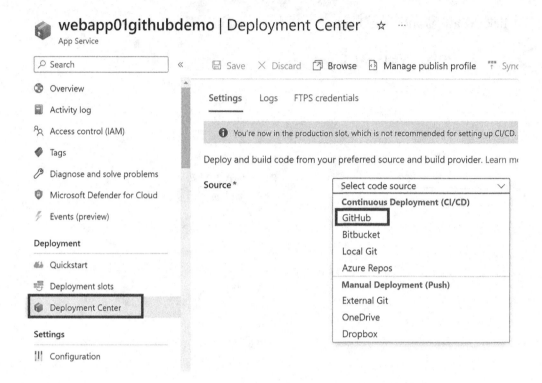

Figure 11-17. *Select GitHub*

Click **Authorize** as shown in Figure 11-18 to facilitate deployment of the application from GitHub to the web app.

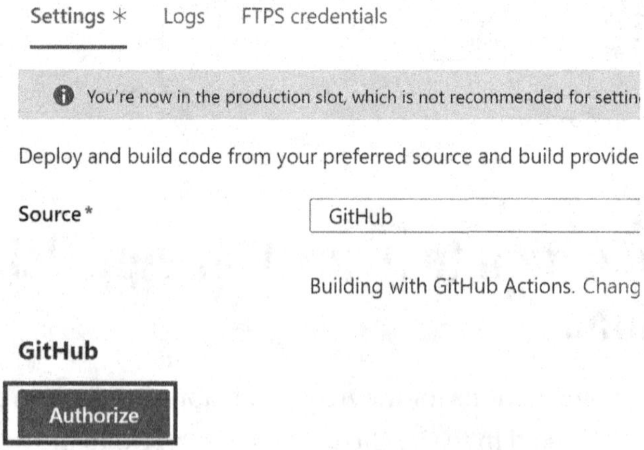

Figure 11-18. *Click Authorize*

Provide your credentials and sign in to GitHub as shown in Figure 11-19.

Figure 11-19. *Sign in to GitHub*

Click **Authorize AzureAppService** as shown in Figure 11-20.

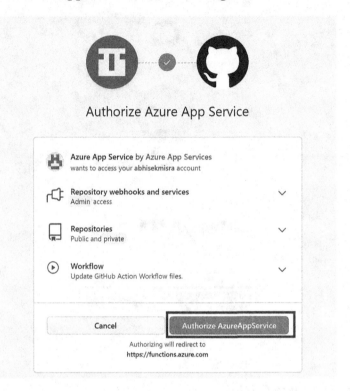

Figure 11-20. *Authorize Azure App Service*

Select the repository and branch details for the GitHub repository as shown in Figure 11-21 and then click **Save**.

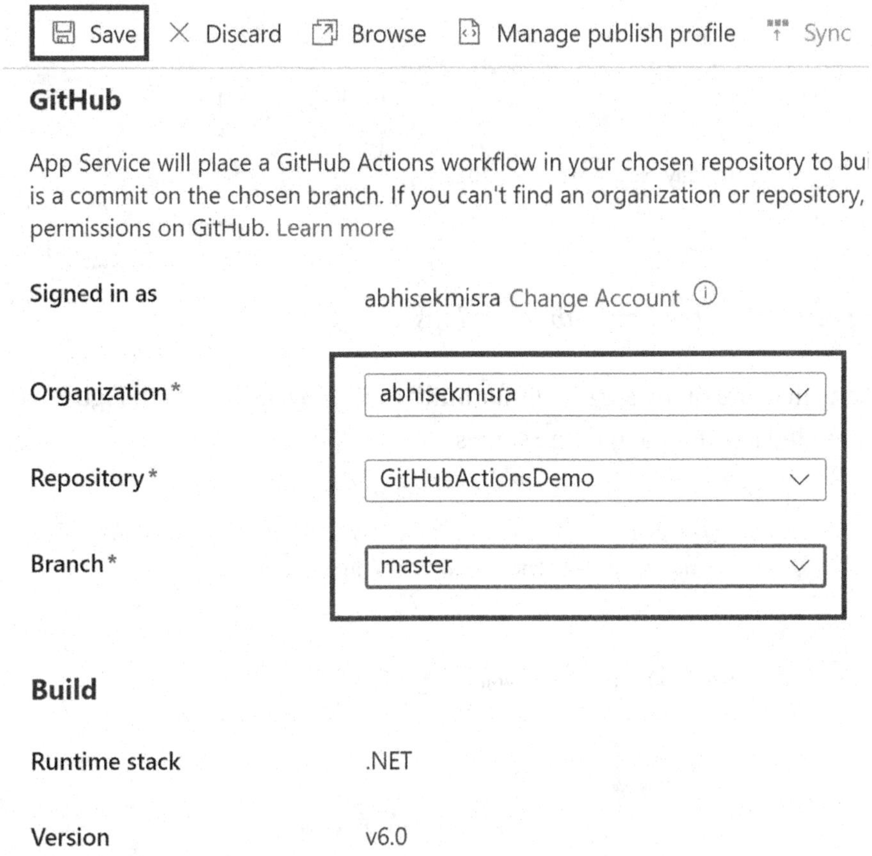

Figure 11-21. *Click Save*

Generic GitHub actions pipeline for building and pushing .NET Core application will automatically get generated. Deployment will get initiated as shown in Figure 11-22. You can click the **Logs** tab to check the build and deployment logs.

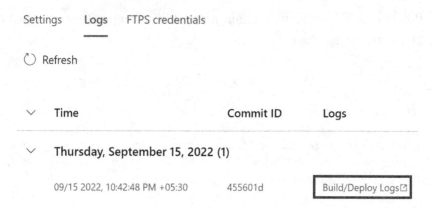

Figure 11-22. *Click the Logs tab to see logs*

You can click one of the stages, either build or deploy, as shown in Figure 11-23 to view the detailed logs for each of the stages.

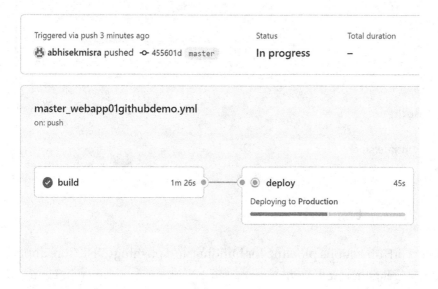

Figure 11-23. *See logs for each stage*

You can see the logs for the build and deploy stages as shown in Figure 11-24.

✓ Add or update the Azure App Service build and deployment workflow

⌂ Summary

Jobs

✓ build

✓ deploy

build
succeeded 2 minutes ago in 1m 26s

> ✓ Set up job

> ✓ Run actions/checkout@v2

> ✓ Set up .NET Core

> ✓ Build with dotnet

> ✓ dotnet publish

> ✓ Upload artifact for deployment job

> ✓ Post Run actions/checkout@v2

> ✓ Complete job

Figure 11-24. *Detailed build and deploy logs*

Once the deployment is complete, you can browse using the URL for the web app, which you can get from the **Overview** tab of the web app. You will see the deployed application rendered on the browser as shown in Figure 11-25.

🔒 webapp01githubdemo.azurewebsites.net

GitHubActionsDemo   Home   Privacy

Welcome

Learn about building Web apps with ASP.NET Core.

Figure 11-25. *Deployed application on web app*

Summary

In this chapter, we explored the basic concepts of GitHub Actions. Then we created a .NET web application and checked in the code to the GitHub repository. We then created an Azure web app and deployed the application to the web app using GitHub actions.

Index

A

AddHostedService method, 47

Advanced Message Queuing Protocol (AMQP), 44, 196

Amazon Web Services (AWS), 2

Application Insights, 192
- create application, 161
- create resource, 158, 159
- provide basic details, 160
- resource group, 160

Appointment.cs, 35, 58

Artificial intelligence (AI), 1, 195, 219

ASP.NET Core Web API, 234, 239

Azure Active Directory (Azure AD), 11, 25, 48, 111, 113, 232
- authentication features, 112
- definition, 112

Azure AD–based authentication
- application scope, create, 118–121
- create application secret, 121, 122
- MathAPI project, 123–126, 128–130
- register application, 113–118

Azure App Service, 7

Azure-based data services
- Azure synapse, 9
- data factory, 9
- Data Lake, 8
- SQL, 9
- storage account, 8

Azure Bot Service, 10

Azure CLI command, 100

Azure Cognitive Services, 231
- computer vision, 220
- decision APIs, 221
- language, 221
- .NET-based desktop application, 225–229
- PaaS-based artificial intelligence, 220
- provision speech service, 221–225
- REST APIs, 220
- speech, 221

Azure Container Apps, 63
- add API/subtract API
  - app created, 141
  - app settings, 138, 144
  - copy application URL, 142, 146
  - create resource, 134
  - environment, 135–137, 143
  - provide image details, 139, 145
  - review, 140, 146
- AKS, 132, 154
- definition, 131
- deploy Math API, 148–151, 153, 154
- Kubernetes cluster, 131
- Math API, 133
- Math microservices, 133
- modify Math API, 147

Azure Cosmos DB, 193, 196, 206

Azure Data Lake, 8

Azure Function, 198, 202

Azure IoT Hub, 195

© Ashirwad Satapathi and Abhishek Mishra 2023
A. Satapathi and A. Mishra, *Developing Cloud-Native Solutions with Microsoft Azure and .NET*,
https://doi.org/10.1007/978-1-4842-9004-0

Printed in the United States
by Baker & Taylor Publisher Services